355

To Mr.
Chas L. Alderman,
my dear friend of
many years and
about whom this
saying applies: "To know
him is to love him."

Sincerely
[signature]
Dallas TX

35,000 DAYS IN TEXAS

THE MACMILLAN COMPANY
NEW YORK · BOSTON · CHICAGO · DALLAS
ATLANTA · SAN FRANCISCO

MACMILLAN AND CO., LIMITED
LONDON · BOMBAY · CALCUTTA · MADRAS
MELBOURNE

THE MACMILLAN COMPANY
OF CANADA, LIMITED
TORONTO

35,000 DAYS

IN TEXAS

A HISTORY OF THE DALLAS NEWS
AND ITS FORBEARS

BY SAM ACHESON

New York

THE MACMILLAN COMPANY

1938

INTRODUCTION

FROM ITS first faint birth cry in 1842, at Galveston, THE NEWS has been a part of Texas, and Texas has been a part of it. Our finite eyes are inadequate to pierce the veil of the future, but, if the past affords a reckoning to go by, the State will continue to be, through all manner of change, a part of the paper and the paper a part of the State.

The baby newspaper that came into being in 1842 was little newer than the Republic of Texas at that time. The independence of Texas had recently been wrought, and every voter was a politician. There were troublous times for the infant Republic as well as for the infant newspaper. Citizens condemned their public officers and condemned the press almost in the same breath. There was an impatience for early development, for a social order similar to that of the older portions of the United States. But Galveston was a village on an island, THE NEWS a strugging hope housed in a flimsy shack. Dreams of future grandeur for Texas were about as insubstantial as dreams usually are, and prospects of a long and accreted experience for the paper were less than brilliant.

But the people who were making Texas then, and those who were to make it afterward, were builders. They had the pioneer instinct for constructiveness. There were bad men among them, refugee desperadoes, adventurers eager for quick fortune and indifferent to methods of acquirement. All this is common to all raw beginnings, but it was in those years that Texas acquired a reputation for lawlessness, a bad eminence too long persisting.

There were Indian wars within the radius of THE NEWS' circulation when its circulation was limited to the few coastal towns within reach of mail facilities. There were bandits, thieves and all sorts of trouble makers. But there were also great and good men, men of vision, men of emprise, statesmen and thinkers. THE NEWS found its way off the island in time, and inch by inch gained a foothold on the mainland. Galveston became a metropolis, and THE NEWS liked to believe it was itself influential in bringing the incoming settlers to look South and see Galveston as their chief port and market dependence. Then came statehood, Texas a member of the Union.

So Texas grew away from its island, its premier port. It grew northward, eastward and westward. Incoming settlers rapidly established themselves in the black lands of Central and North Texas. A railroad was slowly building toward what was the Indian Territory, nearly four hundred miles from Galveston. Fine local market towns, future little cities were rising at the railside. The publishers of THE GALVESTON NEWS, knowing the infinite possibilities of their State, saw the importance of the newer and richer field to the north. They decided, after investigation and deliberation, to establish a newspaper at Dallas. They regarded Dallas as the best promise in northern Texas. And they planted at Dallas THE DALLAS NEWS.

They did not leave THE GALVESTON NEWS orphaned, however. They did what had never been done before. They combined the two papers, 315 miles apart, by telegraph and railroad. Each office of the twin publication served its own territory. Both prospered. Finally, after years of joint publication, THE GALVESTON DAILY NEWS was sold to Galveston interests. THE GALVESTON SEMI-WEEKLY NEWS was not sold. It was brought to Dallas and continued to all readers from the Dallas office. Thus the continuity of the first NEWS, in 1842, was mitered into THE DALLAS NEWS of 1885, and through the intervening years to the present.

Coming up out of the turbulence of war and revolution, THE NEWS was political in its opinion columns. It wished to be always a newspaper first, and so it remains. But it did not withhold its views on public questions. It commended when commendation seemed due, condemned when convinced that condemnation was in the public interest. Naturally it has been an object of enmity and bitter criticism at times. There have been months when it lost circulation by thousands because of its forthright stand on a question of the day. It has often been accused of subserviency to "the interests," a vague entity never exactly defined. But the only interest to which it owed allegiance was the public interest. And never has it departed from its conviction to win a transitory popularity.

Although often charged with disloyalty to the Democratic party and hostility toward the party's heroes, THE NEWS has seldom been accused of vindictiveness. It has never been an unquestioning servant of the Democratic party, and has worn no collar, although it has mainly favored and supported that party, in good faith and with whatever fervor the occasion warranted. But never has it surrendered its independence, nor failed to exercise it.

In a business long established there has grown up a certain body of tradition that attaches to the institution through long association of those who compose its working force. While THE NEWS acquires new talent from time to time, it nevertheless retains its older men in all departments, sometimes from youth into advanced age. There are indeed members under the present roof who served at Galveston in the earlier day, and half a dozen or so who joined the new enterprise during its first year or two in Dallas, more than fifty years ago. The publication office becomes home to them, and the silvern cords of sentiment bind them without chafing. In its long experience, THE NEWS has had almost no "labor trouble." Written contracts with those in the mechanical departments are lived up to with exact loyalty on both sides, and those without contracts are considered fixtures as long as they serve with fidelity and adequacy. The result is a very light "turnover" in personnel. This serves to make acquaintance among all, and personal peculiarities, anecdotes and legends have attached to individuals of the group from one decade to another.

Colonel William G. Sterett was a vivid type, and on occasion could emit floods of words carrying a flotsam of miscellaneous luridity. The Colonel was unique in that his handwriting was very difficult to read and his typewriting no better. He was long the paper's Washington correspondent, and at other times a staff correspondent, editor of "State Press," and political feature writer. In a long and informed article on dipping vats, when those instrumentalities were new in the anti-tick campaign, he wrote about "movable vats" in which the cattle were dipped. It came out "marble vats" and the conscientious author gasped for air. But the gasping was immediately succeeded by vocal outbursts that reverberated upstairs, downstairs and in the business office.

The composing room was presided over by Harvey M. Campbell, foreman, whose imperturbability was almost equal to that of a marble statue. When Colonel Sterett reached the foreman the outpouring of invective and fancy objurgation was cataclysmic. Mr. Campbell listened while sorting copy and marking "takes." When the Colonel came to an explosive end Mr. Campbell turned serenely and said, "Bill, have you got any chewing tobacco?" That was the composing room's reply to the writer's high dudgeon, and the complainant retired heavily, saying the printers had made him a laughingstock throughout Texas and that every lasting one of them ought to be consigned to perdition without benefit of clergy.

. It was the same Harvey Campbell who once helped W. M. O'Leary, then city editor, out of a desperate situation. O'Leary was a genius with some of the erraticisms of his tribe. He came in late one night with an important story to write and found his desk three feet away from the drop light. He couldn't see well and was greatly provoked. Then Mr. Campbell came by, looking for copy, and Mr. O'Leary explained to him that he couldn't write because his desk was in the dark, away from the light. "Why don't you move the desk under the light and see how it works?" the visitor suggested. "A fool can say things a smart man may profit by," replied the excited editor, who then shoved his desk back to where it was before the janitor moved it while sweeping the floor.

About thirty years ago, there was a young artist on the staff who was also a trap drummer in a band. He preferred the audible to the visible arts and gave a great deal of time to his drum. On one occasion he went away on a tour with the band, leaving his drawing board unattended. When he returned he found another man at the position he had temporarily deserted. The successor was a young man named John Knott, who had been drawing pictures of harness and horse collars for a leather goods manufacturer. This John Knott is now John Francis Knott, Litt.D., formally speaking, but just John to the office. He became in the course of years and experience one of the Nation's foremost cartoonists, and remains so to this day. Incidentally, he has a son following in his footsteps.

Cartoonists have their bad moments, like all of us. A young staff writer several years ago wrote a feature story on the subject of cartoon errors. He showed that Dr. Knott had drawn a chariot team of three horses with thirteen legs. There was no denying it, for the picture was reproduced with the legs and the story. Also our cartoonist, not having worked around a cotton gin, made a practice of putting only four hoops on his pictures of a cotton bale, although he sometimes put six or seven, if it happened to be a big bale. He insisted that an artist doesn't have to conform to mechanical standards. During the World War he drew a picture of the Kaiser under a press, being painfully squeezed, according to the war lord's look. But John drew the press screw with the threads running the wrong way, so that the poor old Kaiser wasn't being pressed but being released.

The most interesting news story the paper ever printed was the acceptance by the German authorities of President Wilson's famous fourteen points—unless perhaps it was the news of Lee's surrender at Appomattox. No doubt the latter information was printed conspicuously, but it took outside news a long time to get to Texas in those days. When the Associated Press wires brought the news from Berlin, via Washington, it was at seven o'clock on a Saturday night. All the linotype machines were running at high speed on classified advertisements for the Sunday paper, and the machines couldn't be released for the wire service. So all the printers except the machine operators were called to the type stands and put to work with hand-set type to get out an extra. The type chosen was twenty-four point and within half an hour or so a full page was up and sent to the press. The extra came out and was being shouted on the streets before the linotype operators were aware of any extra being in the works. THE NEWS seldom issues extras, but the one here mentioned created a heavy demand from all over the circulating territory.

In a business establishment where those of long tenure know and appreciate those of similar service, there is a sort of comradeship more often shown in the wordy breach than in the spoken observance. It was told of the late E. B. Doran, who was a zealous and vigilant reporter, that he once got the news of a fire in town,

and press time being near he sat at his machine and wrote a running account of same, by telephone information. After he had his
pages together and got them into the composing room he asked of
a fellow worker, "Where was that fire?" He had named the location, with details and descriptions from the telephone, but after his
story was off his hands he couldn't remember where the fire
occurred. He was always a reporter rather than a moralizer.

Old-timers used to tell of an occasion when a visitor applied to
Harold Ward, building manager, for some information about the
new State of Oklahoma. Mr. Ward, a born and bred Englishman,
answered politely but not very satisfactorily. After the inquirer
was out of hearing the building manager remarked to some one
standing by, "Hoklaoma, Hoklaoma, 'ow the 'ell should Hi know
hanything about Hoklaoma!" At least that was the story the
bystander told.

Innumerable stories reflecting the mellow tones of long-time
association and the exchange of compliments, left-handed or
right-handed, could be written from the recollections of the men
who literally grew up with the paper. The reference in this preface
has been mainly to the men. But the dramatis personæ include
feminine names, although none of the ladies in the office appreciate being called old-timers. We have it from a candid old-timer,
W. H. Benners, that when he came aboard in 1892 there were only
four women employed in the business, and now there are ninety-
six. Less than one-sixth of the total payroll members, but doing a
full proportion of the work. The paper can live with them, but
could hardly live without them.

It would be so easy to extend these somewhat disconnected
thoughts that it requires some resistance to forbear from prolong-
ing this introduction. There are so many faithfuls, so many men
and women excellent in their various assignments, that all deserve
mention in a history of THE NEWS. But the historian's space was
not sufficient to include all those worthy of inclusion, and this
foreword is only a scanty preview of the full volume that follows it.

From what has been said here, the reader might suppose THE
NEWS is manned by graybeards. That of course is by no means
the case. Infusions of young blood are frequent. They carry on

after the older members weaken or retire. And it is not improper for one worker in the ranks to say of all his fellow workers that no body of employees in any establishment anywhere could exhibit an assemblage of finer types, men and women of better principles or a finer fealty to the house they serve, and which serves them in turn, than are the more than six hundred who make the newspaper which is the subject of the book herewith presented.

> *"Those friends thou hast, and their adoption tried,*
> *Grapple them to thy soul with hoops of steel."*

—J. J. TAYLOR.

Dallas
April 21, 1938

CONTENTS

ILLUSTRATIONS

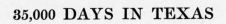

35,000 DAYS IN TEXAS

CHAPTER I

BIRTH OF "THE OLD LADY BY THE SEA"

1817–1842

"THE STORY of THE NEWS is the story of Texas."
How often through the years has this been said of the
oldest publishing institution in the State. Yet, it is as true today
as when first uttered. Under three flags, through five wars, across
seven cycles of panic and prosperity, it has moved steadily as a
recording eye on one of the great trail drives of the American
people.

This progress of a people has elements that are romantic as well
as amusing. But THE NEWS has never been content merely to
publish the record; from the first, the paper asked to be taken into
the outfit as a full-fledged partner, ready to share, and share alike,
in the fortunes or disasters of the enterprise, to take its turn at the
lowlier as well as the more showy tasks of empire. If there were
responsibilities to be shared in times of danger, there was also fun
when the going was good. And, ever mindful of its assignment
as scout and guide, it has rarely failed to speak out in warning
when the times demanded. In short, THE NEWS itself has been
one of the chief characters in this chronicle.

With a slight presumption, Anglo-Americans tend to date the
history of Texas from their own arrival on the plains early in the
Nineteenth Century. This view ignores, of course, some three
centuries of earlier, Spanish and French penetration—a vast and
glamourous epoch, rich in the pageantry of plumed, mail-coated
horsemen, explorers, soldiers, conquerors, Indian agents, traders,

1

administrators, together with humbler friars on foot, spies, scape-grace noblemen with some of the proudest names of Spain, hardy colonists who dared as much as those who sailed on the *Mayflower*. An exciting struggle against great odds—from Indian treachery to be found in innocent looking thickets to cut-throat jealousies within the early Texans' own ranks—characterizes this more remote period. But, in these long decades, there is no record of a printing press ever having been brought to Texas. The diary of this far northeastern province of New Spain can be unearthed only in old friar's tales, in the charts of the conquistadores, and in the interminable files of official correspondence between governors, inspectors-general, fiscales, viceroys, and the kings themselves.

But, at the dawn of the last century a new, slightly nasal cry of discovery was heard to the east. The sound was human, if hardly Spanish. The Yankee had discovered Texas.

Samuel Bangs, who was to father THE NEWS, holds a place in history as one of these first Americans to invade Texas. Since little is known of this pioneer printer's life, he moves along the horizon as a somewhat mysterious, even legendary character. His short, stodgy frame, with large, almost bald head set well into the shoulders, appears like a half realized figure in some charcoal drawing. The nose is smudged to a bulb, and the left eye squints. Tradition had it for years that Bangs was a pirate. It is true that he first touched on Galveston Island just before Jean Laffite set up his rendezvous on the same sand bar. But he was not a pirate.

Boston-born in the early years of the American Republic, Bangs followed in the footsteps of a more famous New England printer. Once his apprenticeship had been served, he journeyed, as did Franklin, to Philadelphia. There he became imbued with the idea of Liberty for the peoples of Spanish-America. The City of Brotherly Love was a filibusterer's paradise in those days. Idealistic dons from Cartagena to Havana floated through the grog shops and taverns on chalky clouds of talk and smoke, finding ready ears among adventurous spirits who were too easily sold on plans to free Cuba or Mexico.

There was much scheming about Texas. Already the ill-fated Gutierrez-Magee expedition to liberate that province had been nursed in the cradle of American independence. So the man who was to launch THE NEWS next appears as a member of the similar Mina and Mier expedition, which sailed from Baltimore early in 1817. The leaders hoped to salvage the cause of Mexican independence, which had been lost six years before by Hidalgo and his followers. They carried with them a small hand press recently imported from England.

Down the Atlantic and around into the Mexican Gulf the ship steered its course, daily nearing the Texas coast, until one evening at sunset it crossed the bar and slid into the splendid but empty harbor on the bay side of Galveston Island. Here the revolutionists halted. Except for a flea-bitten band of coast Indians, there were no regular inhabitants on the island. Bangs could scarcely have imagined that such desolate ground would call him back twenty-odd years afterwards to help settle the fate of a nation. But there was immediate work at hand. He set up and printed the manifesto of the expedition, a call to Mexican patriots to take up arms against the Spanish tyrants. This document in Spanish was the first printing on the island and among the first on any Texas soil.

After a few weeks of rest the expedition sailed on, bound this time for Tampico on the south, where its members debarked and began their march inland. But the sons of Mexico failed to rally to their banner, and Royalist forces swooped down like so many mountain eagles. Trapped, the filibusterers were massacred, almost without exception. Bangs was one of the few whose lives were spared, solely because he was a bird rarer than any eagle, a practical printer. For the next few years he served his captors well, and, on the final winning of Mexican independence in 1821, was acclaimed a hero. Receiving now the patriot's reward, he was appointed official printer for the new State of Coahuila—to which was soon added the territory of Texas. Bangs became one of the prominent citizens in the capital of Saltillo. He suffered only one minor mishap; when he was baptized into the Catholic faith by a padre somewhat deafened from years of frontier service, he heard himself rechristened José Manuel Bancs.

☆

When Bangs camped on Galveston Island in 1817, virtually all Texas was barren of the white man. Only San Antonio, two hundred miles to the west, Nacogdoches on the north, and a few other presidios and villas testified to the white man's intention to settle it—if and when he got around to the task. But, after the Austins gained lawful entry into the province for themselves and party in 1820-21, a steady, ever-widening stream of settlers trickled in from the United States. Within nine years the flow had become so menacing that Mexican authorities tried stubbornly to check it. But, it was too late. No such breach in the levee could be fixed while the westward surge of the Americans neared floodstage. Then, at the end of 1835, the flames of revolt broke out in Texas, adding horror to havoc in the eyes of the Mexicans. Soon Santa Anna's army was rolling northward from Querétaro and Saltillo to stamp out the rebellion.

The State printer of Coahuila-Texas now suffered the tortures of divided loyalty. He saw a nation that had honored and profited him bent on slaughtering his own blood brothers. Unable to take either side in Texas' quarrel with Mexico, Bangs returned to the United States. He settled in Mobile, took unto himself a wife, and proposed to rebuild his fortune through his craft. Thus he heard only from afar the story of the swift, bloody course of events in Texas in the spring of 1836—the fall of the Alamo, the massacre at Goliad, the panicky retreat of the Texas army under Sam Houston; then the miraculous reversal of arms in which the Texans, turning savagely on their pursuers at San Jacinto on April 21, routed and destroyed an army twice their number.

The winning of Texas freedom is a drama in the classic sense, which calls for the art of the poet and the historian. Before this tale of heroism the stoutest cynic pauses in respect. But what came after San Jacinto is another matter. For all of its noble poses and grander dreams, mixed in with many real achievements, the

Republic of Texas at times barely missed becoming a farce. Heroes and villains who survived into this sequel soon lapsed into less heroic moods, and in the rebound of normal human passions and behavior, it is not always easy to tell them apart. Characteristic American frenzies came into their own again; chief among these politics, which, forced underground for the duration of the war, soon reappeared.

As might have been expected, jockeying for political place caused a rash of newspapers to blossom overnight, once a treaty had been extorted from the morose Santa Anna. One of these, the *Telegraph and Texas Register,* proved exceptional. It had been founded on the eve of the Revolution at San Felipe de Austin by Gail Borden and his brother Thomas. It became the official organ of the patriots, and, after the fall of the Alamo, its fate was welded to that of Houston's fleeing army. Halting at the temporary seat of government at Harrisburg, editors and printers had only put the forms to press on April 14, exactly one week before San Jacinto, when Santa Anna's advance guard entered the town, captured the unlucky printers and dumped press and type into Buffalo Bayou. The editors managed to escape with a few copies of the issue.

When the Republic formally organized at Columbia late in 1836, a grateful Congress bought the publishers a new press, from which the reborn *Telegraph* was soon publishing the country's laws as well as chronicling the acts and speeches of its statesmen. In April of 1837, the *Telegraph* ended its odyssey, moving for the last time to the city of Houston. This first permanent seat of government had been laid out some months before by developers who persuaded the Republic to choose it over Columbia. But the *Telegraph* was sold shortly afterward by its founders when Thomas Borden became collector of customs at Galveston and his brother Gail started his trek to greater fame as inventor and founder of America's first condensed-milk industry.

The new owners were Jacob Cruger, a contracting printer with a flair for knowing the Right People, and Dr. Francis Moore, Jr. The latter, a school teacher recently arrived from New York State, was to become the first notable newspaper editor in Texas. His story impinges on that of both THE NEWS and the *Civilian,* the

two other newspapers of the first rank which were spawned in the
Republic of Texas.

☆

As the Hero of San Jacinto and unanimous choice for first president, Sam Houston in 1837 had good reason to consider himself
the George Washington of Texas. But, like the father of the common country, he was never, in the eyes of his contemporaries, an
unqualified hero above party or partisanship. Opposition, in fact,
to this star pupil of Andrew Jackson supplies the one unfailing
source of political controversy, not only during the ten years of the
Republic but during the next twenty years of American statehood
as well. How THE NEWS came into being as a by-product of this
squabble is a necessary part of the prelude.

Next to Houston himself the most striking figure of the Republic
is none other than that fine, gallant and highly lyrical son of the
Old South, General Mirabeau Buonaparte Lamar. Since he was
the spearhead of the anti-Houston party and became, in a sense,
godfather to THE NEWS, it is necessary to salute his genius in passing. For genius he had, of a sort. Commander of the cavalry at
San Jacinto, Secretary of War in the provisional cabinet, second
President of the Republic, and founder of the public school system
of Texas, his claims on the gratitude of a people are valid. If
posterity sometimes smiles at this "Troubadour" who, despite the
charges of his enemies, did not pen verses to dark-eyed señoritas
while his incredible Santa Fe expedition foundered in dust and the
credit of the nation evaporated under the brilliancy of his dreams,
it would be unfair to forget his more solid accomplishments. And,
despite his flowing, majestic, at times even florid prose style, he
should never be confused with his first cousin, the Hon. Gazaway
Bugg Lamar, famed blockade runner of the Confederacy.

Lamar's first success was won as a journalist. In 1826, while
still in his native Georgia, he founded the Columbus *Enquirer*. It
was ushered into the world as "a literary as well as political paper
. . . attached to the republican creed as exemplified in the administration of Thomas Jefferson." That he gave it a firm foundation is seen in the fact that the journal thrives after a full century.

But this scion of one of the truly distinguished families of the South had another early penchant, that for history. Perhaps he drew this, as well as other intellectual interests, from his uncle, an eccentric bachelor scholar who lived with Lamar's parents on their Warren County plantation. This recluse, for some reason, was allowed to inflict a preposterous succession of names on the male children born to simple John and Rebecca Lamar. Thus, through the birthdays of Lucius Quintus Cincinnatus Lamar, Levoissier LeGrand Lamar, Jefferson Jackson Lamar and the Texas hero, the curious may reconstruct a lifetime of delightful, if somewhat disordered, reading. At that, Gazaway Bugg Lamar escaped the same uncle's preoccupations.

In 1835, the year in which Bangs left Mexico to return to the United States, Lamar set out for Texas. His express purpose, odd as it may seem, was to write the history of that future empire. His first wife had died shortly before, he had recently been defeated for Congress, and his profits from the *Enquirer* encouraged his desire for historical research.

Only the outbreak of the Texas Revolution forced Lamar to lay aside pen for sword, to suspend the writing of history in favor of its making. His bravery at San Jacinto, together with a strong political bent, conspired further to delay his satisfaction of Clio's demands. The Georgian was raised to the vice-presidency with almost as much enthusiasm as that which placed Houston in the chief executive's chair in the closing days of 1836. From the first, little love was lost between the President of the Senate and the President of the Republic. Before the prairies were green again Lamar's plans were forming to capture the first office in Texas. Barred by the Constitution from succeeding himself, Houston was equally determined that Lamar should not gain this honor.

If any public man ever believed in the power of the press, it was the first vice-president of Texas. Lamar used to be a newspaperman himself, as the insufferable phrase has it. And he clearly saw that, with the *Telegraph* and most of its struggling contemporaries bound by ties of patronage to the Houston Administration, he must find editorial support in other quarters. Lamar acted. As early as October, 1837, an old associate on the Columbus *Enquirer* was expressing the hope that "your Press may promote the cause of Liberty and Truth in Texas and that you may shortly occupy the highest station in the State."

Whether Lamar ever owned any Texas paper outright under a dummy editor, or otherwise, is questionable. Yet, there is no doubt that he materially aided more than one aspiring moulder of public opinion to set up shop. This became obvious when his campaign for the presidency opened in 1838; new papers sprang to his support in Richmond, Brazoria, Nacogdoches, Houston and elsewhere. Sam Houston threw his influence, though, behind one of the other two candidates, and the issue hung in the balance. But journalism was not to decide it. Midway in the race, one opponent plunged without warning to his death from a boat in Galveston Bay; the second shortly afterwards killed himself with a shot through the temple; and Lamar was elected without opposition.

Lamar's worry about press support was only one among many that beset his administration. The United States had spurned the first offer of the Texans to join the Union. The new President set about, therefore, to make sure that Texas should remain forever free and independent. To this end he created a new capital at Austin, won recognition from England, France, Belgium and Holland, and began formulating elaborate plans for a University of Texas. But dismal red figures showed up unaccountably on the other side of the ledger; both the Santa Fe and Yucatan expeditions proved ghastly failures, Lamar's merciless war against the Indians turned General Houston's stomach, and all the while the country listed more and more perilously toward bankruptcy.

A deadly stream of criticism of these measures came from Galveston Island. It was fired from the columns of the Galveston *Civilian* which, although born in Houston in the spring of 1838, had been moved fifty miles to the new port city before that year was gone. Its artilleryman was the fiery young Kentuckian, Hamilton Stuart, life-long idolator of General Houston from the moment he heard of his victory at San Jacinto. The paper, at its start in Houston, had been financed partly by Dr. Francis Moore, Jr., of the *Telegraph*. Stuart selected the name on his own responsibility. It was his protest against the practice of saluting practically everybody in Texas, even General Houston's enemies, with such titles as captain, major, colonel or general.

Galveston, as a matter of fact, was beginning to assume importance in the life of the Republic when Lamar took office. It had been laid off in 1836 on a league of land at the east end of the island, for which the promoter had paid $50,000. The new seaport by 1839 was outstripping the older port of entry at Velasco farther west on the mainland. Lamar saw that it would become vastly more important, and set about building his political fences there, accordingly. Above all, he wanted a journal to offset Stuart's *Civilian*. He dickered with John S. Evans, whose defunct *Commercial Intelligencer* had given the island its first newspaper for a few fitful months during the campaign year of 1838.

"So you think it would be politic for me to establish at this time a Commercial and Political Paper upon the island," Evans plaintively wrote Lamar in June of 1839, adding that "if so, would our Friends at Houston aid in sustaining the enterprise?"

☆

But before Evans could get his answer, Samuel Bangs returned, unannounced, to Texas.

Along with his wife, Caroline, and her two brothers, George H. and Henry R. French, the forty-five-year-old printer landed at Houston with a small hand press, a quantity of type and little other baggage. He saw there was no outlet for his talents in the crowded newspaper world of the capital city of Texas. Perhaps he did not so much as talk with the President of the Republic, but it is a significant fact that Bangs continued without unpacking to Galveston where, on April 15, 1839, he began publication of a clamorous, pro-Lamar organ, the *Daily Galvestonian*. His two brothers-in-law served as editors of this immediate predecessor of THE NEWS of Texas.

Bangs could have had few illusions about the ability of Galveston alone to support a daily paper, populous as the place might seem in comparison with his memory of it twenty-two years earlier.

(The *Civilian* and all other local rivals were weeklies.) At the time the island city had not 1,000 inhabitants, including slaves. A friendly observer noted that, in the whole town, there were only 300 buildings "which a bold person would or might call houses." Only one brick chimney was visible in the sprawling assembly of clapboard structures, each of which sat on wooden blocks about two feet off the ground. Even the stores struggled to keep chins above the mud in rainy weather. Citizens shared the poorly defined streets with pigs, "whose ears and tails were cropped by dogs roaming at will."

In reality a village on the bay side of the island, Galveston was certain, however, that its superb, almost land-locked harbor guaranteed a great city. The town calaboose was a half-sunk hulk of an old clipper, and the first wharf was merely a planked, double-file footwalk, which jutted one hundred and fifty yards from shore to channel. But citizens banked heavily on the future; a spirit of enterprise and commercial venture took for granted that more impressive buildings and other proofs of civic growth were imminent. With the daring of a people who were convinced that they commanded a future cross roads of the oceans, they had challenged London itself by naming their principal street the Strand. Perhaps some Englishman suggested it, for already the nascent cotton and shipping center had attracted more than one subject of the girl queen of Great Britain.

The *Galvestonian* managed to continue publication through most of Lamar's two-year term of office. But, when an anxious populace in 1841 returned Sam Houston to the presidency, partly in rebuke of the Georgian's extravagances, the paper passed into troubled waters. Its timbers shivered, then it sank with all hands on board. Fortunately, the waters were shallow.

Texas itself needed a skilled pilot as 1842 opened. With its "redbacks" almost worthless, its credit exhausted, and Mexico threatening to reconquer the land momentarily, the prospect was indeed gloomy. Six years had passed and the United States had merely recognized, not guaranteed, the independence of Texas. President Houston at this point swaggered up and took a hand in the great game of international poker. He was a past master at the art of bluffing. For, he made it clear, Texas could call on powerful friends across the water, even if the American Union were indifferent. Since annexation to the United States seemed a dead issue, the Republic would entertain offers of a protectorate from Great Britain.

Instantly there were bitter realignments in Texas. Lamar, whose dreams of a Southwestern Empire overshadowed even Aaron Burr's "conspiracy," would ultimately demand annexation. England's "notorious," oft-repeated policy of fostering the abolition of Negro slavery, at all times and in all places, became a red herring which the anti-Houston party dragged across Texas. Southern slave owners, led by John C. Calhoun, rose as one man in Washington in behalf of the émigré planters of Texas. They, too, demanded annexation of an adjoining territory which, it was believed, was capable of growing more cotton than all the rest of the United States.

In this state of alarm and dissension, Bangs launched his second and more famous journal on Galveston Island—THE DAILY NEWS —in the spring of 1842. In more ways than one, it seemed merely a revival or continuation of his *Daily Galvestonian*.

There was little in the puny, four-page sheet appearing on the morning of April 11 to give promise of either a long life or a prosperous one. The date itself seemed inconsequential. Bangs least of all had any premonition that April 11, 1842, would go down in the annals of Republic and State as the birthday of the oldest business institution in Texas, the first of more than 35,000 days in the life of a newspaper. Nothing about the mite suggested its future as the imperious "Old Lady by the Sea," or its present day expression in THE DALLAS MORNING NEWS. No copy of that first issue is extant. But from one for April 19 which came to light many years ago, its exact birthday has been fixed.

THE NEWS was born in a one-room, unpainted shack on the Strand near its juncture with Tremont Street. It is known that it came into being in the same building and on the same press that had served the lamented *Galvestonian*. The actual scene may be reconstructed in imagination. Throughout the preceding night, Bangs and one of his brothers-in-law, George H. French, probably worked at the delivery. The air must have been thick with tobacco smoke and the smell of printing, while sperm candles probably gave the only light in the room. In this tipsy flare the figures of the two men cast huge grotesques against the walls as they bent over the type cases, or fed and worked the old style Washington hand press. But at dawn they were able to present the offspring to a world which, it must be admitted, was perhaps not greatly interested.

Bangs did not bother to stamp his paternity openly on this quarto measuring only eight and one-half by twelve inches. The only name listed is that of the editor, his favorite brother-in-law, George H. French. What, then, had become of the brother Henry? An advertisement in the same issue revealed that this editor of the late *Galvestonian* had deserted journalism in favor of more tangible public service:

The subscriber having cut out the business of catering for the literary tastes of his friends, has taken up the more agreeable one of providing for their appetites, and that he may be prepared to receive them in proper style has taken the shanty

NO. 3 TREMONT STREET

where his friends will always find a *cordial* welcome and a *pie*-ous gratification.

—HENRY R. FRENCH.

The new organ, as might have been expected of a Lamar partisan, sharply opposed England and had little good to say of the administration of President Houston:

Almost every arrival from the United States brings accounts of new difficulties arising between the United States and Great Britain [begins the first or lead editorial] and from the tone of the press of that country it is evident that the people are anxious for a war with England. . . .

In the present crisis of affairs Uncle Sam has but one course to pursue, and that is to fight. John Bull is eager for it, for he has already forgotten the drubbing he received some twenty odd years ago. . . .

Then the editor with even more sanguine words washed away all doubts of his true Texas sentiments by adding:

After the difficulty between the United States and Great Britain is settled, the former country should take Mexico in hand, provided Texas does not settle her hash in the meantime, for the contempt with which she has treated the Star Spangled Banner.

An atonement is required and nothing but Mexican blood will wash away the disgrace.

The editor next cracked down on General Houston on the annexation question in a shorter comment:

We have said, and we repeat without fear of contradiction that the Commissioners who have been sent to the United States to forward the interests of Texas are not the right sort. It is a matter of astonishment to us that they have not been recalled some time since.

News in this earliest extant issue was less timely. The lead story on page 1 gave the text of a tariff act of the Congress of Texas, approved eighty-two days earlier by President Houston. But it was considered important enough to fill three columns.

Other news was handled more briefly. An example:

We learn that Hon. James Reilly, chargé d'affaires to the United States, has written to Mr. Webster upon the subject of the mails between the two countries.

Even pithier is this item which, as in the case of all others in the issue, lacked the dignity of a headline:

There has been another terrible fire in New York. Amount of loss, $119,000.

But, in the rush of important foreign dispatches, local news was not slighted. The editor knew that both crowds and the weather make news; he reported, therefore, that "our city is full of people and our streets would look more animated and busy but for the old fashioned norther which has been blowing for the last two or three days and has caused stoves and Mexican blankets to be in considerable demand." Nor were the fine arts neglected: "Col. Sefeeld and Lady will give another concert at the Tremont House on Wednesday evening. We bespeak for them a full attendance of the ladies, and the gentlemen will attend as a matter of course."

In the role of ship news reporter the editor was not overburdened that day, there being but one arrival, the schooner *Falcon* from Velasco, and one clearance, the sloop *Phoenix* for Corpus Christi. A larger boat, the *Neptune,* had arrived from New Orleans a few days earlier. Its list of "27 passengers, 22 volunteers and 15 Negroes" was still a topic for news and editorial discussion.

☆

Advertisers took a large share of the available white space. With only twelve columns to the issue, approximately seven were filled with their notices. These ranged in size from the single inch squares of attorneys and counsellors-at-law to the eight inch spread of M. Garcia & Co., who listed without price their stock of new goods. These embraced sperm candles, French prints, gunpowder and claret wine, "just received per brig Francis Ashby, 20 days from New York." Much of the advertising was not directly revenue bearing. Horace Greeley's year-old *Tribune,* published from "No. 30 Ann Street, New York City," was publicized at half-column length, followed by an equal notice of Sam Whiting's *Austin City Gazette.*

Bangs himself required more than half a column of advertising space. Here, in the boldest of black-faced type, he offered his services as "book, job and newspaper printer to the citizens of this Republic." Under his Mexican alias of José Manuel Bancs, he also offered to sell two "first rate leagues of land" which the State of Tamaulipas had granted him in Texas before the Revolution. Advertisers paid $1 for the first insertion of each "square" and one-third of that amount for subsequent insertions. The cost of the paper to readers might seem high—6½ cents a copy. Both sources of income might bring in a gross income of $200 to $300 a week. But the joker lay in the fact that this was in Texan currency. Before the end of the Republic, the exchange rate with the American dollar fell to as low as two cents.

Such was the paper published in the infancy of THE NEWS. It might well have been merely one more of the fly-by-night ventures which characterized early-day newspapers on Galveston Island,

then, and for many years afterward, noted as the graveyard of
Texas journalism. In the period of the Republic alone, eighteen
newspapers were started in that city. Bangs and French continued
daily publication for only two months. In June the paper slowed
down to tri-weekly publication, the form most frequently followed
by Texas newspapers until the end of the Civil War.

Bangs and French tired of THE NEWS and transferred it within
a few months to Michael Cronican and Wilbur F. Cherry. These
practical printers leased the type and press from Bangs for $4 a
month and the shack on the Strand from J. P. Davie for twice that
rent. Bangs stayed on the island for a year or so longer, starting,
among other journals, the *Texas Times,* the *Independent Chronicle* and the *Daily Globe.* On the outbreak of the Mexican War he
moved on to Corpus Christi, where, in January, 1846, he issued
the *Gazette,* first of the peripatetic "war journals." In a few
months he was at Matamoros, publishing the similar *Reveille,* after
which he fades into obscurity as he trails General Taylor and his
army across the brush country of Texas and northern Mexico. He
had little cause to imagine that his journalistic progeny would perpetuate his memory for more than a century.

Once Bangs cast off THE NEWS, its young life became more
precarious. Cronican sold his interest to Cherry, who thought he
had solved his problems when he hired a promising young New
York stater, George D. Sebring, as editor. But Sebring died within
a few months, before he ever got into harness. Competition was
keen from Bangs himself, not to mention Stuart with his powerful
Civilian. Cherry almost despaired of continuing publication when
B. F. Neal, founder of the ill-starred San Luis *Advocate* on the
lower end of Galveston Island, proposed an exchange of his equipment for half interest in the paper. This was a fateful move, for
it was through Neal that there was attracted to the enterprise the
man who would breathe new and enduring life into it—Willard
Richardson, the true founder of THE NEWS.

CHAPTER II

TEXAS ENTERS THE UNION

1843–1859

WILLARD RICHARDSON, who saved THE NEWS from extinction in its crucial second year, took the editorship in March, 1843. He at once launched his first crusade, that in behalf of the annexation of Texas. Not every novice could expect to be half as successful.

When Richardson began his long rule over the paper, it was an insignificant little sheet with a circulation of not more than 200, shaky both in business management and editorial policy, ready to flicker out at a moment's notice, as did all the other journals started by Samuel Bangs. Becoming owner as well as editor in 1845, he built it steadily in the fifteen years which led to the Civil War so that during the 1850's it emerged the most widely circulated, the wealthiest and the most influential paper in Texas.

This true founder of THE NEWS was able to gain these ends because of the temper of his mind and the steady flow of energy generated by it. Physically he was far from robust, but every ounce of bone and muscle counted. Tall, spare of build, with a mop of brown hair that early turned gray, he commanded the respect of his fellows more by the force of his intellect than by flashier surface qualities. His manner was quiet and tolerant; his manners, gravely courteous. A contemporary later described him as being "prudent, persevering, cool and indomitable, never caught by surprise nor unnerved by adversity." It is noteworthy that the principles and policies of newspaper direction first laid down by him have, with only minor changes, persisted throughout the history of THE NEWS.

☆

Like Bangs, Richardson was a New Englander by birth. Born in Massachusetts in 1802, of English and Irish stock, he was fully as adventurous. But where the printer went filibustering, the other youth enlisted in a more exciting war of ideas. Richardson ran away while a boy, seeing much of various cities and States, until he finally reached Sumter, South Carolina. There, during formative years of his life, he found a spiritual home. And, with the zeal known only by the convert, he swore allegiance to the social and political creed of the tidewater, planting South. Entering South Carolina College in 1827 as a junior, he was graduated one year later. In that atmosphere he became a lifelong disciple of John C. Calhoun and other spokesmen of the States' rights school.

The man who was to become "the First Journalist of Texas" began his career as a school teacher. For nine years he followed that calling. More important, perhaps, he fell in love. The object of his affections was Louisa Blanche Murrel, one of the belles of Sumter. Both were ambitious and headstrong, and there were quarrels. In 1837, at a moment when the course of true love seemed hopelessly blighted, the young school teacher saddled his horse and rode away to the new Republic of Texas.

One of the first friendships which Richardson made on reaching the new country was with Mirabeau B. Lamar, then its vice- president. Inevitably, their like ideas and common background drew them together. As a Lamar partisan and follower of Calhoun, Richardson found himself opposed to the more Jacksonian General Houston. And when Lamar advanced to the presidency, the school teacher turned to surveying and other government employ. In the meantime he had patched up the quarrel with his sweetheart by means of long, fervent letters, and at last she consented to marry him. But the mails were uncertain between Texas and the United States, and Richardson's service for the government caused him to travel far to the west in the unsettled country. One day in the summer of 1840 President Lamar opened a letter from "A Lady in Distress."

"I trust the purport of this letter will excuse in a measure the liberty I take in addressing you—it is written solely to ascertain the fate, if possible, of one who has ever represented you to me as a most gallant soldier and sensible man. Indeed I should presume from the manner in which he has invariably mentioned you in his letters, that he has the honor of a personal acquaintance with you. Should this be the case, I feel satisfied that his extraordinary merits and talents would be sufficient to recommend him to your sympathy and protection should he need them.

"This person, Sir, is Mr. Willard Richardson. He is very dear to me as an esteemed friend and from the fact that he was frequently corresponding with me until the 1st of November last, leading me more than ever to expect letters often, and since which time I have written nine letters to him . . . and having received no answer—I have great cause to apprehend that some serious misfortune has befallen him. I am racked with suspense and anxiety and conjecture. Sometimes I think he accompanied Col. Johnson and shared his dreadful fate. The recent hostilities of the Comanches lead me to fear he may be a prisoner. He surely would write if he could. . . . That you will comply with my request [for information] I have no doubt. A gentleman of your standing and character cannot resist the appeal of a lady in distress."

This was the sort of mission of state which, we may be sure, appealed to the romantic President of Texas. That Lamar responded gallantly and effectively may be taken for granted, for the lovers were soon in communication once more, Richardson returned a little later to bring Louisa Murrel to Texas as his bride, and Lamar remained until his death one of the most intimate friends of the family.

☆

Meanwhile, history was being made in Texas. When Lamar stepped out of the presidency in 1841, Richardson followed him into retirement. The younger man moved to Houston, where he opened a school for boys, while Lamar took up residence on Galveston Island. From the precincts of private life both were soon viewing—with the customary alarm—the course of Houston's second administration. In the summer of 1842, Dr. Francis Moore, Jr., was forced to visit his old home in New York State for a few months, and he invited Richardson to try his hand as editor of the *Telegraph* in his absence. The schoolmaster scored an instantaneous success on the editorial tripod. The clarity, vigor and polish of his writings attracted wide attention.

If the future of the infant NEWS was uncertain in the early part of 1843, that of Texas was equally precarious. Houston's complicated moves to force the hand of the United States on the annexation question, largely through threats to accept a British protectorate, had thus far been fruitless. To no one did they seem greater folly than to Richardson, who took Houston's pro-British sentiments at face value. He considered it providential, therefore, that he was asked out of a clear sky to become editor of THE NEWS at Galveston by B. F. Neal, his old friend from days in West Texas. He accepted with the full endorsement of his mentor, General Lamar.

Like a knight of old, Richardson rushed to the defense of what he believed to be the most sacred institution of America, Negro slavery. "In fact," Richardson confessed later, "it was mainly for the purpose of using our efforts to prevent the success of this abolition policy of England," in so far as Texas was concerned, that he accepted, "although we were embarked upon our dubious enterprise with many misgivings whether we should be able to sustain ourselves for one year or even one month."

With his views, Richardson was not extended a cordial reception in Galveston. The *Civilian* was now entrenched on the Island, and its pro-British editor enjoyed a wide popularity. Business and civic leaders tended to see their interests served better under at least the shadow of the Union Jack, rather than under the folds of the Star-Spangled Banner. Capt. Charles Elliott, the astute *chargé d'affaires* whom Her Majesty's Government had sent to Texas, spent most of his time in the seaport. He repeatedly assured his Prime Minister that Stuart's *Civilian* was "by far the best conducted Journal and of the most influence in the country." It was openly the organ of the strongest group on the island, the pro-British party which the envoy from the United States characterized as "proud, overbearing, impudent and ferocious."

But the new editor slashed away, denouncing the perfidious

aims of Albion in every issue. In December Lord Aberdeen admitted publicly what Richardson and the world had long professed to know—England was "constantly exerting herself to procure the general abolition of slavery throughout the world." Richardson was more racked with anxiety than before, and, after the new year, Lamar joined him in a demand for annexation.

The issue neared its climax as 1844 opened. Anson Jones, Houston's Secretary of State, has often been called "the architect of annexation." He had just taken office as the last President of Texas. Naturally, he continued Houston's same game, while the spotlight shifted rapidly between Texas, London, Mexico City and Washington. President Tyler on March 6 named John C. Calhoun as his Secretary of State. The South Carolinian now declared annexation to be an article of true faith for all Southerners:

"To our section," Calhoun said, "the present issue is a question of absolute self-preservation; so much so that it were infinitely better for us to abandon the Union than to give up Texas to become a colony of Great Britain." Let Stuart and other critics howl, Richardson could have basked in no greater approbation!

Victory came in 1845 when the Democratic party, led by James K. Polk and George M. Dallas, swept to triumph on the issue of Texas annexation. Now that "the aims of England to obtain control of this vast cotton producing region independent of the slave States of the Union" had been defeated, Richardson believed that slavery was safe forever in Texas.

In its elation THE NEWS was willing to forgive old foes in the glorious new era—all but one, General Houston. Its antagonism to Houston was revived by his prompt offer to serve Texas in the United States Senate. Houston asked for the office on the claim that he had brought about annexation.

"This is not true," Lamar declaimed in the columns of THE NEWS on November 22, recalling all his antagonist's moves since 1841. Then he added:

"I can perceive in this conduct nothing but a cold blooded betrayal of the people of Texas and a most insulting contempt of all official and moral obligation. . . . If [it] be not treason, I do not know what can constitute crime. General Houston, himself, is . . .

now endeavoring . . . to avert the odium which he perceives is about to overwhelm him. . . . The crowning act—consistent only with himself—is the climax of audacity. Does he blush at the exposure of his treason? No. He makes a merit of his guilt and, turning to the people he has dishonored, as if in mockery of all human virtue, he demands the patriot's reward for the traitor's crime."

But Houston, rather than Lamar, received the patriot's reward at the hands of the first Legislature of the State of Texas, and he hurried off to Washington to take his seat in the Senate. Any further evening of the score belonged to the future.

Entry into the American Union failed to lift all the worries of either Texas or THE NEWS. While the inflow of American currency cleared the commercial atmosphere somewhat, the outbreak of the war with Mexico retarded the arrival of new settlers in large numbers. The war itself was reported as well as the frail facilities of THE NEWS allowed; its only memorable dispatches were those of George Wilkins Kendall, a Texas ranger, who was America's first war correspondent. These were reprinted from Kendall's own New Orleans *Picayune,* two days by boat from Galveston. But it was not until about 1850 that the benefits of union began to be felt in Texas.

Immediately, however, politics of the United States came rolling over Texas, complicating the highly personalized disputes within the former republic. THE NEWS found itself confronted with the question: would it be Whig or Democratic? The latter party, obviously, stood in the higher favor in Texas. Richardson's own convictions were identical with those of its Southern leaders. But the editor made a novel answer. The time had come, he thought, to shunt political issues aside in favor of more important questions. The economic and cultural progress of the people cried out for first consideration. Whig or Democrat, THE NEWS would have neither of them; instead, "the true interests of the new State will be better promoted by keeping aloof from party contests." Then he laid down a policy of independent journalism, rarer then than now in Texas, which remained the basic attitude of the paper ever afterward. Summarized in the editor's own words during the first years of statehood, this creed read:

Independent of existing political organizations, we shall endeavor to do each even handed justice. The days of ultra-partisan journalism have passed; men of intelligence have discovered that the organ of party leaders or of political caucuses is not the most entitled to their confidence. We have never been able to learn that political discussions have any other effect than to make all parties still more obstinate and tenacious by holding to the opinion previously entertained by them. The same amount of talent, energy, zeal and personal sacrifice applied to objects of public enterprise and improvement would confer a degree of prosperity on the country exceeding anything heretofore known.

But Richardson, in the same confession of faith, did not climb too far out on the limb; he reserved full right, what with General Houston and other politicos abroad in the land, to speak up in meeting whenever he thought the occasion demanded:

Yet we have never pretended to publish what is called a *neutral* paper. We believe it our duty to have decided opinions upon all public questions and to declare them frankly, giving our reasons for them, regardless of whether they are considered as favoring one party or the other.

An era of great expansion in Texas opened in 1850, and Richardson was ready to put his theory of non-political journalism to the test. The State at that time received $10,000,000 from the United States in payment for territory to be used later in creating parts of the States of New Mexico, Arizona and Colorado. Texas also retained her public lands, in excess of 125,000,000 acres, which thus became a huge potential reservoir for the encouragement of internal development. Now there was a deluge of newcomers, most of them from the Old South, drawn to this last major cotton-growing area where Negro slavery was not only permitted but encouraged. As a result population nearly tripled—from 212,000 in 1850 to 604,000 at the end of the decade. Galveston, by the time of the outbreak of the Civil War, would rank as the chief gateway and business nerve center of the State. Although first in size with 6,000 inhabitants, it was trailed closely by Houston, whose lack of deepwater transport was its main handicap.

Richardson called first for a settlement of the old debt of the Republic, now that Uncle Sam had paid cash into the State's treasury. The debt, he argued, should be settled "on terms creditable to Texas and equitable to her creditors." This was vital to effect a softening of the harsh credit terms exacted of Texas merchants because of this past due obligation. When the total sum of $11,500,000, scaled down to $8,500,000, was finally liquidated, The News was satisfied and inclined somewhat to pat itself on the head. "A great many of our fellow citizens have differed with us on this question," the paper said, "but we feel assured that time will establish the correctness of our views."

An even more important reform sought by Richardson was the repeal of the State prohibition of banks. This Jacksonian distrust of the financier had been brought over bodily from the Constitution of the Republic. The issue came to a head when an ambitious young attorney general won a $100,000 suit in a lower court against R. & D. G. Mills, the oldest firm of cotton factors and commission merchants in Galveston, who were charged with the crime of circulating notes of the State Bank of Mississippi as currency in Texas. The News branded both suit and law as absurdities, since similar paper for years had been circulating by the hundreds of thousands of dollars in all parts of the State. Opposition to repeal found its strongest voice in the Austin *State Gazette,* edited by the magnetic, but highly personal, John Marshall, who was also chairman of the State Democratic Executive Committee.

The *State Gazette* [commented The News] is hunting through the writings of the last century for arguments against banking and produces some extracts from Thomas Jefferson and Albert Gallatin, who knew as much about the modern system of banking as they did about power presses and the magnetic telegraph.

This slur at the possible human frailty of the immortal Jefferson infuriated the defenders of the status quo, and one of the statesmen of Western Texas, addressing the Travis County Democracy, charged that "but for The Galveston News we should have heard nothing about banks. That paper can be bought at any

time for six-bits." In reply THE NEWS reproduced this comment
"for the amusement of our readers" and added that the politician
"gives our six-bit paper undue importance on the subject of banking." Shortly afterward THE NEWS reprinted an article from the
Dallas *Herald,* a paper started in 1849 in the frontier village named
in honor of George Mifflin Dallas, with the observation that "this
paper seems to understand the subject much more clearly than
some other journals of larger pretensions which we might mention." The repeal movement was soon engulfed, though, by the
greater issue of slavery and secession—out of which maelstrom,
curiously enough, banks were to emerge, at last, legitimate in
Texas.

☆

Closer to Richardson's heart than either the debt or banking
questions lay the problem of railroad building in Texas. With a
river system not navigable much beyond tidewater, the State must
have rail lines if there was to be any unified growth of the vast
prairie country.

The Republic of Texas had chartered numerous railroad companies, but it was not until 1851, when there were already thousands of miles of steel highways in the older sections of the United
States, that construction took tangible form in Texas. First construction was on the Buffalo Bayou, Brazos & Colorado, today a
thirty-minute ride on the transcontinental system of the Southern
Pacific. By 1855, thirty-two miles had been built from Harrisburg
on the bayou to Richmond on the Brazos, and its first locomotive,
the General Sidney Sherman, was hauling a fleet of cars on a regular daily schedule. A year later Houston citizens voted a one-cent
tax on themselves to build the Houston Tap Railroad, an eight-
mile connection with the B. B. B. & C. Railroad.

Largely through the enterprise of Paul Bremond, a pioneer merchant of Houston (who ultimately was rewarded for his enthusiasm by bankruptcy), work on the State's second common carrier
was started northward from Houston in 1853. This was the Galveston & Red River, which had Colbert's Ferry 400 miles away

on the border with what was then the Indian Territory as its objective. The backers soon changed its name to the Houston & Texas Central, serving notice thereby that they would not carry its terminus southward to Galveston.

THE NEWS reported the first railroad accident in Texas on June 10, 1856. It was on "Paul Bremond's Road," at a time when it operated only twenty-five miles out of the city. Its one locomotive was the Ebenezer Allen, named for an attorney general of the Republic.

"The train was returning from Cole's Stand on the 8th instant," Galveston readers learned, "when three cars were thrown off the track by a fence rail laid across the rails. There were quite a number of persons on the cars, perhaps seventy-five or one hundred, about half of whom jumped or were thrown from the cars. Fortunately no one was dangerously hurt. We hope the perpetrator may be discovered and summarily punished."

Small as these two carriers were, they began to divert to Houston cotton and other traffic which Richardson believed should flow to Galveston. His fellow townsmen were slower to take up the new fad of railroads; they could not see rail lines for the water surrounding the island. But, by 1855, the editor of THE NEWS persuaded Galvestonians that they must meet this competition from Houston. Consequently, building of the Galveston, Houston and Henderson Railroad was started from Virginia Point, immediately across the bay on the mainland. It would not extend the fifty miles to Houston until the end of the decade, and its value to Galveston was further lost by the failure to build a bridge or causeway to bring trains into the city proper.

Although railroads were proposed lavishly in other parts of Texas (even hamlets such as Dallas and Tyler proposed to connect themselves with bands of steel), most of them remained largely on paper or in the dreams of their promoters. Their advocates at last turned to the State for subsidies, and the Legislature responded with donations of eight sections of land for each mile of line completed. Still building lagged. Then the railroad men returned, urging that the grants be doubled. Again, the Legislature complied, but to the State's disappointment construction still faltered.

Richardson grew impatient. Settlement of the interior within a 300-mile radius of Galveston failed to wait on railroad building. Particularly were the north-central prairies, with their rich, black-waxy soil, becoming a new Eldorado equally capable of producing wheat and cotton abundantly. Dallas, Fort Worth, Sherman, Waco, McKinney, Waxahachie, and Denton were but a few names of settled communities in a region which had been cleared of the Indians only about ten years before. "Dallas bids fair to become a considerable inland town," one of its prophets reported to the editor of THE NEWS in 1859. Dependent chiefly upon slow and costly ox-team freighting, this whole area was rapidly being cut off from the Texas seacoast by the costliness of its transportation. Richardson was shocked to learn about this time that fully half of the 300,000-bale cotton crop of the State was already moving overland to Red River points, Shreveport and Jefferson Landing on Caddo Lake, thence by water to New Orleans, "where it is not known as Texas cotton at all."

When, therefore, railroad promoters converged on Austin for the third request in 1856, demanding an additional bonus of a State bond of $9,000 a mile, THE NEWS went on the warpath. Richardson had lost all faith in the ability or intention of "the railroad men," and he was tired of their delays and excuses. Now he produced instead his own solution, a scientifically designed plan for a network of 1,200 miles of railway, to be coordinated with a river-and-intracoastal canal system, which the State of Texas itself would build and own.

Richardson opened his campaign for this State system with a seven-column map on the first page, April 22, 1856. Then he followed up with a running fire of news stories, editorials and special articles. It was such a crusade for internal development as fired the soul of the editor and proprietor. He combed the State-owned railroad experience of the world for support, citing the examples of Prussia abroad, and of Georgia closer at home.

An inevitable consequence resulting from this peculiar character of ownership [said the editorial in ascribing Georgia's position as the

Empire State of the South to its publicly owned rail carriers] is that the roads are managed economically, honestly and efficiently, the directors being immediately responsible to the people, their neighbors and fellow citizens, who as the stockholders are vigilant supervisors and guardians of their own interests. . . . The railroads of Georgia are model works. They are owned exclusively by the people of the State, so that whatever profits are realized by them inure to the benefit of the home population and are not sent out of the State to swell the fortunes of foreign capitalists.

So enthusiastic did the editor become that, leaving others in charge at Galveston, he went to Austin to lobby in person before the Legislature. But his State Plan met powerful opposition beside that of the railroad promoters. In 1854 Dr. Francis Moore, Jr., had been succeeded by another able editor of the Houston *Telegraph*. This was the aggressive E. H. Cushing, who soon ranked with Richardson and Stuart as one of the chief editors of Texas. The alert Cushing at once pointed out in his paper that Richardson's plan, as the map showed clearly, would make Galveston the hub of this perfect transport system. In trip-hammer style Cushing pounded the prejudices of the interior against the largest city of Texas, declaring that "the people of Galveston have little right to claim the benefits of railroads. The only work they have done was to plan and issue immense schemes which they intended to lay upon the shoulders of the State to work out, while they would not touch any practical work with so much as their little finger."

Thus the State Railroad Plan went down to defeat at Austin as the Legislature adopted the bond loan plan instead. Deeply disappointed, Richardson was not disillusioned; a year before he had seen the bill to create a State University—such as his friend Lamar had advocated—lost because "the railroad men consider that $2,000,000 School Fund as their own money." The editor predicted then that "the noble project of a State University will fall between the fire of other forces contending for the spoils of the Treasury and the public domain." In such pessimistic mood he counseled Galvestonians to nurse their wounds and to remember that "although Galveston cannot now do much to advance herself beyond pointing to the advantages of her position, the day will yet come when she will not be so feeble in regard to State enterprise or legislative influence." But defeat and the *Telegraph's* taunt had their result—the citizens of Galveston promptly voted tax funds with which to build the railroad bridge to the mainland by a score of 741 to 11, "the most decisive vote ever given in this city."

☆

The paper which Willard Richardson published both to reflect and to influence the life of Texas during the 1850's was a more impressive organ than the near-folder issued by Samuel Bangs.

The main edition of State-wide circulation was the weekly, a four-page paper whose sheets were slightly larger than a standard newspaper page of today. Physically, the edition was four times larger than the original NEWS and carried ten times more news, editorial, and advertising matter. Printed in six-point type on a good grade of rag paper, it was issued each Tuesday morning at the publication office in Tremont Street between the Strand and Mechanic, where the plant had been moved in 1845. The weekly was largely an accumulative edition of material carried over in type from the smaller tri-weekly editions which served readers primarily in Galveston and immediate vicinity. To print it more readily, a power press was bought in 1855, thus relegating to the job office the original hand press inherited from the paper's infancy.

For all of Richardson's devotion to progress and internal development, he made the gathering and presentation of news his first and major objective. But there were few newsgathering facilities of the kind common today in Texas before the Civil War. With only a few miles of disjointed railroad and no working telegraph either within the State or connecting with the outside world, mail boats and stage lines furnished the speediest channels. The eastern half of the United States had been fairly well laced together by trunk telegraph lines by the middle of the century, and New Orleans, accordingly, became the nearest center of wire news for Texas. By weekly, then tri-weekly mail boats, THE NEWS, the *Civilian* and the *Telegraph* were enabled, simply by culling from the newspapers of that city, to present the latest telegraphic intelli-

gence some forty-eight or fifty hours later. Toward the middle of
the decade the time between New Orleans and Galveston was
almost halved, due to the westward progress of the New Orleans
& Opelousas Railroad. When this line reached Berwick's Bay (at
what is today known as Morgan City) Cornelius Vanderbilt put
a line of steamers in service from that point to Galveston, Indianola
and Powderhorn. By this combined rail-and-water route, passengers and mail could now reach Galveston from New Orleans in
the record time of twenty-two and one-half hours—a great saving
over the all-water route still followed by Charles Morgan's rival
fleet of steamers.

Richardson's first circulation war came with Cushing and the
Telegraph. In 1858 the Houston paper began reaching up-State
points before its rival. The editor of THE NEWS investigated, only
to learn of a new trick in journalism.

"The Postmaster at Houston replies to the strictures of THE
NEWS," Richardson explained to his readers, "that the *Telegraph*
is printing its Wednesday issue on Tuesday."

It was a game that two could play at, but Richardson preferred
to scoop his competitor more legitimately. Soon Cushing was
squawking.

"The *Telegraph* does not like to see such an arrangement of the
mails as enables THE NEWS to publish the Governor's message
before it was received at Houston, one day nearer the seat of government," wrote Richardson. "There is nothing like enterprise,
neighbor, to surmount the difficulties of the season."

Richardson displayed his news conservatively. Headlines might
be several banks deep, but they were rarely more than a column
in width. Usually they bore such one-line titles as "The Banking
Question" or "A Most Melancholy Death." General and commercial news held the right-of-way in the paper. But THE NEWS
faithfully reflected life in Texas, and that life was not wholly concerned with the price of cotton, the repeal of banking or even
railroad construction. Crimes, as well as the lighter sides of
existence, had their interest to contemporaries; and Richardson
reported them adequately.

Because distance, perhaps, lends glamor, news of violence got a better play in Richardson's journal the farther from Galveston it originated. Grimes County obliged frequently in this matter. Under "Fatal Affray," one might read of a murderous *rencontre* between two gentlemen, in which, "as usual, whiskey stimulated the bloody work." Or, under the heading, "Murder at Prairie Plains," the reader could read of the affair at the race track near Kellum Springs in which two other gentlemen literally cut each other to pieces "in regard to the bets."

Nearby might be the eye-catching headline, "A Reverend Scoundrel." This item from a town on the northern frontier of Texas told of the impostures of one Christopher Columbus J——. He pretended, it was said, to be a gentleman of the cloth and inflicted his "prolix, verbose and arrogant sermons" upon the good people of the town for almost a year, until he disappeared one day, taking along the wife of one of his flock. The next issue of THE NEWS, for those still interested, reported that the scoundrel had been caught, tried and freed in an adjoining county, only to be shot dead by his victim's brother as he left the courthouse. This rustic avenger delivered himself up to the law, but he went unpunished because "public opinion was in his favor."

More fatal than the accident on Paul Bremond's railroad was this intelligence, reprinted from the Rusk *Democrat*:

DEATH FROM TEXAS WHISKEY

Mr. John A. C. W——, agent for a patent plow, died on the 4th inst. at the Verandah House in this place of *delirium tremens*. Such occurrences are not rare here of late. Such whiskey as is retailed throughout the country generally is bad and poisonous enough not only to produce *delirium tremens* in the human subject, but villainous enough to insure *hydrophobia* in a dog—But a few weeks ago several gentlemen were poisoned near unto death in San Augustine by drinking some of the miserable stuff.

THE NEWS issued its first extra on Sunday morning, May 31, 1857. It gave details of the burning of the Charles Morgan steamer *Louisiana,* with a loss of fifty-six lives. The tragedy occurred in sight, only five miles off Galveston on the Gulf side, just before midnight. On November 17 of the same year Richardson issued

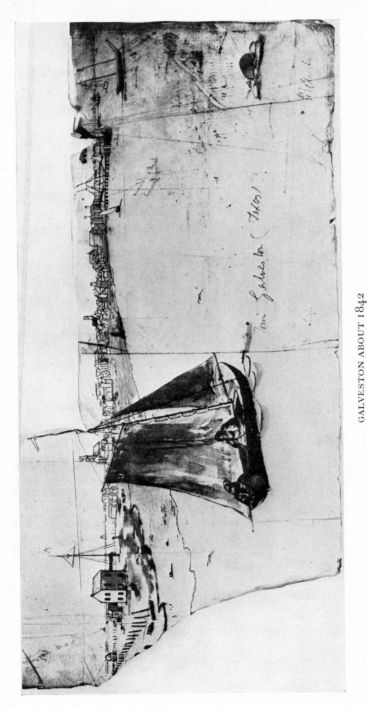

GALVESTON ABOUT 1842

A contemporary sketch by William Bollaert. Courtesy of the Newberry Library, Chicago, from its Edward E. Ayer Collection

THE NEWS AT ITS FOUNDING IN GALVESTON

Facsimile of the first page of the earliest known issue, No. 8 in Volume 1, from which the origin of the institution has been fixed as of April 11, 1842 another extra. This related the frightful intelligence that the steamer *Galveston* of the Vanderbilt line to Berwick's Bay had been rammed on the high seas by her sister ship, the *Opelousas*. The first vessel sank within twenty minutes with an even greater number of casualties. The best known casualty was General James Hamilton of South Carolina, en route to Austin in connection with the settlement of the debt of the Republic of Texas—which debt he had helped to contract through Biddle's Bank in Philadelphia almost twenty years before.

Between reports of violence on one side, and of civic and commercial progress on the other, Richardson still found space to chronicle the social and intellectual movements of the period.

Society in the capital letter sense rarely paraded in the newspapers; the canons of good form did not permit it. Sometimes, however, these affairs took on such public importance, as when Col. Michel B. Menard, the founder of Galveston, and his "lady" entertained, or the Artillery Company gave its second anniversary ball, as to make them matters of public record. Even then, no woman guest was ever identified in print more openly than as Miss L—— or Mrs. Col. W——.

The Texas of the 'Fifties had its theatricals, and Richardson believed in encouraging such entertainment in spite of the objections of blue-nosed readers. Blakeley's troupe of minstrels, "just returning from a triumphant tour of Western Texas"; Mr. Stephen Massett, the celebrated vocalist and composer in concert; these and others found a welcome in his columns. When Mrs. Ada Logan opened the dramatic season in January, 1859, with a gala performance of "Agnes de Vere," followed by a farce, "The Irish Tutor," the editor gave up mere pleasantries of reporting to write his first serious criticism:

We found the low comedian to be humourous without vulgarity; the chamber-maid pert and lively, with perhaps just a little too much swing; the juvenile tragedy, correct and gentlemanly; and the other characters in their respective roles well up to the requirements of the occasion. Altogether, it is a very pleasant little company and we wish them every success.

One of the great attractions of the decade, a howling success from New York to New Orleans, played Galveston in the same period. This was Donetti's Troupe of Acting Monkeys, Dogs and Goats, to which "collection of learned animals,"—the press agent "assured the most fastidious" upon his word as a disciple of Barnum—"they may lend their countenance with entire safety and propriety." Richardson found the monkeys, especially, entertaining. In his account, entitled "Dogs, Monkeys and Men," he conveyed much of his amusement:

. . . Do humans eat, drink, laugh, chatter and cheat each other? So did the monkeys. . . . In a word, they did everything that could be expected of sensitive and well bred ladies and gentlemen in such a place. . . . Were it not for the caudal adornment so universal among them, we might commiserate their wild and senseless heathenism, as we do that of the inhabitants of New Zealand and the South Sea Islands, whom they so much resemble. We might commission regiments of missionaries, like Donetti, for instance, to teach them the arts and vices of civilization. . . . It is even possible that Donetti, by applying all his powers to the education of one monkey, might at last render him fit to run as a candidate for the Presidential chair—provided the said chair had a hole bored in the bottom of it.

If the editor of THE NEWS seemed at times flip and even cynical, he could be graver on more serious matters. Except for the subject of slavery, the one topic tabooed in the South, he believed in the widest possible freedom of speech and intellect. He encouraged all sorts of public lecturers, including the itinerant "professors" who revealed the mysteries of spiritualism, phrenology and other manifestations of new thought. His attendance on and report of these open forums brought down criticism on his head from at least one rival. When a certain Professor Fowler arrived to speak on mental and physical hygiene, the conductor of THE NEWS was pleased with the series. Stuart in the *Civilian* had held his tongue while THE NEWS allowed the humbug of spiritualism to be outlined in its columns, but now, the editor of the *Civilian* was convinced, Richardson had grown "reckless of truth, morality and the decencies of life;" he had openly espoused these health talks, which had been given before mixed audiences of men and women! The News made its own defense:

We attended several of these lectures and found them highly instructing and interesting, especially those which treated of the general physiological laws of health, the moral and intellectual education of the young, of the various causes of domestic and social unhappiness and of the proper means of securing the refined enjoyments of the home. . . .

We are told that it is highly indecent for the ladies of Galveston to attend lectures on female complaints, to learn of the laws of health and the proper means of preventing the afflictions under which so many are suffering. But while our Contemporary thinks it so improper for our wives and daughters to know anything of their complaints and their appropriate remedies, he does not hesitate to recommend to them such books as "The Anecdotes of Love," by Lola Montez!

The advertising in Richardson's paper, both in volume and form, was a marked advance over that in the original News. It was, likewise, vastly more revenue bearing.

While patent medicines occupied a fair part of the space, they were not predominant. It is noteworthy that Boston, which supplied most of the medical copy, was not far behind in the amount of advertisements of its book publishers. If Dr. J. C. Ayers' "Pills That Are Pills" were urged upon readers of The News with the endorsement of Senator Edward Everett, the Bishop of Boston and the Chief Justice of the Supreme Court of Massachusetts, Little, Brown & Co. took even more space to urge the latest work of Louis Agassiz, or a new law book endorsed by Chief Justice Roger Taney of the Supreme Court of the United States. If S. Swan & Co. of Augusta, Georgia, were heavy and consistent users of space to advertise their many lotteries, Albert Weber of Philadelphia, C. Meyer of New York and T. Gilbert & Co. of Boston required even more white space to publicize their grand, parlor grand and square pianofortes.

There is a strangely modern note in much of this antebellum copy. Who, for instance, could resist this sales appeal?

A Perfumed Breath—What lady or gentleman would remain under the curse of a disagreeable breath when using the "Balm of a Thousand Flowers" as a dentifrice would not only render it sweet but leave the teeth white as alabaster?

Many persons do not know their breath is bad and the subject is so delicate their friends will never mention it. Pour a single drop of the "Balm" on your tooth brush and wash the teeth night and morning.

Advertising by the middle of the decade was producing a gross revenue of about $10,000 a year for the weekly. Circulation had risen steadily to some 3,500 subscribers. In December, 1857, as a bold defiance of the panic then raging throughout the country, THE NEWS raised its advertising rates 20 per cent. Yet such was the momentum and value of the paper to readers and advertisers that it had no visible effect on business or news carried in its columns.

Richardson alone could not carry the full burden of this expanding business. In 1852 David Richardson, a native of the Isle of Man (and no relation), joined in the partnership of W. & D. Richardson, which lasted until the second year of the Civil War. The newcomer took over the functions of both advertising and circulation managers, traveling most of the year in the interest of one or the other jobs.

There were more additions to the staff. In 1855, L. K. Preston, who had struggled against the pole-chopping tendencies of farmers to operate a telegraph line between Houston and Galveston, gave up the fight and joined THE NEWS as second traveling representative. If David needed an assistant, so did Willard, and intermittently the editor was aided by one C. D. Morgan, a competent reporter but one burdened with poor health and a bilious sense of humor. One of Morgan's articles, written from the popular health resort at Sour Lake where he had been sent to recuperate, managed to slip by the editor's attention. A purported exposé of how and why the mineral waters got their taste and odor, the article so incensed the resort owner that Morgan was forced to take an extended leave of absence in the North.

☆

So prosperous, indeed, was THE NEWS as the decade neared its end that Richardson built a new plant in Market Street between Twenty-second and Tremont. It was one of the four-story, iron-front buildings—with sides of brick imported from England, and trimmed with genuine marble—which were a source of civic pride to all Texans.

Here in its new home THE NEWS took a fresh lease on life, installed its second power press, and prepared for the even greater responsibilities which it expected the 1860's to bring it. The paper knew from whence it had started, and it was equally confident of where it was headed. Only, it could not anticipate the twists of fate itself, as Richardson was soon to find out.

CHAPTER III

GENERAL HOUSTON AND "THE TEXAS ALMANAC"

1845–1861

THE DULL red glow from the embers of the slavery question lights the story of Texas and THE NEWS from annexation onward.

For a time the subject of abolition did indeed seem extinguished, settled presumably by the Compromise Measures of 1850. But soon it was smouldering again, with smoke and sparks growing ever more plentiful as the 1850's advanced, until the agitation finally burst into the flames of the Irrepressible Conflict itself.

On one subject Richardson was fully in accord with Hamilton Stuart—the untouchability of the South's "peculiar institution." This taboo extended even to trivialities such as, for instance, comment on a trashy novel. One day the editor of THE NEWS picked up a new romance, "Mabel Vaughn," and skimmed through it with interest. But, in hurrying to find out how the tale ended, he skipped two pages near the conclusion. Then he wrote his review. Richardson was overwhelmed to learn in the next issue of Stuart's *Civilian* that he had approved a book charged with abolitionist sentiment. For, embarrassingly enough, he found on rechecking that he had overlooked page 427, on which a minor character denounced in passing the institution of slavery. "Of course," Richardson hastened to correct in the next weekly issue, "this is enough to condemn the book utterly with Southern readers."

The blind spot obscured a more fundamental principle. As early as July 8, 1856, THE NEWS reported a mass meeting of citizens who deliberated "the propriety of permitting Lorenzo Sherwood," a member of the Texas Legislature, to defend his Austin activities before a Galveston audience. The result was a communication to Sherwood signed by Hamilton Stuart, Col. M. B. Menard and others, delivered through the press of the city:

. . . Your right, in common with every other citizen, to free opinion, free discussion and the largest liberty of self-defence, is fully recognized [the letter stated] and will be respected.

But there is one subject connected with your course in the Legislature—that of Slavery—on which neither you, nor any one entertaining your views, will be permitted to appear before the community in a public manner. That your views on that subject are dangerous and unsound is the fixed belief of this community. Your introduction of the subject in any manner will be the prompt signal for consequences, to which we need not allude.

The one lawmaker of Texas whom neither THE NEWS nor the *Civilian* nor any citizen could ever intimidate was the senior United States Senator, Sam Houston. He was already annoying many of his constituents with his anti-secessionist, with what they construed as his anti-slavery, acts and sentiments. And THE NEWS was more than willing to revive its old quarrel with the Hero of San Jacinto. (Richardson had said that he refused to publish a *neutral* paper.)

Senator Houston told his fellow townsmen of Huntsville in September, 1856, that he voted to abolish slavery in the District of Columbia because "I did not desire to see the Federal metropolis a slave mart." Outraged as was the Huntsville *Item*, which declared "a Texas Senator who will thus cater to the fanatical sentiment of abolitionists . . . is unfit to hold his position any longer," THE NEWS more calmly called the statement to "the candid attention of Southern men" and asked their reflection upon it. Houston, for his part, replied by voting in the Senate to allow Kansas to decide whether it would be slave or free territory. This set the blood of many Texans to boiling, and the columns of THE NEWS, specially those for letters from readers, became more agitated.

It was the Senator's turn to be annoyed, and in October before an audience at Livingston in Polk County he denounced THE NEWS as a "filthy, lying sheet." He went on to say that "its editor has done everything mean and contemptible except stealing. He would have done that had he had the moral courage and had the nights been long enough to conceal his thefts." To which THE NEWS replied, with a show of good humor :

. . . As regards the abuse bestowed upon us on this and so many other occasions, we have only to reply by reminding General Houston that he appears to verify his own favorite and oft repeated anecdote about the butting ram. There is even now but little of him left beside the tail.

This last taunt struck home, for Houston had hoped that year to win the Presidency of the United States. He had failed to get as far as the Democratic nomination, since James Buchanan was chosen instead ; somewhat desperate, he had flirted for a time with the new American, or Know Nothing party. THE NEWS from the start had opposed the Know Nothing movement as subversive of the true spirit of Americanism. Beside its own editorial campaign, it published a series of articles by Anson Jones, the last President of the Republic, then living in Washington County. These exposures of "the Anti-Catholic, Anti-Foreign and Anti-Slavery movement in the United States" had done much to check its spread in Texas. Nor would THE NEWS lose any chance to tar the Senator with his alleged Know Nothing connections. But Houston refused to concede victory to his enemies in Texas. As if in response to the taunt, he announced early in 1857 that he would be a candidate for Governor. When the Democratic party nominated Hardin R. Runnels, instead, he decided to appeal from the party convention to the people themselves, offering himself as an independent Democratic candidate. He did not resign as United States Senator.

Joined by the Houston *Telegraph,* if not the Galveston *Civilian,* Richardson opposed the election of Houston. At first, THE NEWS was mild in its manner. As late as May, it confessed that while its support of Runnels was open, "the salvation of the State does not depend upon a choice," and that it would not devote much space to the campaign since "the people are quite as competent as we can pretend to be to make a choice." Houston brought his canvass into Galveston on the eighteenth of the same month. THE NEWS reported the speech in part as follows:

According to previous announcement, General Houston addressed a respectable assemblage last night at Morian Hall. His speech was characterized by his usual egotism and personality. He entered into a labored defense of his course upon the Kansas-Nebraska Bill. . . .

He was especially troubled about THE GALVESTON NEWS and threw forth insinuations in relation to its conductors which . . . were gratuitous . . . and which were so pronounced to his face. . . . General Houston's indecent attack upon the senior Editor of THE NEWS would do no harm in this community except to himself—it was as vulgar as it was un-Christian.

But the war was on and THE NEWS now gave Houston more than he had asked for, opening its columns to a remorseless analysis of all his public errors. From the Dallas *Herald* it reprinted Houston's campaign speech in northern Texas in July, in which the Senator was reported to have "denounced and villified" General J. Pinckney Henderson and other patriots of the Texas Revolution. From other points in the campaign, it related other hot-tempered denunciations. Then, on July 25, under the heading "Choose Ye," THE NEWS made a final, pre-election appeal. By this time, the paper felt that "such a calamity as the election of Sam Houston to the Executive Chair and the consequent endorsement of his recent votes and speeches in the Senate . . . is too much for our credulity to entertain." It concluded by predicting that "the people of Texas will rise in the majesty of their power on the Third of August and pronounce a just and righteous verdict."

And when the third of August rolled by, THE NEWS' prophecy was borne out. For, when the returns trickled in, it was seen that Runnels had won over Houston by some 10,000 votes majority. Richardson and his journal took much credit for this first, and only, defeat of Houston on an appeal directly to the people of Texas.

In the closing hours of the campaign, newspaper readers of Texas were startled to learn that General Thomas J. Rusk, Houston's colleague at Washington since 1846, had killed himself in his home in Nacogdoches on July 30. An extra of the Nacogdoches

Chronicle brought first details of this "Most Melancholy Event" to Galveston. Rusk's wife had died only a few months before, and he had never recovered from the shock of it. Immediately Richardson's attention was drawn to the necessity of having a biographical sketch of Rusk, the first major Revolutionary survivor to die, prepared for the 1858 TEXAS ALMANAC. In fact, with the campaign behind him, he had a great deal to do in completing this forthcoming volume.

THE TEXAS ALMANAC, the first volume of which had appeared in January, 1857, was peculiarly the embodiment in more permanent form of all that Willard and David Richardson had been trying to accomplish in the weekly and tri-weekly editions of THE NEWS. It was to serve first of all as a yearly report on the material and social progress rapidly being made in Texas "from the seaboard to the mountains and from the Red River to the Rio Grande." Conceived originally as a substitute for older almanacs of the United States, whose calendars of planting, details of longitude and latitude and other features were poorly adapted to Texas, it soon outgrew these simpler pastoral functions. THE ALMANAC at once became a cyclopedia of Texas, valuable alike to planter and business man at home and destined by wide distribution throughout the United States and foreign countries to encourage immigration to Texas.

Willard Richardson, like his friend Lamar and so many other early day Texans, had a weakness for history. Even Houston, who preferred to make it, ended by devoting much time, thought and energy to preparing a proper chronicle for posterity. And, among the seven aims of THE NEWS listed daily in the masthead, were its dedications (1) "to miscellaneous articles in reference to our past" and (2) "to biographical sketches of great men of this and other countries." Carried over into the design of THE ALMANAC, this historical interest suddenly became entangled in the long controversy between Richardson and General Houston, with a result which was extraordinarily bitter. Never before nor since would Texans witness such an acrimonious dispute between a journalist and a statesman.

The first edition of THE TEXAS ALMANAC had contained a

running summary of Texas history from La Salle's landing in 1685 to the coming of the Austins. The edition sold 10,000 copies, and a greater number was promised for 1858. In the meantime, the biography of General Rusk, which touched off the explosion, was completed. It was written, most probably, by General Sidney Sherman, a member of the anti-Houston party then living in Galveston. Characteristically, Richardson made the sketch do double duty; he ran it first in the columns of THE NEWS in the fall of 1857.

Widely disseminated, the sketch created a State-wide sensation, for it ripped directly into General Houston's reputation as the Hero of San Jacinto. It began, conventionally enough, with regret over "the sudden and untimely death" of Houston's colleague in the Senate. But soon it was plowing up old memories, recalling the retreat of Houston and his army after the Alamo had fallen and after the massacre of Fannin and his men.

. . . General Houston intended to proceed beyond the Trinity and perhaps as far as the Sabine in that direction [the sketch related] but the rank and file of the army, as well as a large majority of the officers, were desirous of meeting the enemy as soon as possible and of putting a stop to his further devastating progress. In this sentiment Colonel Rusk participated, and although inclined to give Houston, as far as possible, the direction of the tactics . . . in this instance he as [Secretary of War] gave orders to take the road to Harrisburg, which Houston did not endorse. . . .

The order was received by the whole Army with the greatest enthusiasm . . . as it gave hope of a battle with the advancing Mexicans—a hope which was gloriously fulfilled at San Jacinto a few days thereafter.

Thus it will be perceived that the most decisive event in the history of Texas was brought about by the wise assumption of responsibility by Col. Rusk at a time when the destinies of the Republic hung in dubious suspense. . . .

Shocking as this interpretation of Houston's Fabian policy of retreat seemed to Houston's partisans, the following account of the Battle of San Jacinto itself appeared more outrageous:

The events of April 21, 1836, are too familiar to all to need recapitulation. The part which Col. Rusk performed upon the battlefield was second to none in point of wisdom, courage and effective service. While the Texian columns were advancing towards the enemy's front, the Commander-in-Chief received a wound in the ankle and immediately called on the troops to halt. But Rusk, perceiving that to halt at that moment would be certain ruin, rode forward and cried, "Push on, boys, push on!" And they did push on, under the lead of this gallant Secretary, shouting "Remember the Alamo!", "Remember Goliad!" And they won a victory in an hour which has secured freedom and prosperity to an empire.

It was the mission of Rusk to win laurels on that day and for other men to wear them. . . .

The Dallas *Herald* among others reproduced the Rusk biography in full. While complimentary, the editor of that frontier journal questioned the account of Rusk's part in the battle. THE NEWS' version, he pointed out, ran counter to that in Yoakum's History, then just recently published. Richardson called on Lamar to settle the question. That Revolutionary figure had been withdrawn from public life for many years and in his home retreat near Richmond-on-the-Brazos had renewed his interest in the writing of Texas history. President Buchanan had just offered him a diplomatic post in Nicaragua, which he was to accept as his last public service, but he paused long enough to say through THE NEWS:

I am as confident as I am of my own existence that General Rusk was never invited to any command at San Jacinto by General Houston, and that the only authority he is known to have exercised on that occasion was when he assumed the responsibility of continuing the battle against the remonstrances of the Commander-in-Chief, who had ordered a halt.

Rushed into THE ALMANAC, the sketch played a large part in the immense sale of that edition. Twenty-five thousand copies were sold prompty and the Richardsons began to plan for an edition of 30,000 in 1859. They also ordered another power press, "expressly for our ALMANAC, so that it will not interfere with publication of our paper."

When the edition of 1859 appeared it was even more critical, in historical and biographical material, of Sam Houston. The summary of Texas history by now had reached the Revolution, and Houston was presented in far from flattering light in it. But a 24-page narrative of the campaign and battle of San Jacinto, written by another eye-witness, Dr. N. D. Labadie of Galveston, proved even spicier. This reiterated most of the attacks on Houston's generalship, adding that the victory was won "almost against the will of the Commander who, when he could no longer put off the action, finally yielded to the incessant demands of both officers and men to be allowed to meet the enemy."

☆

Goaded beyond endurance by these attacks in THE NEWS and THE ALMANAC, Houston finally gave his answer. He needed little incitement since the Legislature of Texas had already pushed him aside as Senator. He chose a spot that should be both dramatic and resounding, the floor of the United States Senate. There, on February 28, 1859, Houston made his farewell address, devoting all his time to an excoriation of "the author of this ALMANAC" and to an impassioned defense of his own conduct at San Jacinto.

Stating that he had been careless in replying to all the false insinuations that had been published about his military career, Houston added that although he was not a writer of history he felt called upon by a recent publication to refute its slanders in behalf of his posterity:

I find a production purporting to be a TEXAS ALMANAC which contains what is said to be a narrative of the Campaign of San Jacinto. . . . The object was to assail my reputation and to show that the Battle of San Jacinto and all the preceding acts of generalship connected with that event had been forced upon the general and that really on that occasion he had acted with a delicacy unbecoming a rugged soldier. . . .

The truth of history has been perverted and the opposite has been asserted. Contributions of material have been made to THE ALMANAC; it was concocted and arranged and then given to the world in such a shape that the dissemination of the calumny throughout the United States must affect the individual to whom it was directed and make some impression upon him and destroy his reputation.

The author of this ALMANAC, Willard Richardson—I must immortalize him—if reports be true, and I have no reason to doubt them, would have been dignified by a penitentiary residence, had he been assigned to his proper place, owing to the peccadilloes with which he has been charged. Although they have not been smothered and done away with, his character is not vindicated to the world. He still goes on from sin to sin, from abuse to slander. . . .

Houston was not ready to end the dispute here. He would give Willard Richardson and all his old enemies a trouncing to remember him by. He returned to Texas, where he announced he would again run for the governorship as an independent, Jackson Democrat. His opponent, Governor Runnels, was even then assured of the regular Democratic nomination. The canvass began early in the spring of 1859. Although the Know Nothing agitation had largely abated, THE NEWS again led the opposition. But other and more far-reaching matters than this historical controversy were taking the center of the stage as 1859 and 1860 crowded on the next decade. "Bleeding Kansas," the Dred Scott decision, John Brown's raid on Harper's Ferry—these were only too palpable signs of danger ahead on the issue of slavery.

THE NEWS believed that Houston's election would be an even greater calamity than in 1857. It professed to see him in the role of demanding that Texans put aside "all the great issues vital to our existence as a nation in favor of the single issue of Houston and anti-Houston." But sentiment was swinging back in favor of the aging Hero of San Jacinto, although the *Telegraph,* with THE NEWS, remained adamant. And when the votes were counted, Runnels joined the company of single-term governors in the face of Houston's victory at the polls in August.

THE ALMANAC came out in 1860 with an even larger volume of historical items, including a reprint in full of Houston's counterattack in the Senate. Richardson was inclined to slow down on the argument, now that the country was rent by graver issues, although he was quick to defend THE ALMANAC from the charge of perverting history. He insisted that he had sought to make THE ALMANAC an impartial compilation of fact, and, in reproducing Houston's speech, he wrote that it was "certainly entitled to rank among the authoritative historical documents of the country." He refused to reply to the personal abuse heaped upon him by Hous-

ton; while it was true, he added, that THE NEWS had never complimented Houston by so much as a single *puff*, the paper had
confined its criticism to his public career, had never reflected on
his private character. And Richardson concluded the row with
a strikingly detached analysis of Houston:

It must certainly be admitted that Gen. Houston possesses some
extraordinary traits of character. In personal address and the power
of obtaining an influence among the masses, he has few if any
superiors. It is to these remarkable traits that he is indebted in no
small measure for the ascendancy he secured and so long maintained
in Texas, in spite of the numerous enemies he made at the outset
among the leading and prominent patriots of the Revolution.

He is still a prominent actor on the stage; and though his more
recent political course has driven from him many of those who were
formerly among his warmest supporters, still he seems to wield his
usual influence in the party with which he has connected himself. . . . Indeed, the controlling influence he has so long exercised
over the people of Texas, all attending circumstances being taken
into consideration, is one of the most prominent features of our
history and will probably task the future historian for an adequate
explanation. . . .

☆

Houston, however, was not to enjoy his triumph for long in
Texas. The election of Lincoln, a "Black Republican," in November of 1860 seemed proof to the more concerned of the Southern
leaders that the North was determined to force the slavery issue
to final settlement.

Already the nerves of Texans were taut from calamities ascribed
to abolitionist fanatics—the atrocity story had been born. On a
Sunday afternoon in July, 1860, the town of Dallas was destroyed
by fire, twenty-five business houses in all being reduced to ashes
at a loss of more than $200,000. The editor of the Dallas *Herald*
sent lurid dispatches to THE NEWS and the *Telegraph* of a reported abolition plot to repeat the Dallas disaster throughout
Texas. Negroes were being organized, it was alleged, in a secret
revolutionary body to work these calamities.

As late as 1858, after the Texas Legislature had authorized the

Governor to call a convention of Southern States to discuss the possibility of seceding from the Union, THE NEWS had urged caution—"with the alarming evidences around us of an approaching crisis, we cannot join in the cry that all is well. But while we shall continue to advise prudent preparations to meet the evils that are threatening us, we shall never be among those who counsel a dissolution of the Union, unless as a measure of last resort for the protection of the rights of the South."

But by the opening of 1861, THE NEWS reasoned that the South had been forced to this last resort. Richardson approved secession. This was his final disagreement with Sam Houston. But THE NEWS refused to exult in the last humiliation of its opponent when the Confederate State of Texas deposed the Hero of San Jacinto from the Governor's chair at Austin.

WILLARD RICHARDSON, SENIOR PROPRIETOR

[1844–1875]

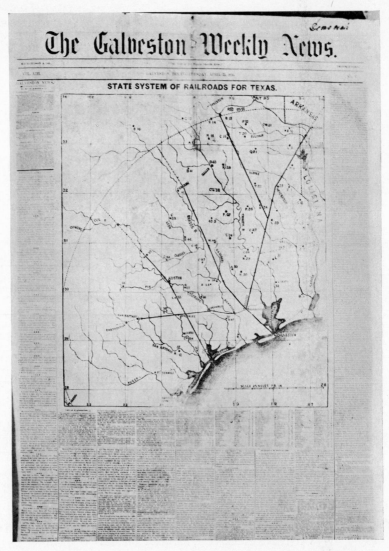

RICHARDSON'S PLAN FOR A SYSTEM OF STATE RAILWAYS

Proposed in THE NEWS of April 22, 1856, the scheme was rejected by the
Legislature of Texas in favor of land subsidies to private railroad builders

CHAPTER IV

WAR, FIRE AND STRAW PAPER

1861–1865

THE CIVIL WAR, it has been said, merely singed the broad acres of Texas. But its people did not escape all of the suffering inflicted with a heavier hand on the Old South. More than 50,000 Texans took up arms in behalf of the Confederacy, and most of them saw service east of the Mississippi in the major campaigns of the war. The resources and products of the State were placed at the disposal of the Richmond Government, and Texas remained an important source of supply until Grant finally succeeded in 1863 in hacking the Confederacy in two by the capture of Vicksburg.

As for Galveston, Houston and the more heavily settled areas on the coast, these felt war at first hand, since they bore the brunt of the successive Federal attempts to invade the State through the seaports extending from Point Isabel on the southwest to Sabine Pass on the border with Louisiana. The Federal blockade of these same gateways paralyzed the trade of Texas and brought on, by the end of the war, an acute shortage of all goods which had to be imported. Particularly hard hit were the newspapers. Cut off from the bases of their supplies of newsprint, ink and equipment, many were forced to suspend as the blockade tightened. The effect of war and blockade on those which did survive was far reaching. On THE NEWS and the *Telegraph* it was revolutionary.

In the first flush of war excitement Galveston assumed more importance than ever in the life of Texas. Confederate military headquarters were set up on the Island, following passage of the Ordinance of Secession at Austin on February 1, 1861, and the

surrender of Federal property and important armed forces by
General David Twiggs at San Antonio. Among officers of the
United States Army stationed in Texas who resigned to serve their
native, Confederate States were Albert Sidney Johnston and
Robert E. Lee, colonel and lieutenant-colonel, respectively, of the
Second United States Dragoons. Charles Morgan's and Commo-
dore Vanderbilt's coastwise steamship lines were pressed into
Confederate service, and the railroad between Galveston and
Houston hummed with the movement of troops and supplies.

By midsummer of the opening year of the war, Galveston began
to feel the pinch of the blockade which had been extended to include the entire western Gulf. When General P. O. Hebert arrived in September to assume command of the military district
comprising Texas, New Mexico and Arizona, he prudently chose
Houston rather than Galveston as headquarters. Galveston citizens became uneasy, then alarmed, over their defenseless position ;
they besieged both Austin and Richmond for defense guns and
ammunition. Although private citizens raised a purse of $5,000,
only one large gun reached their island, and the two small forts
erected at each end of the thirty-mile strip of land had to be tricked
out with Quaker, or dummy, guns cut from cypress and oak trees
in an effort to fool the blockading squadron. Finally, to the disgust
of many, the new Confederate Governor of Texas, Francis R.
Lubbock, ordered all civilians to leave the island. With their commerce choked off and in despair of relief from either Austin or
Richmond, the townspeople began an exodus.

☆

Willard and David Richardson decided at the opening of 1862
to obey the evacuation order. Loading presses, all available paper
stocks, files, office records and other movable assets on flat cars of
the Galveston, Houston and Henderson Railroad, THE NEWS
moved bag and baggage to Houston, where a temporary building
was leased on Market Square. David continued on to Austin,
where, the partners agreed, THE ALMANAC for 1863 could better
be compiled. But less than four issues of the weekly paper had

been printed at Houston when a fire broke out in the plant early in February and reduced contents to ashes and twisted iron.

The loss was such a body blow as would have knocked out a less determined person than Willard Richardson, then a man of sixty, without a penny of insurance. But "Old Whitey," as his more familiar contemporaries called him, refused to take the count. Realizing what cash and credit he could in the midst of a war, he was aided by the loan of newsprint from Cushing of the *Telegraph*. Hamilton Stuart concomitantly decided to suspend the *Civilian* for the duration of the war and sold his press to Richardson. This left only one publisher on Galveston Island, Ferdinand Flake, who soon began issuing *Flake's Bulletin* for such remaining readers as could not read his German-language weekly, *Die Union*. By April 8, THE NEWS, from its place of refuge in Houston, was enabled to resume publication.

Reduced to a single sheet and printed on both sides, THE NEWS that rose from the ashes was hardly a shadow of its former self. Less than half a column of advertisements was to be seen, most of them from fellow refugees from Galveston who began their announcements with "On Account of the Blockade" or "Having the largest part of my stock of merchandise temporarily in Houston." The news columns were stripped for action, all leaded editorials and special articles were thrown overboard, only the smallest type was used so as to pack all vital news into the smallest amount of space.

As of old, New Orleans continued to be the chief outside source of news. The twenty-two and one-half hour connection by way of Berwick's Bay had been disrupted by the water blockade, but New Orleans papers could still reach Houston within four days. This was made possible by the recently completed Texas & New Orleans Railroad extending from Houston to Beaumont. There remained only a two-day gap by stage between Beaumont and the western terminus of the New Orleans and Opelousas Railroad. But New Orleans was soon to be isolated from Texas, for the same papers which told of the Battle of Shiloh in April, with its depressing report of the death of General Albert Sidney Johnston, also gave the alarming news that Federal gunboats had run past the lower Mississippi forts and were even then threatening the imminent capture of the city. This was, in truth, bringing the war close to home. THE NEWS called for conscription in Texas.

The *Picayune* and other papers arriving in Houston on May 6, 1862, confirmed the fall of New Orleans before the gunboats of David Farragut, flag officer of the Western Gulf Squadron. THE NEWS wailed over this surrender of "the First City of the Confederacy"; it was a calamity affecting the people of Texas most seriously "because of our proximity to New Orleans, our long continued intercourse with that city and our dependence upon it for much of our trade and all of our intelligence from the seat of war and from all parts of the world." Richardson pondered in public about the receipt of future news. "How it will come, we cannot foresee. All we can say is that we shall give our readers all that can be had from whatsoever quarter it may come."

Fortunately, two main river crossings above New Orleans remained for a year more in Confederate hands—Vicksburg and Natchez. As yet there was no telegraph connecting Texas with any other State. But, by two overland rail-and-stage lines, communication was promptly set up with these river gateways. The first led from Houston, by way of Shreveport, to Vicksburg. Thirty-five miles of the route, or from Houston to Navasota, could be traveled in the cars of the Houston & Texas Central Railroad. The second, more southerly route, lay across Texas to Beaumont and the Louisiana border, thence northeastward to Alexandria and Natchez. Here, again, the first leg from Houston was by train as far as Beaumont. Thus by the middle of 1862 these two channels were furnishing, "By the Central Train" and "By the Beaumont Train," enough information to justify THE NEWS and the *Telegraph* in issuing morning and evening editions of their tri-weekly editions and a mounting number of extras. This news—true as well as false—was always from seven to fourteen days old.

Texas readers become fearful over news of closer origin as the summer of 1862 gave way to fall. The capture of New Orleans had served notice that Galveston and other Texas ports might expect the same fate. "The Lincolnites may take our ports," THE NEWS admitted in August, adding acidly that "they might as well have them now for all the good they are to us." Richardson rode to Galveston on a military pass on the railroad about this time, found business at a standstill and less than 2,000 persons on the island—"what a contrast to the life and bustle of former days!" Then, on October 4, the United States Gunboat *Harriet Lane,* two other ships of almost equal size and five auxiliaries, all under the command of Commodore W. B. Renshaw of the Western Gulf Blockading Squadron, moved across the Galveston bar, quickly reduced the fort on the eastern end of the island and came to anchor in the harbor with their guns commanding the streets leading from the waterfront. Sending a detachment of marines ashore to raise the United States flag over the customhouse, Commodore Renshaw received a delegation of citizens aboard his flagship *Westfield* and told them that he had come to hold Galveston "until the end of the war." Confederate forces had withdrawn without a struggle six miles westward on the island and then crossed the railroad bridge to Virginia Point on the mainland. There they dug in to resist any further movement of the Federals toward Houston.

The editor of THE NEWS at first was speechless, chiefly because "the papers have not been permitted to speak." But, on October 18, he defied military censorship and opened the columns of the paper to a review of "the late disgraceful abandonment of Galveston by our troops and its surrender to the enemy." Under the caption "Who's to Blame?", he continued:

The military authorities were "either imbecile or neglectful," and no attempt was made by them to procure guns to defend the place, nor indeed to defend it with the guns procured by the citizens. . . .

We know that it is not considered prudent to expose the mistakes and errors of those in high places, but when it becomes a question between them and the citizens as to who should bear the blame, it is time that gentlemen who ride about in ambulances behind sleek mules and call themselves "the Government" should be brought to their responsibilities.

The fall of the chief seaport of Texas aroused the people of the interior. Governor Lubbock hurried from Austin to confer with military authorities at Houston and Virginia Point. The angry protest reached even Richmond. As a result General J. Bankhead Magruder, hero of the recent victory at El Bethel in Virginia, was assigned to Texas as the new district commander. Arriving in Houston at the end of November, he began rebuilding the Texas defenses so energetically that within a few weeks THE NEWS was gratified to find that "everybody seems favorably impressed with our new commander. General Magruder is evidently a working man and by his untiring energy is inspiring confidence in all."

On New Year's Day, 1863, General Magruder justified this confidence by carrying out a brilliantly planned and executed attack on Galveston by land and water. Sending two small cotton-clad steamers filled with picked troops down the bayou from Houston, Magruder at the same time moved Confederate troops across the railroad bridge from Virginia Point under cover of night and deployed them around the city. At dawn the bayou steamers entered Galveston harbor through East Bay; with the nerve of terriers they at once attacked Uncle Sam's seadogs. Simultaneously the land forces began the assault on the Federal troops holding the city. The small ships rammed themselves against the *Harriet Lane* and boarding parties scrambled on her deck for a few minutes of furious hand-to-hand fighting. First the ship's commander, Captain Wainwright, then the second in command, Lieutenant Lea, lay mortally wounded, and the flag was struck in surrender.

Commodore Renshaw tried to bring the *Westfield* to the rescue, but, in turning, grounded his ship on Pelican Spit, the low sand bar on the northwest side of the harbor. Meanwhile the Federal troops, mainly the 42nd Massachusetts Infantry, had been driven to the water's edge and had barricaded themselves behind Kuhn's Wharf, where they soon surrendered. Renshaw now ordered his other ships to move out of the harbor. He effected the escape of

his sailors, including all the crew of the *Westfield,* except himself
and a volunteer party of six who remained with him to blow up
the ship. All seven were killed in the explosion.

Throughout January 1, THE NEWS and the *Telegraph* at
Houston were issuing extras filled with wire reports of the

GLORIOUS NEWS!
RECAPTURE OF GALVESTON
FROM THE YANKS!
Together with 600 Yanks and
The Gunboat *Harriet Lane.*

This counter-assault, the most exciting military event in Texas
since the Battle of San Jacinto, had an incalculable influence on
the press of the State. For the first time the telegraph was brought
into play to relate a big news story while it was happening—the
military telegraph line between Galveston and Houston which had
been taken over at the outbreak of the war after only a year's
operation as a private company. From it may be dated the birth
of modern newspaper reporting in Texas. Ferdinand Flake acted
as Galveston correspondent of THE NEWS and sent reams of able
and colorful "copy." It was Flake who first gave movement, order
and perspective to the action, while his follow-up stories were
splendid examples of interest in the human side of the conflict.

Notable among Flake's dispatches were those on the death of
Lieutenant Sidney Sherman, mortally wounded in the Confederate charge, and the death and burial of Lieutenant Lea of the
Harriet Lane. Lieutenant Lea had been fatally injured in the
attack by the bayou steamers. But it was not known until later
that his father, Colonel A. M. Lea of the Confederate Engineering
Corps, himself a West Pointer, had reached the wharf front in
time to see his enemy-son fall in the hand-to-hand fighting on
shipboard. He had hurried out by skiff after the ship's surrender,
only to see his son breathe his last. The next day Colonel Lea read
the Episcopal burial service for him and Captain Wainwright.
Before taps were sounded at the grave, the Confederate officer
added:

Allow one so sorely tried in this his willing sacrifice to beseech you
to believe that while we defend our rights with our strong arms and

honest hearts, those we meet in battle may also have hearts as brave and honest as our own. We have buried two brave and honest gentlemen. Peace to their ashes; tread lightly over their graves. Amen.

Magruder and his troops returned to Houston, where they were acclaimed heroes of Texas. The Legislature at Austin voted the thanks of the State, while the citizens of Houston built a triumphal arch of flowers for the hero and set aside a holiday in his honor. Old Sam Houston, from his sickbed at Huntsville, wrote Magruder that "you, Sir, have breathed new life into everything, have introduced a new era in Texas by driving a ruthless enemy from our soil. It gives me great pleasure to mingle my congratulations with the many you have received."

For a moment the Hero of San Jacinto held the public eye again. THE NEWS faced the fact that, once more in connection with the approaching gubernatorial campaign, he was riding high in popular favor. In March Houston was well enough to visit the city named for him. He received what was to be a final welcome from the people of Texas. THE NEWS was not fulsome, but it did remark that "General Houston's sentiments were patriotic and entirely free from personal abuse." A few weeks later Houston, in a letter to George Robinson of the Huntsville *Item,* eliminated himself from the campaign, stating that "having noticed for some time past the agonizing distress of some of the press of Texas, I am disposed to relieve them from their painful apprehensions." Two months later Houston lay dead in his "Steamboat House" home at Huntsville. THE NEWS said farewell to this old antagonist in this language:

> The sudden death of a man who has filled so large a space in the past eventful history of Texas cannot fail to be received by the public with a feeling of painful surprise. That General Houston has been one of the most remarkable men of the age will not probably be denied by any.

The year 1863 saw a second and more decisive defeat of a Federal force seeking to invade the populous areas of Texas, the victory of a small force of Texans under Captain Odlum and Lieutenant Dick Dowling who, at Sabine Pass in September, blocked the landing of the Nineteenth Federal Army Corps under General Franklin. More widely heralded than the Galveston vic- tory—the defense of Sabine Pass elicited the formal thanks of the Confederate Congress—this second success heartened Texans greatly; it compensated in their eyes somewhat for the more seri- ous disasters to the Confederacy that year, the fall of Vicksburg and the defeat at Gettysburg.

Mexican and French news also distracted attention momen- tarily from these larger reverses. THE NEWS learned from its corre- spondent at San Luis Potosí that the Superior Junta of royalists had formally invited Prince Maximilian of Austria to be Emperor of Mexico. Although invading French troops had been turned back the year before at Puebla by General Zaragoza in the Battle of Cinco de Mayo, Marshal Bazaine now made the invitation possible by leading the troops of Napoleon the Third into Mexico City. Authorities at Richmond uncovered a plot—said to have originated with the French Consul at Galveston—whereby Texas was to secede from the Confederacy and resume an independent status, this time under a French protectorate. But THE NEWS and the people of Texas were satisfied with the Richmond Govern- ment and merely laughed at the proposal.

Soon, however, the effect of the fall of Vicksburg began to be felt harshly in Texas. Regular mail service became impossible, despite the best efforts of the Postmaster General, a Texan himself, John H. Reagan of Palestine. Newspaper readers, on the other hand, were demanding more and fresher news from the distant war centers. Printing supplies were getting lower. In the midst of these perplexities, David Richardson without warning an- nounced dissolution of the old partnership in THE NEWS and claimed full ownership for himself of THE TEXAS ALMANAC. Terming this act "an unparalleled audacity," Willard Richardson denounced it from Houston, with the result that no regular TEXAS ALMANAC was issued during the remainder of the war. The dis- solved partners were also to remain enemies for the next four years.

In these circumstances, the editor of THE NEWS felt he could only congratulate his rival when Cushing of the *Telegraph* announced that he had completed arrangements for a Pony Express to expedite the receipt of news from east of the Mississippi. Richardson was indignant, however, when it was disclosed that Confederate military authorities rather than Cushing were subsidizing the Pony Express, together with a telegraph line which had just been strung from Houston to Beaumont. Flake in Galveston joined Richardson in disputing Cushing's exclusive right to dispatches through this new service. A row in the grand manner ensued and was settled only after the military agreed that all papers should have equal access to such information. The authorities also improved communication with headquarters of the Trans-Mississippi department at Shreveport by a through telegraph line early in 1864. Still, no wire connections were made east of Shreveport or Beaumont during the war, so that word of the closing events of the great conflict reached Texas from one to two weeks after they had happened.

The staff of THE NEWS grew in the latter part of the war. A business and news office was opened at Shreveport with Dr. M. Estes in charge. L. K. Preston did more work as correspondent than as traveling agent, and W. P. Doran served as war correspondent on the Texas fronts, particularly along the southwestern coast, where the Federals had been able to lodge themselves in footholds at Indianola, Corpus Christi and in the border section around Brownsville. General N. P. Banks had captured the latter city for the purpose of stopping trade across the Rio Grande between Texas and Mexico. His border blockade became increasingly effective. Adding to the shortage of supplies was the relentless inflation of Confederate currency. The most acute shortage of newsprint occurred in 1863. Richardson, for a time, was forced to reduce THE NEWS to the size of a dodger and to print it on yellow, straw wrapping paper. Subscription rates soared to as high as $48 a year, Confederate currency. There was also a period in which butter, eggs, poultry and other produce were accepted in barter. But in May, 1864, both Richardson and Cushing were forced to ask specie payment, the subscription price being $8 a year, gold.

Although newsprint became more plentiful in 1864, due to greater success in running the blockade with supplies, it was quickly consumed in the growing number of editions and in supplying the enlarged list of subscribers. By November the issuance of free extras had become so onerous that THE NEWS, following the lead of Flake and Cushing, began issuing and selling a daily Bulletin. An associate editor of THE NEWS, the Rev. J. E. Carnes, formerly of the *Texas Christian Advocate,* was added. Then on February 21, 1865, THE NEWS as a six-day-a-week issue was born, emerging from its chrysalis of *The Bulletin* as an enlarged but still a single sheet of paper printed on both sides—truly a war baby.

The desperate and hopeless prospect of the Confederacy became apparent to many Texans as 1865 got well under way. Sherman's march to the sea through "the Empire State of the South" was in progress, and THE NEWS could only caution its readers to remember that military reasons prevented correct reports from being published. "We need not look for any correct information," wrote Richardson, "till Sherman reaches the coast or is forced to surrender." The situation in Virginia, with the Capital under siege, was known to be graver. The spirit of Texans began to sag. But THE NEWS reminded its readers that "right or wrong, we must support our government throughout this struggle, or all is lost." Pointing out that for more than three years no man had been more popular throughout the Confederacy than President Jefferson Davis, THE NEWS saw no reason to lose faith in him "because of our recent disasters."

On April 2, while the eyes of Texas were focused on the campaigns to the east, military authorities at Houston handed THE NEWS and the *Telegraph* transcripts of important conversations held closer home. These were discussions begun March 11 at Point Isabel between Major General Lew Wallace, sent to Texas on a warship by General Grant, and Confederate officers on the Mexican border. The future author of "Ben Hur" had proposed that the whole Trans-Mississippi Department give up the contest. Wallace had made the offer as attractive as possible to Texans by urging that Confederate and Union forces unite and cross into Mexico, join the Juarez faction to expel the French troops, depose Maximilian, and thus preserve the Monroe Doctrine. Although the Confederates refused the offer and made the conversations public in an effort to bolster morale, a virtual armistice resulted between the opposing forces on the border. This lasted, with one notable exception, until the close of the war.

THE NEWS was inclined to take hope from Wallace's overtures. Richardson construed them as "a favorable omen for the South that the enemy are driven to such disgraceful a resort to stratagem, treachery and deception to divide us against one another. We believe the insulting proposition will only serve to arouse our people to a more determined resolution never to submit to such an enemy."

So earnest was Richardson in his desire to uphold the morale of his readers that he persuaded even himself there was yet hope for the Confederacy. Thus, when the last big story of the war, Lee's surrender to Grant on April 9, reached Houston nine days later, he refused either to believe it or to publish it. Less conservative but professing equal skepticism, Cushing at once issued an extra of the *Telegraph*. The latter warned his readers that it was based on "Yankee sensation dispatches" seeping into Texas from New Orleans. The next day Richardson commented on these same dispatches in which "the downfall of the rebellion is for the hundredth time pronounced certain."

But two days later, on April 21, the twelve-day old catastrophe at Appomattox was confirmed by wire from General Kirby Smith at Shreveport. It was doleful intelligence to be received in Texas on this the twenty-ninth anniversary of the great Texan victory at San Jacinto. Detailing the capitulation of Lee and the Army of Northern Virginia, Smith pleaded with the Army of the Trans-Mississippi to "stand by your colors; maintain your discipline; protract the struggle. You possess the means of long resisting the enemy."

At first the spirit in Houston was to protract the struggle. General Magruder at a large mass meeting declared that "there is nothing in the recent bad news that should make us despair for a moment of our final success." In Galveston the Second Texas Cavalry resolved itself into a convention and pronounced that "rather than bow in submission to the 'Stars and Stripes,' we will die as freemen upon the field of honor, or become voluntary exiles from the home of our maturity." In the midst of these deliberations, on April 28, THE NEWS learned by wire from Shreveport that Abraham Lincoln had been assassinated. Richardson could be forbearing in the death of Sam Houston; he did not find it in his heart to be equally charitable with the "Black Republican":

We do not propose to speculate upon the probable results of Lincoln's death. No one can say whether it be for the weal or the woe of our nation. Providence takes care of those things and to his will we submit.

It does look to us, however, that an avenging Nemesis has brought swift and inevitable retribution upon a man stained with so many bloody crimes. On the Fourth of March Abraham Lincoln made his inaugural address. Our country was bleeding and suffering from the war that his party waged against us, and with deliberate malice he gloated over our sufferings and visited them upon our own heads.

In the plenitude of his power and arrogance he was struck down, and his soul ushered into eternity with innumerable sins and crimes to answer for. He sowed the wind and has reaped the whirlwind. We accept the result as one of the inscrutable decrees of Providence.

In the meantime, the morale of the Trans-Mississippi Department was cracking. Troops began to get out of hand. The State government withered away at Austin, despite the inability of THE NEWS "to believe that a Confederacy of eight millions of freemen, covering a territory nearly equal in area to all Europe, is going to collapse in a day merely because we have lost one of forty or fifty able commanding generals." There was talk already of the Reconstruction which Lincoln had planned for the Southern States. THE NEWS quoted Nathan Bedford Forrest's definition of that plan: "not only destruction; it is degradation and disgrace as well." But, by the twenty-fourth of May, THE NEWS was forced to admit that "if our people are not prepared to undergo the dangers and privations of such a protracted struggle, the sooner we give up, perhaps the better."

While the talk rolled on at Houston the last battle of the Civil War was fought on May 12 at Palmito Ranch between Brownsville and Point Isabel in southeast Texas. The Federals, having learned of Lee's surrender, moved in the light of the armistice to accept the surrender of the Confederate garrison at the ranch. Ignorant of the end in northern Virginia, the Texans in gray gave battle, losing five of their men and killing thirty Unionists as they drove them across the Rio Grande.

At that moment Confederate authorities at Shreveport, as if in response to the advice of THE NEWS, were considering the best means of surrendering this last remaining Department of the Confederacy. They ordered Colonel Ashbel Smith, commander at Galveston, to open negotiations on May 30 with officers of the blockading squadron offshore. Colonel Smith was received on shipboard by Edmund J. Davis, the only Texas Unionist who had reached the rank of general in the Federal Army. Smith and another commissioner were taken at once to New Orleans to treat with General Phil Sheridan.

But reports of the more bellicose reaction of Kirby Smith, THE NEWS and various Texans to Lee's surrender had reached New Orleans ahead of the peace commissioners. Ashbel Smith found Federal officers preparing to send an army of 100,000 into Texas and, consequently, much surprised that this new conquest would not be necessary. The New York *Herald* on May 27 had explained these plans fully:

The rebel Trans-Mississippi generals—Kirby Smith, Sterling Price and Magruder—have probably now within call armed forces of 50,000 to 60,000 men. These forces, largely composed of border ruffians, bush-whackers and veteran guerrillas, are among the most desperate fighters and reckless adventurers of modern times. They are headed by desperate military and political leaders, ready for any enterprise that will save them from "submission to the Yankee government." The great body of the planters of Texas are possessed of the same implacable spirit. The whole batch of them, leaders and followers, soldiers and civilians, are in a state of hot excitement for continued war. The government, according to our advices, fully comprehends.

But by now the government comprehended otherwise. Ashbel Smith returned from New Orleans with the terms of surrender, which were finally ratified on board a gunboat in Galveston Harbor on June 6. The war, so far as Texas was concerned, was officially over. The next day THE NEWS also bowed to the verdict:

We have laid down our arms, disbanded our troops and surrendered our whole country. Our military having thus given up all means of self-defense, it would only expose a journalist to ridicule and contempt to talk any longer of resistance. . . . By the terms of surrender we cease to be free men, and whatever of life, property and personal security we can now claim are just such as our rulers may grant us, and no more.

Newspaper sensationalism? Hardly. The curtain would now be raised on Reconstruction in Texas.

CHAPTER V

RECONSTRUCTION

1866–1873

T HE END of the war, with its lifting of the blockade, brought on a boom in Texas. THE NEWS was still being published in Houston. Returning to Galveston from Houston in June of 1865, Willard Richardson was astounded by the great inrush of goods and people, the first evidence of the trade revival which would raise the population of the city from the war-time level of 2,000 to more than 15,000 within a year and one-half. A great jam of cotton, wool and other products now rushed to the port, seeking bottoms in which to be carried to the markets of the world. Matching this was the inflow of manufactured goods to satisfy the long-denied wants of Texans. More than fifty vessels lay at anchor in the harbor when he reached Galveston, proving that "shipping is now four times as large as ever before."

The truth is [wrote Richardson] Texas has the inherent power to recuperate from the effects of this war beyond any State in the South. If the government at Washington should adopt a liberal and humane policy, Texas may become a source of vast revenue to the United States. But under a contrary policy—a military government —Texas is certain to become a burden and a tax upon the Federal government.

We are now looking with the most intense anxiety to see what policy will be pursued in reference to this great State.

Neither Richardson nor the people of Texas was kept long in suspense. On June 17, President Johnson appointed A. J. Hamilton, a Texas Unionist, as provisional governor, and two days later General Gordon Grainger landed at Galveston with 1,800 Federal troops. The general's first act was to proclaim the emancipation of the Negroes of Texas—the origin of the "June-teenth" holiday.

AN OLD BLIND HORSE ON A TREADMILL POWERED THE PRESS OF THE
NEWS IN 1863

Difficulties of publishing at Houston during the Civil War forced the paper
to adopt this expedient. Drawn by Glenn Moore from an eyewitness account
by J. D. Padgitt, now of Dallas.

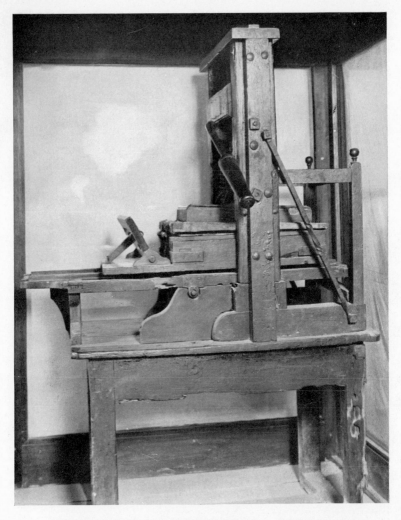

ORIGINAL ARMY PRESS CARRIED TO TEXAS AND MEXICO BY
SAMUEL BANGS

Courtesy of the State Museum, Monterrey, Mexico, and
Mr. E. Borton, Monterrey

Thus was ushered in the first military government of Texas, which would hold sway until the middle of 1866.

Caught in the current of this post-war boom, THE NEWS was forced to expand rapidly. First Galveston, then New Orleans, and finally eastern advertisements began crowding back into its columns, so that by August 31 the daily edition had to be doubled from two to four pages. Richardson felt he should spent most of his time in Galveston preparing for the earliest possible return of his paper to its home base. Left in Houston as Associate Editor, Carnes was equal to the swelling duties of the editorial office, but the counting room began to suffer from neglect. Late in the fall of 1865, therefore, Richardson inserted a small want ad in THE NEWS for a competent bookkeeper. From this advertisement came one of the most significant additions. For, the applicant who saw it, came promptly to Houston and got the job was Alfred H. Belo, a 26-year-old North Carolinian recently arrived in Texas.

Colonel Belo, who was to affect the subsequent history of the institution profoundly, was born at Salem, N. C., in 1839, two years after Willard Richardson emigrated to the Republic of Texas. Member of a family which had found political and religious refuge in the Piedmont section of America before the Revolution, he was an unusually fine specimen of the young manhood of the South which had entered light-heartedly into the Civil War. His parents were well to do, according to the standards of their hill country, and he had been prepared for a college education which was interrupted by the outbreak of war. He at once raised the first company of the Forsythe Riflemen and at twenty-two was named a captain when the famous Fifty-fifth North Carolina Regiment was organized near Raleigh early in 1862. Within two months he commanded a battalion.

The regiment, after several months of intensive training and a baptism of fire near Washington, N. C., was combined in October with three others from Mississippi to form General Joseph R. Davis' Brigade. Then, as a part of Longstreet's Corps, they

were soon sent to hold the lines near Suffolk, Va. Belo's regiment
was commanded by Colonel John K. Connally, a fine tacti-
cian and exceptionally strict disciplinarian. The regiment boasted
a seventeen-piece band led by a German "professor" who had
studied at Heidelberg. The company ranks were full, the men clad
better than the average, the officers resplendent in their new
gray field uniforms. None was more proud of the regiment than
Major Belo. Of more than medium height, well set up and hand-
some of face in a serious, aristocratic way, the young officer looked
the part of a commander. The broad forehead, the firm blue
eyes set wide apart, the strong, straight nose contributed to the
impression.

Young Belo soon proved his mettle. One evening about dark
near Suffolk the Unionists, in a surprise sortie, captured a heavy
piece of Confederate artillery. This was in the spring of 1863.
Two brigade officers reported that the gun had been captured from
the Fifty-fifth North Carolina Regiment. Colonel Connally protested the erroneous report, but in vain. Since the honor of the
regiment was thus impugned, he demanded satisfaction for the
slander. The colonel himself challenged the first of the brigade
staff officers. The lieutenant colonel, Maurice T. Smith, was
next in line to challenge the second offending officer. But Smith,
a Presbyterian elder, "was conscientiously opposed to duelling"
and excused himself. Whereupon, Major Belo issued the second
challenge.

Principals and seconds in the two affairs of honor met the next
morning in separate parts of the same field. Colonel Connally's
opponent had chosen doube-barreled shotguns, loaded with buck-
shot; Major Belo's antagonist, the Mississippi rifle at forty paces.
Major Belo's first shot plugged his opponent's hat, while the return
fire missed him. On the second exchange Major Belo missed his
target, but a bullet tore through his coat just above the shoulder.
Once more the count began, only to be halted by a shout from the
opposite side of the field—friends of the duellists had found an
honorable settlement. Colonel Connally's antagonist, "a gallant
officer and true gentleman," having become satisfied that he had

erred in laying the blame on the Fifty-fifth Regiment, "withdrew the cause of offense."

☆

There was need for unity, for the enemy lay ahead. The Fifty-fifth North Carolina, together with the Mississippi regiments in the brigade, crossed the Potomac in the Army of Northern Virginia in the latter part of June, and on the morning of July 1 marched down the Chambersburg Pike into the battle of Gettysburg. Quickly deploying into line, they got an order to advance. Colonel Connally grabbed the battle flag from a wounded color guard and stepped in front of his men. This drew the enemy's fire at him and he slumped to the ground, severely wounded in arm and hip.

"Are you badly hurt?" shouted Major Belo, hurrying to the side of his superior.

"Yes, but don't pay any attention to me," replied the Colonel. "Take the colors and stay ahead of the Mississippians." And the Tar Heels stayed ahead.

But before the sun sank on the first day of battle, Confederates in this section were pushed back. The Fifty-fifth North Carolina covered the retreat of the brigade through a cut in an embankment. A Federal officer reached the embankment and seeing Major Belo in the cut, threw his sword at him, yelling, "Kill that officer and that will end it." The sword missed Belo but struck a soldier behind him. "Shoot that Yank," commanded the battalion officer, which was done. The Federal charge was thus checked for a time and the brigade managed to withdraw to a stronger position. But late in the day Lieutenant-Colonel Smith was killed while reconnoitering, and, in a counter-charge at sundown, Major Belo fell seriously wounded.

Thus none of the three field officers was left in action two days later when the remnants of the Fifty-fifth North Carolina immortalized themselves in the climax of the battle—the final, fatal charge at Gettysburg. Three of their number, according to the well-authenticated claim of the regimental historian, Charles M. Cooke, reached a point near the Benner barn, "the farthest to the front," the most advanced point reached by any assaulting column in "this high water mark of the struggle for Southern independence."

With the wounded colonel captured on the field, the lieutenant-colonel dead and Major Belo incapacitated, command of the regiment passed for a time into other hands. But, by January, 1864, young Belo had recovered enough to return as the colonel of the regiment. From the Wilderness to Spottsylvania he saw action again, but at the second battle of Cold Harbor in June, while leading a charge, he was struck by a bursting shell. The bone of his left arm was shattered between the elbow and the shoulder. Although the arm was finally saved by surgeons, he was not able to rejoin his command.

The loss of Colonel Belo to the regiment [Cooke later wrote] was irreparable. He had been with it in all its hard-fought battles and had the confidence of every man in the regiment. He was cool and intrepid. He never lost his head in the midst of the fiercest conflict nor failed to discover and seize the advantage of position. He had a genius for organization and appreciated every detail that contributed to the effectiveness or character of a military organization.

Colonel Belo was recuperating in North Carolina when Lee surrendered at Appomattox. He appealed to General Beauregard and had just been given another command when General Johnston's Army surrendered. But, instead of bowing to defeat with it, Colonel Belo, with a Captain Lillington, set off for the Trans-Mississippi Department, where they hoped to continue the fight with Kirby Smith's Army. By the time he reached Shreveport he found that the army could no longer protract the struggle and that Generals Smith, Sterling Price, Magruder and Governor Pendleton Murrah of Texas had gone into exile in Mexico. He also thought of accepting refuge in the Empire of Maximilian but halted instead in South Texas on a Waller County plantation. There he exchanged tutoring of the planter's children for board and bread until the day he saw the advertisement in THE NEWS for a bookkeeper.

☆

Taking the counting room job at Houston, Colonel Belo promptly showed unusual business judgment and skill at organization—two qualities which were to continue to be outstanding throughout his later career in the guidance of THE NEWS. Richardson daily laid heavier responsibilities upon his new business office associate, and a few months later, on March 1, 1866, admitted him to partnership. Notice was given in THE NEWS on March 14:

A partnership in THE NEWS' office having been agreed upon dating from the first instant, it has become necessary to close up the past business to that date as soon as convenient. The business hereafter will be conducted in the name of W. Richardson & Company until further notice. Col. A. H. Belo, for some months past in charge of the books of the office, is authorized to settle all previous existing accounts with the office, as well as to attend to any further business under the present firm name.

The senior editor of THE NEWS had other concerns than the business office. Early in 1866 the skeleton telegraph system set up by military authorities was extended to the State capital and to San Antonio. More important, it was also extended eastward from Shreveport to Jackson, Mississippi, where it tapped the New York-New Orleans trunk line then recently reopened. With this connection, THE NEWS, the *Telegraph,* Flake's *Bulletin* and the San Antonio *Herald* formed the Texas Associated Press, a loose, cooperative organization patterned after the similar expense-sharing agreement among newspapers in the New Orleans Associated Press. The Texas group had its own correspondent at Jackson, D. Flanery, who was entitled to take off and relay such news budgets from the trunk line as he thought best.

Then, on March 23, 1866, THE NEWS returned to Galveston and resumed publication there after four years. The business office was in the old building on Tremont Street, but editorial and mechanical rooms were located on the third and fourth floors of a new brick structure which Richardson had under construction on Market Street. One week later, "due to the increase of advertising," the four-page daily expanded from seven to eight columns. This issue reflected the rapid expansion in news-gathering facilities and in the staff during the first twelve months since the war; the paper had already made great strides toward recovering the place formerly held in Texas journalism but lost during the war to the *Telegraph* at Houston. In May David and Willard Richardson met, buried their old disagreement and agreed to revive THE TEXAS ALMANAC in 1867. David did not become a partner again but became national advertising agent at No. 6 Wall Street in New York, where he remained until his death, in 1871.

While THE NEWS and Texas were enjoying a business revival, political affairs in the State were not equable. Reconstruction at first did not seem onerous, although Governor Hamilton hardly commanded the support of a majority of his subjects. He was roundly criticized by THE NEWS and struck back by recommending to President Johnson that Willard Richardson be denied a pardon for his part in the late rebellion. In the growing contest at Washington, THE NEWS had come to believe that Johnson, then fighting the Radicals in Congress, was "the only friend the South has." THE NEWS accordingly had supported him and his reconstruction policies. Richardson heard rather directly, it was intimated, from the President.

"Judging from an official paper in the possession of the said Richardson for a considerable time past," Richardson replied in THE NEWS to Hamilton's threat, "President Johnson has better authority than Governor Hamilton to satisfy himself as to the loyalty of our citizens. The inference to be drawn from said paper is that the President knows the course THE GALVESTON NEWS is pursuing, and that he does not look upon its opposition to such men as Governor Hamilton, Thad Stevens, Sumner and other Radical leaders as opposition to the Government."

So, under the conciliatory policies of Johnson, the Conservatives of Texas met in Constitutional convention at Austin in February, 1866, and proceeded to restore civil government. Hamilton Stuart, whose *Civilian* was revived as a daily paper that year, offered the resolution, "cordially and fully accepting the terms and conditions laid down by the President for the restoration of the State to the Union." The new Constitution recognized the abolition of slavery in Texas. It was adopted on June 4 when J. W. Throckmorton of McKinney, a leader of the Conservatives, was elected Governor over E. M. Pease. Richardson journeyed by rail and stage to Austin for the inaugural on August 9, and when President Johnson two days later proclaimed that Reconstruction in Texas had been completed, the editor of THE NEWS and most other Texans believed that they might face the future with a measure of confidence.

But far from being ended, the ordeal of military Reconstruction in Texas had scarcely begun. The Congressional elections of 1866 turned in favor of the Radicals instead of President Johnson. Scarcely had the new Senators from Texas, the venerable David G. Burnet and O. M. Roberts, reached Washington in December than it became evident that the Radicals would not seat them. After a visit to the White House, Burnet informed Richardson that "the Ultra-Radicals are fully intent on abolishing our State governments and on territorializing the several 'rebel' States. The President is discouraged, and I don't wonder at it."

The full force of this prophesied disaster struck Texas on July 30, 1867, when General Phil Sheridan at New Orleans, under Congressional Acts reducing the South to five military districts, removed Throckmorton as "an impediment to the reconstruction of that State" and named his defeated opponent, Pease, as the second military Governor of Texas. Shortly afterward, the military removed the justices of the State Supreme Court. Among the substitute appointees was Edmund J. Davis, the same general who had received Ashbel Smith in Galveston Harbor.

Texas now passed into the darkest hours of her political history. Five long years of oppression followed, during which bitterness and suffering never dreamed of during the war were engendered. With its leaders disfranchised, the State turned instinctively to the Conservative press, of which THE NEWS was the leading organ, for guidance toward ultimate delivery from bondage. The lowest depths of this civil horror were reached after Edmund J. Davis, supported by the military commander of Texas, seized the executive and legislative power in 1870 by means of what THE NEWS called "a vile combination of the brigand and the bayonet."

This Davis victory, THE NEWS swore, must be made the "last of many reverses." Offering no apology now for devoting so much attention to political affairs, "since politics are now the main consideration," the paper called for "wise, prudent, far-seeing and independent action" to wrest the affairs of Texas from the hands of "the alien, the scallawag and the thief." In July, 1870, Hamilton and Pease, disgusted with the military despotism of Davis and his Radical Legislature, joined Throckmorton and other Conservatives at a mass meeting in Austin to denounce the usurper's latest outrage. This had consisted of the postponement of election of Texas Congressmen which should have been held in November of the same year. The convention memorialized President and Congress "to guarantee the people a republican form of government in Texas." Grant, who had succeeded Johnson in 1869, turned a deaf ear, as did Congress, and the Radicals at Austin, backed by a newly created State police, carried degradation into almost every community of the State. Grant signed a bill in 1870 readmitting Texas to the Union, and he proclaimed that the second military government of Texas was ended; but, under the circumstances, this supposed restoration of civil authority under the Davis regime was as farcical as it was tragic.

Early in 1871, Texans met at Austin to perfect a formidable reorganization of the State Democratic Party. Still refusing to be "the organ of any set of Democratic office-seekers," THE NEWS gave its wholehearted support, however, to the party as the engine of deliverance. "We support the Democratic Party," Richardson continued, "because it is right." Continuing its opposition to the Davis regime, the newspaper was amused to read the outcries of Horace Greeley in the New York *Tribune* because a Democratically controlled Legislature in that State had refused to seat a

Republican from New York City. "Our Governor, from whom most of our present ills flow," remarked THE NEWS, "was foisted on us in the very way the *Tribune* complains of so bitterly."

Horace Greeley, as a matter of fact, was read and widely quoted throughout the South, more so than any Republican publicist. The supreme phrase-maker of his day, he was even in Southern eyes—as THE NEWS called him—"the first journalist of the age." Despite his cutting words for the section both before and during the war, he had shown unexpected generosity by going bond for Jefferson Davis. His original advice in 1861, moreover, to "let the erring sisters depart in peace" had not been forgotten. When the citizens of Houston in 1871 invited Greeley to open their second State Fair in May, THE NEWS heartily seconded the motion. "We wish we could persuade him to come among us and tarry a short time," the paper commented. "He would find that we Texans, like a certain sulphurous-smelling personage, are not nearly so black as we are painted." And, to the surprise of virtually everyone, including Greeley, he accepted.

As the old journalist set out for the Southwest, Texas began preparations on a grand scale for his reception. THE NEWS felt called upon to warn its fellow Texans "not to make fools of themselves as New Yorkers do when a live lord comes about;" for while the distinguished guest might appreciate the respect and attention of his hosts, "he will not be pleased with flummery." Greeley arrived in Galveston May 18 aboard one of Charles Morgan's steamers from New Orleans. Then for ten days he was entertained as vigorously and enthusiastically as Texans knew how. He was feted continuously by large, curious throngs during what became a tour of triumph over the southern part of the State. More than 15,000 cheered his address at the opening of the Houston Fair.

The guest of the two major railroads of Texas, Greeley rode by special train over the Houston & Texas Central northward to Hempstead and Calvert, thence westward to Brenham and back to Houston. Next, he was carried westward as far as Columbus on the Buffalo Bayou, Brazos & Colorado. Perhaps THE NEWS had been mistaken about his dislike of flummery; "the pleasant look-

ing, elderly gentleman in dark coat, white pants and straw hat"
seemed to relish the attention showered upon him by reception
committees and the more democratic mobs which swarmed aboard
his train or milled through his hotel rooms. The frequency and
obvious pleasure with which the journalist responded in speeches
belied Richardson's concern that "we have Barnumized him too
much." In fact, the single, rude jolt which Greeley experienced in
Texas was given by THE NEWS itself on the day of his arrival in
Galveston. It was in this lead editorial:

The visit of Mr. Greeley is in many respects a remarkable event.
Mr. Greeley is a private citizen and yet his voice is more potential
than that of any public man in the nation. He comes as the representative of a party that has forced its principles and policy on the
South at the point of the bayonet. And he comes, too, as an honored
guest. We have asked you, Mr. Greeley, to come to the State whose
name has been a byword and a reproach, to see how mistaken you
have been and still are. We want your goodwill, your esteem, your
respect. Come, look at us, and if we are as other people, go home
and tell the world what manner of men we are.
    It is perhaps the first time in the history of the nation that the
people of a State have stepped from their daily round of duty to do
honor to a public enemy. Yet the people of Texas know exactly
what they have done.

"A public enemy," indeed! Greeley lost no time to answer. At
a dinner in his honor he used the editorial as a text for his remarks.
While he had come to Texas (he said) to make no talks "upon
subjects on which the people have been so much at variance," he
felt it proper, since a morning newspaper had greeted him as a
public enemy, to make a reply. Then, "in a fraternal and kindly"
spirit, he reviewed the war and its aftermath, pleaded for a dis-
missal of "the dead issues" and called upon North and South to
unite their energies in behalf of the common country. More sensa-
tionally, the Radical Republican journalist spoke out in behalf of
relief for the white men of the South:

The result of the war made it essential that the blacks should have
the ballots but amnesty and the right to elect their own rulers should
be restored to all classes to prevent a conflict of races and to preserve
the whites.

When Greeley returned to New York he was greeted by a large group of fellow Republicans gathered in Union Square to congratulate him upon "his safe return from his journey to the far Southwest." And now Greeley went further than in his Galveston speech:

I hear it suggested that I went to Texas with too much parade and circumstance and that I was too often found making speeches from the platform of cars and from the balconies of hotels. Though all I did say was said in the hope of promoting a clearer and better understanding. . . .

I did say that I regarded the policy of excluding the leading men of the South from office as a very great mistake, and a very great injury to the National cause and to the Republican party. . . .

Well, gentlemen, the thieving carpetbaggers are a mournful fact; they do exist in the South and I have seen them. They are the greatest obstacle to the triumph and permanent ascendancy of Republican principles at the South and as such I denounce them.

Meanwhile the leading white men of Texas acted through the Democratic Party. Under threat of losing all representation at Washington, Davis at last was forced to call a special election in October of 1871 to chose the Congressmen who should have been designated a full year before. He issued, however, a famous election order which so hedged the exercise of the ballot as to arouse the fighting spirit of Texans. Richardson presided over a mass meeting in Galveston which issued a firm and unmistakable protest to the Governor. Other mass meetings followed, culminating in a State-wide Tax Payers Convention in Austin in September. It was composed of outstanding leaders in the business and agricultural life of Texas. John J. Hand, by this time an important member of THE NEWS' organization, was one of the two representatives from Galveston. After exposing the gross extravagance and mismanagement of the Davis regime, the convention called upon citizens to resist illegal tax collections by resort to the courts and thus to dry up the sources of the usurper's power. Again Hamilton and Pease, as well as Throckmorton, joined in this last and mightiest protest against the administration of Edmund J. Davis. The protest was translated into sweeping action in the October special election when Democrats won each of the three contests, including a victory by D. C. Giddings in the Third Texas District, which embraced both Houston and Galveston. The Democrats followed up a month later in the regular election for legislators by winning a clear majority in both houses.

THE NEWS was relieved and greatly encouraged by these triumphs. Thus far, as the newspaper viewed it, Texans had been "seeking in vain to free themselves from the grip of the most remorseless wretches that ever committed murder or robbery"; now all Texas could take renewed hope, for, with the capture of the Legislature, the back of Radicalism in Texas had been broken.

Never since we commenced our editorial career in the publication of THE NEWS now more than thirty years ago [wrote Richardson] has our whole soul been so earnestly directed to any cause as in our late efforts to overthrow the Radical Party. And the reason is obvious; for we can truly say that never before in the history of this country have we seen its liberties in such peril.

Shortly afterwards Greeley had a chance to prove the sincerity of his conversion to the cause of justice in the South. When Giddings appeared in Washington to represent the Galveston-Houston district, the Republican incumbent, backed by Governor Davis, contested his seat on the grounds of an illegal election. Greeley now came through magnificently, insisting in the columns of his *Tribune* that Giddings be seated. This the House of Representatives finally did, unanimously. "To Horace Greeley's pen more than to any one other thing," said John H. Reagan a few months later, "do the people of the Third Texas District owe it that they are represented by their own representative rather than by the creature turned out by the unanimous vote of the House."

☆

Texans, on the other hand, were soon given an opportunity to show their gratitude to the first journalist. A liberal wing of the Republican party, meeting in Cincinnati, named Greeley as a candidate for the Presidency in opposition to Grant. When the Democratic National Convention met in Baltimore in July of 1872, a suggestion that Greeley be made its standard bearer as well —a suggestion unanimously endorsed by the Texas delegation headed by Reagan—swept the floor. And soon Greeley was accepting this second, fusion nomination "in the confident trust that the masses of our countrymen, North and South, are eager to clasp hands across the bloody chasm which has too long divided them. . . ."

THE NEWS was also ready to forget the word enemy, at least in so far as Horace Greeley was concerned. It gave its full editorial support to the Greeley ticket. The junior partner, Colonel Belo, now dividing much of his time between New York and Washington since David Richardson's death the year before, had covered the Baltimore convention, the first time any Texas newspaper had its own wire correspondent at a national gathering. He was optimistic over the outlook: "the enthusiasm is spreading and it now seems as if every thing must yield to it," Belo wrote in the summer. "Many suppose that Grant will be unable to carry ten States. I tell them that Texas will give Greeley a majority of fifty thousand."

Less imbued with the optimism of youth and more realistic, Richardson in Texas knew that Grant's re-election was a foregone conclusion. But he was convinced of one beneficial result from the Greeley fusion ticket—"through all this passive Greeley movement," he said in an interview given to the editor of the Dallas *Herald* in July, "the Democratic party will be preserved for future usefulness." And if, in the election, Greeley rather than Grant failed to carry five, much less than ten States, the electoral vote of Texas was delivered in full to the old journalist. Tired and deeply hurt by the ballot box disaster, Greeley died in New York a few weeks afterward. THE NEWS in farewell now apostrophized him as one of Texas' greatest friends and as one of "the grand spirits of the earth."

The final overthrow of Radicalism in Texas was accomplished in 1873. In November of that year Richard Coke of Waco received a clear-cut majority over Governor Davis. When the Democratic victor arrived to take office in January of 1874, Davis refused at first to give way. He appealed to President Grant for Federal troops; but the military figure in the White House turned a deaf ear, and, after considerable gun play on both sides, the last Reconstruction Governor of Texas abdicated. The State was now finally freed, THE NEWS believed, from "the dense league of fraud, incompetence and rapacity"; it was the end of the rule by "the alien, the scallawag and the thief."

CHAPTER VI

TOWARD "THE DALLAS NEWS"

1874–1885

OPPRESSIVE AS Reconstruction had seemed, it merely retarded rather than halted the economic growth of Texas. Each year from 1865 until the Panic of 1873, THE NEWS saw a steady advance in population and in the production of new wealth. Indians and the rising cattle barons still divided vast stretches west of Fort Worth and San Antonio, but more than 200,000 new settlers, most of them from the bankrupt sections of the Old South, moved into the eastern half of the State before 1870. The majority chose, THE NEWS noted, that tier of north-central prairie counties, the "great wheat region" which so long had held the interest of Willard and David Richardson, the future cotton kingdom of which Dallas would become the capital.

Revival of THE TEXAS ALMANAC AND IMMIGRANTS' GUIDE in 1867 had the encouragement of new settlement as its main purpose. While THE NEWS was giving its whole soul to the political redemption of the State, Willard Richardson and his growing body of associates fostered the economic expansion through this year book. The resultant shifts on the population map early set up a newspaper publishing problem which had to be met finally; it would be solved at last through "a daring experiment," the establishment of a duplicate edition of THE NEWS at Dallas.

Willard Richardson's old dream of a railway system for Texas began to materialize in this same period. Before the Panic struck in 1873, mileage had been tripled to 1066—virtually the size if not the exact routes of the rail system proposed by him seventeen

77

years earlier. The editor was specially elated at the resumption of
a northward march by "Paul Bremond's Road"; from its war-
time terminus at Navasota the Houston & Texas Central pushed
on to Calvert, to Hearne, to Corsicana, then Dallas, finally reaching its goal on Red River at Denison in the spring of 1873. There
it met the newly arrived Missouri, Kansas & Texas Railway which
had been building southward from Sedalia, Mo., and would soon
have connections into Kansas City and St. Louis. Texas at last
had uninterrupted rail connection with the rest of the United
States.

The News' great concern over the progress of the Central Railroad grew out of the fact that it would tap "the great wheat
region." Here, in the post-war period, it was realized that a new
farm economy was possible, one in which Negro slavery and the
plantation system might be forgotten. A single farmer, aided by
two or three sturdy sons (as The Texas Almanac alluringly
pointed out) could soon make himself independent, provided he
would forget that cotton had been king, content himself with 200
or 300 acres, and turn his strength to growing grains. Already, by
1866, this area had raised 6,000,000 bushels of wheat, compared
with a total of only 50,000 for the entire State in 1850. And that
despite the failure of railroads to reach the promised land. A writer
in The Texas Almanac for 1867 thus described it:

The traveler in the great wheat region is struck with the great
difference in the appearance of the country arising from the different
modes of farming—in place of the cotton gin, the melancholy me-
morial of the great system of labor which has passed away, are seen
barns, mills, agricultural machinery, piles of straw, together with all
the evidences of a prosperous country inhabited by the white man.

A year later another Almanac writer reported that this section
was "the only part of the State which has had any accession to its
population during the gloomy period":

But even now, October, 1867, they are pouring in by every thor-
oughfare and every crossing of the Red River. They are a good class
of people—sturdy farmers from Missouri, Tennessee, Kentucky and
other states, who have been ruined by strife at home. Though they
do not bring much money to Texas they bring what is much more

ALFRED HORATIO BELO, PRESIDENT

[1865–1901]

JOHN J. HAND
[1867–1888]

THOMAS W. DEALEY
[1870–1906]

HAMILTON STUART
[1873–1894]

R. G. LOWE
[1874–1906]

DONALDSON C. JENKINS
[1873–1900]

valuable: muscle, intelligence, enterprise, energy and agricultural skill.

The editor of THE NEWS was more than impressed with these reports; Richardson soon became convinced, and so stated publicly in THE ALMANAC, that "northern Texas shall in the course of time contain the largest population of any equal extent of territory in the State, and as a consequence this section is destined from this time forward to be the seat of the wealth and the center of the popular power in Texas." How THE NEWS acted on this prophecy before it was borne out will be seen.

Dallas, a town of only 2,000 people, in 1868 was acknowledged by THE ALMANAC to be "the heart of this beautiful section so often alluded to." Its citizens looked forward hopefully to the day when railroads would finally reach them. Already they were assured that the northbound Central would cross the westward-building Texas & Pacific at their city. With two wool-carding machines and fifteen small flour mills, it aspired to be a manufacturing center. In trade, though, lay its chief hope. Although Dallas, as its pioneer *Herald* pointed out, "does not now control the trade of more than twenty miles in the shape of a crescent," its leaders believed that the first snort of the oncoming iron horses would be the signal for a boom. There were even some souls visionary enough to predict that, with railroads, Dallas might some day challenge the position of Jefferson, the miracle trade center of northeast Texas. This old landing on Caddo Lake had risen during and after the war to be the second largest city in the State, with a population of 15,000 and a trade of more than $10,000,000 a year.

Another contemporary view of North Texas communities is furnished by THE TEXAS ALMANAC of 1872 which reported:

Dallas, Sherman, Paris, Clarksville, Bonham, Sulphur Springs, Greenville and McKinney, county towns respectively—are all elegant little towns with enterprising and refined populations, abounding in churches and first class schools, neat public buildings, capacious houses of business, tasteful private dwellings, together with all the appliances which go to make up the successful interior village.

Indeed, Dallas, Sherman and Paris are each beginning to put on the airs of a city whilst Bonham in the race of improvement and prosperity is rapidly striving to overtake them.

Richardson was among the leaders of Texas invited to ride into Dallas on the first train when the Central reached there July 16, 1872. Due to a faulty train connection at Houston, he did not arrive in the north Texas town until several hours after the ceremony. But he had time to study the teeming village, to call on his colleague Jossyln of the *Herald* and to appoint a wire correspondent for THE NEWS, Nat M. Burford, now that Dallas had at last been linked by telegraph as well as railroad with the rest of the State. He continued on over the graded roadbed eighty miles farther to the terminus on Red River, crossing over into what is now Oklahoma, then the Indian Territory, for a fleeting glimpse of that land, before starting homeward. He was back in Galveston by July 25, when he reported to his readers on his memorable seven hundred mile journey:

We made the trip to the Indian Nation and back to Galveston in just eight and one-half days, spending one day in Corsicana, a day and two nights in Dallas, a half day in McKinney and had a comfortable rest and sleep every night. In fact the whole journey was performed with scarcely any fatigue. In a few months more, with the extension of the Missouri, Kansas & Texas, our citizens may get on the cars in our city and proceed by steam all the way to St. Louis, Chicago and even to San Francisco.

It has been our first visit to northern Texas, and though we have always heard that country represented as the garden spot of the world, yet it exceeded our expectations, not only in the remarkable richness of the soil but in the number of farms scattered over it and in the large crops of wheat, corn, oats and cotton we saw everywhere——

Though we missed the celebration at Dallas, yet we have been more than compensated for the journey by the pleasure it has afforded us in seeing one of the most beautiful regions anywhere to be found on earth.

☆

With advancing years Richardson relaxed his grip somewhat on the reins of THE NEWS. Both returning prosperity and the efficiency of the staff assembled by him and Colonel Belo made this possible. He found time not only to visit the black-waxy prairie country of North Texas but also to journey to more distant parts.

In 1868 he and his wife returned for the first time in thirty years to their old home in South Carolina. Then he went East, spending weeks in New York with his old partner David Richardson. Shortly after General Dodge completed the Union Pacific Railroad he ventured all the way to Sacramento and San Francisco. The postwar boom enhanced Richardson's personal holdings on Galveston Island so that there were extra funds with which to indulge his old passion for the theater. Almost single-handedly he imported the French Opera Company from New Orleans in 1868, so that Texans might hear M. Gounod's newest work, "Faust," and other productions. The old newspaperman bought more land in The News' block in Tremont Street and erected the Tremont Opera House, on the southeast corner of Tremont and Market Streets, the first modern theater building in Texas. It was opened in 1871.

Meanwhile, under the drive of Colonel Belo's youthful enthusiasm and passion for organization, The News was regaining its old primacy in the State. Following the war, Cushing sold the Houston *Telegraph,* and its new proprietors could not keep pace with the Galveston rival. It became more evident, as The News phrased it, that the war, plus the coming of "the costly, troublesome yet essential telegraph," had indeed revolutionized journalism in Texas.

No longer [said the senior editor of The News] do the people ask for opinions and elegantly written disquisitions; but they are imperative and insatiate in their demand for news.

And The News met this new demand to an amazing degree during the blackest part of Reconstruction. Not content with the embryo Texas Associated Press, it built up its own separate system of news-gathering, so that there were soon a hundred local, or wire, correspondents in the important centers of the State. Daily weather forecasts from Washington and daily market reports from New York proved expensive innovations by telegraph but justified themselves in the Statewide approval by, and value to, business and farming interests. In this period, with a daily and tri-weekly circulation of 8,000 and the weekly entering 7,000 other homes, the paper could boast "circulation more than double any paper in

Texas." It could truthfully claim that "our field is the whole State. Neither Houston nor Galveston alone, nor combined, could support a journal like this."

The proprietors of THE NEWS took advantage of improvements in the mechanical field—a flat stereotype foundry, improved presses, folding and mailing machines. In 1873 they were hearing of "a wonderful type-setting machine invented by Mr. Delcambre which, to use the vernacular, takes the rag off the bush." It was alleged that the machine could set 3,000 to 4,000 ems of type an hour, a claim laughed at by expert typesetters in the composing room. Richardson refused to join in the skepticism. "Do not let us laugh at him," pleaded the man who had seen the advent of the power press and the magnetic telegraph. "Either he or some other man will find the key to this much desired but most difficult invention." But even Richardson's faith in inventive progress was strained a year later:

The wonderful discoveries of the last half century have almost prepared us to believe anything [he wrote]. But we must admit that our credulity is put to rather a strong test when we are called upon to believe in the reported invention by a Chicagoan named Elisha Gray of an instrument called a telephone, by which sounds are said to be transmitted.

Despite this strain on credulity, Colonel Belo on a visit to the Centennial Exposition at Philadelphia in 1876 was to see and hear a workable telephone. Credit, incidentally, for the invention of the telephone finally was given to Alexander Graham Bell, whose first patents date from 1876, but the pioneering work of Gray, Thomas A. Edison and others is recognized. Two years later Colonel Belo installed the first telephone in Texas, a private line between THE NEWS' office and his home. The first commercial telephone exchange in the State began operation in Galveston in 1879. The subscriber with telephone number 1 was George Dealey, tea and coffee merchant, whose sons and grandsons were to play an unforgettable part in the subsequent history of THE NEWS.

The staff continued to grow into a large family connection. In July of 1868 Colonel Belo married Nettie Ennis, member of a well-known South Texas family. The bride's father, Cornelius

Ennis, had been one of Bremond's associates in the building of the
Central Railroad, as the city named in his honor testifies. The
marriage ceremony was performed in the newly finished Trinity
Episcopal Church and brought out, THE NEWS reported, "the
beauty and intelligence, the worth and wealth" of the island, all in
tribute "to the social eminence of the fair bride and her family, as
well as to the deserved popularity of the bridegroom." The year
before John J. Hand had been brought on from the New Orleans
True Delta to head the then established large job printing office of
THE NEWS. Within three years he became the third partner. As a
result of the Panic of 1873 Hamilton Stuart ended the career of
the Galveston *Civilian* and joined THE NEWS as its first State Press
editor.

One day in the latter part of 1874 as Willard Richardson was
passing through the counting room, a new face caught his attention. It was the English lad who had become the new office boy on
October 12. He stopped the boy and asked what salary he was
making. The answer was three dollars a week. The old man patted
the youth on the head in a kindly fashion and said, "Never mind,
George, sometime you will get more."

Speaking in prophecy, Richardson little realized how significant
that moment was in the long story of THE NEWS. For the new
office boy completed the triumvirate of those who were, in turn, to
bear the greatest single responsibilities throughout the first century
of the institution—the 72-year-old Willard Richardson, the 35-
year-old A. H. Belo and the 15-year-old G. B. Dealey. It would be
more sensational, perhaps, if it could be recorded that Richardson
gave the office boy a raise at that time, but he did not. The management was frugal, and raises few and far between. Illustrating
how thrift was practiced by the head of the business, two copies of
THE GALVESTON NEWS were delivered each morning to Richardson's home several blocks from the office; after he and his wife had
read them, the publisher carefully folded the papers again and
brought them back to the office for resale. It has been said that a

nickel in those days looked about as big as a five-dollar bill does
today.

With his parents, four brothers and four sisters young George
B. Dealey had arrived four years earlier from England. Two of
the brothers, Thomas, who was his senior by four years, and James,
who was two years his junior, were also to leave a lasting imprint
on the paper.

The new office boy had been born in Manchester, England, on
September 18, 1859. The full name was George Bannerman Dealey, the middle name that of a close friend of his grandfather. The
family moved to Liverpool when the boy was only six or seven
years old. Thus life in the great English textile center during the
crisis of the American Civil War left only fleeting impressions on
him. The father, George Dealey, was a steady, God-fearing man
with a strong idealistic, humanitarian strain dominant throughout
his life. The mother, Mary Nellins, was born in Clones, County
Monaghan, Ireland, the daughter of an officer who had served
under Wellington in the Napoleonic wars. When financial reverses
overtook the family in 1870, she agreed with her husband that they
should break all ties in England and strike out for the New World.
Because of relatives already there, Galveston became the logical
destination. And, toward the end of Spring, they took passage on
an old style sailing vessel, the bark *Herbert*—a six weeks' crossing
which turned into a glorious adventure for the children. Then one
fine day the ship came in sight of the low lying Island of Galveston.
Boats of this size could not enter the harbor in those days because
the bar had not been dredged; the *Herbert* anchored, therefore, in
Bolivar Roads and was soon met by steam lighters which "light-
ered" passengers and cargo to the docks in the harbor.

Young George was eleven years old when the Dealey family
reached their journey's end. Thomas at once got a job as office
boy in THE NEWS. In spite of Reconstruction, Galveston was far
from bankrupt. There were many pleasing aspects of the new
environment, such as attractive homes and gardens filled with
semi-tropical vines, shrubs and flowers. There were also names
and faces and customs surviving from the days when "the British

party" ruled the island, which helped smooth the edges of strangeness in a new country.

For a short time young George attended what was the first free school in Galveston, established in 1870 under the State-wide system authorized by the Constitution of 1869. This historic institution was then operated by George D. Briggs, father of Clay Stone Briggs, who was later to serve the Galveston district in Congress. Among his teachers were Hans Ans and wife, the former an instructor in German. The school was then located on Post Office Street near 22nd Street. The boy also later attended night sessions of the Island City Business College operated by Joss and Bemish.

But all this time young George had an "eternal itch" to be at work; at last he got a part-time job in the new Trinity Episcopal Church, officials of which hired him to ring the bell and to pump the new pipe organ. This latter assignment gave him entry many years later into the unique association of Former Organ Pumpers of America. When the faithful had assembled and the opening music of the service played, the boy rested behind the organ. Sometimes he went to sleep during the sermon. On such occasions the choir leader had to leave the choir loft and rouse the pumper before more celestial sounds could be heard from the organ.

Organ pumping lost its appeal, however, and young Dealey sought other employment. Between 1870 and 1874 he held jobs, successively, in a cotton broker's office, in a candy manufacturing concern, in a hotel, in two saddle and harness manufactories, in a fruit store, a leather and shoe findings establishment, as a Western Union messenger boy and then as an employee of Ranger & Company, at that time the largest cotton buying concern in the world. Thus he brought a varied experience to his first permanent job, that offered him in 1874, when his older brother Thomas was promoted in THE NEWS from office boy to clerk in the mailing room. Colonel Belo hired young George because of his satisfaction with the older brother. In THE NEWS G. B. Dealey found his life work and began the unbroken connection with the same publishing concern that would establish a new record of its kind in American journalism. On October 12, 1938, he would begin his sixty-fifth year with the institution.

The personnel of THE NEWS in 1874 numbered fifty-seven persons; looking over it, Richardson recalled the time "when one man could fill his newspaper; now it requires a brigade." One of Richardson's and Belo's most trusted lieutenants in later years also joined THE NEWS in 1874. This was Colonel R. G. Lowe, a Scotsman who had commanded a Louisiana regiment from Shreveport during the Civil War. A year earlier Donaldson C. Jenkins had been persuaded to desert journalism in New Orleans to become editorial writer for THE NEWS at Galveston. The division of labor had been carried to military lengths. There were now sub-departments even in the editorial office, with local, commercial and news editors. But all divisions, business, advertising and mechanical as well as editorial, were organized, it was stated, "on the principle which demands efficiency at a liberal price as the best economy," and THE NEWS could boast that "it brooks no idlers or incapables and has no use for amateurs."

Willard Richardson's strength faltered under the attack of a serious ailment. His old energy flared for a moment as the enormity of the Panic of 1873 bore in on Texans. THE ALMANAC was suspended, but "Old Whitey" had the satisfaction of seeing THE NEWS, under the skillful direction of his lieutenants, barely dip its colors to "the financial gloom that has had no parallel in the recollections of men."

A shadow fell over the railroad outlook in 1873—that cast by a weird new movement among the small farmers which called itself the Grange. THE NEWS had a paternal interest in the steam carriers and felt called upon to analyze "the meaning and force of this rural movement" which had launched attacks on the railroads. In so far as the Granges sought fair freight rates by non-political means, the newspaper held them to be praiseworthy. "But when we see the steady-going farmers yielding to the temptation to dabble in politics, to control legislatures," THE NEWS warned, "we regard the movement with suspicion; we fear the germ of communism." THE NEWS sent a staff man to consult John H. Reagan at Palestine. The future chairman of the first Texas Railroad Commission explained that "we have no need of any such organization in Texas, yet I am not surprised at such a thing springing up where the interests of the people are very different and a different political party has sway."

Richardson's editorial contributions came less frequently and were mainly reminiscent. When the Austin *Statesman,* created in 1871 by the Democratic State caucus, attacked the political course of THE NEWS, he reviewed the attitude of his paper since 1843. The question of fidelity to true Democratic principles depended, he wrote, "altogether on what shall be accepted as such principles." Pointing out that THE NEWS had always been a disciple and exponent of the Jeffersonian Democracy of "Mr. Calhoun and his compeers of 1832-33," the Galveston paper had remained "true and single to its creed of Democracy in the long years of its weakness as in the days of its strength," a fact which he denied to many of the platforms and candidates who before 1861 had been styled Democratic. While wishing the Democratic Party of Texas full wisdom and success in the future, Richardson for the last time reaffirmed his old creed of a newspaper that should be "outside of party, laboring for the material prosperity of the people of Texas —an Independent, Democratic Journal."

Speaking more generally of the past, Richardson about this time could add:

A generation has almost passed since the senior proprietor of THE GALVESTON NEWS entered upon that which has been his life's work— the management of an honest, an upright, a truthful journal. In reviewing that life's work as written in the files of this journal, he is proud to aver that he has always battled for the right, been the foeman of corruption in high place and the uncompromising advocate of the material advancement of the people of Texas.

Willard Richardson died at his home in Galveston on July 26, 1875, after an illness of several months. Truly, his life's work had been written in the files of his journal and in his long influence on the life of Texas. There was no need now for an extended eulogy.

On the afternoon of the funeral "members of the editorial staff, attachés of the counting room, composing room, job room and press room" attended in a body. The pallbearers included Colonel A. H. Belo and John J. Hand, "surviving partners," and Donaldson C. Jenkins, R. G. Lowe and Hamilton Stuart.

Richardson's death was the occasion for numerous editorial expressions both in and out of Texas. Two representative comments will suffice. Only a short time before the New York *Times* had lost its own founder, Henry J. Raymond. It remarked on "the Galveston dispatch of last night announcing that Willard Richardson, founder of THE GALVESTON NEWS, died yesterday morning. Mr. Richardson was an unusually successful journalist, having built up the largest and most profitable newspaper in Texas and having no rival in point of circulation in that State."

With the insight of proximity, the San Antonio *Herald* concluded its remarks by saying: "Willard Richardson's history is almost the history of Texas; the history of his paper is really the history of Texas."

☆

So firmly had the institutional character of THE NEWS been molded during the last ten years of Richardson's life that his death caused no disturbance or upset, nor even momentary turning from its course. Colonel Belo, second in command since 1866, now took full control, buying the interest of the Richardson heirs in accord with the belief that active ownership should vest with those engaged directly in conducting the paper. The new partnership was styled A. H. Belo & Company. John J. Hand remained the partner in charge of the mechanical department. D. C. Jenkins was added to the partnership as editor-in-chief. Announcement of "this partial change in proprietorship" on October 1, 1876, led Colonel Belo to add:

The senior and principal proprietor under the present management is deeply sensible of the responsibility he has undertaken. His lamented associate, Willard Richardson, had the experience of a long life in the business of conducting a newspaper. The value of his

assistance and the strength of his name to THE NEWS were always
appreciated, and now that he is gone, no less is felt the want of counsel
from "his good gray head which all men knew."

But there is this reflection to reassure and sustain the present association in the conduct of THE NEWS—that their hope and their efforts will continue to be in the line of his well-known aspirations as a
journalist, citizen and patriot. For no new line of departure is to be
undertaken; but if possible, redoubled energies will be applied to the
task of accomplishing the previously conceived ideal, not only of a
journal valuable as a property, but above all a journal greatly useful
as a public influence in our day and generation.

Regarding political parties, public men and specific public
measures, Colonel Belo reaffirmed that:

Hereafter as heretofore, THE NEWS will avoid all embarrassing
pledges and entanglements calculated to destroy its independence
and impair its usefulness. Avowing Democratic principles in the wide
and generous sense—its aim is to hold itself free to combat abuse of
power wherever found.

THE NEWS has been blessed up to this time with a general success
unexampled in this State and scarcely surpassed anywhere in the
country. Yet we feel confident that it is but at the outset of its career.

But no dead hand, however wise, was to lie heavily on THE
NEWS. This was as Richardson would have had it, for new times
and conditions called for adaptations and growth. A firm hand
and keen eye, looking well to the future, were necessary during the
first years of the new regime. It was not until the end of the 1870's
that Texas, like the rest of the country, climbed out of the financial
debris left by the crash of 1873, and THE NEWS could not prosper
more than its readers and advertisers.

As the economic distress of the decade dragged on—eighty-four
railways totalling one-tenth of the nation's mileage went into
bankruptcy in 1876-77 alone—THE NEWS became restive under a
national policy confined to mere watching and drifting. Particularly did it score the "skinflint contraction policy sponsored by
Northern statesmanship of the gold-eagle stamp" which had forced

the country to return in 1869 to a single gold standard of money. It joined other Southern and Western journals in criticizing the "gold fetich worshippers" and called for the repeal of the act which required specie payment. The newspaper also demanded a paper currency based on bonds and automatically self-adjustable "to the wants of business," so that there might be a safeguard against future financial crises. So far, in fact, had the depression deepened that THE NEWS came to believe it to be "the urgent duty of statesmanship to interfere" by means of measures designed to counteract the deflation. The Federal Government should adopt "a liberal public policy with regard to railroad construction and other forms of improvement as a means of reopening the springs of a general prosperity partially or wholly frozen up by the hard times." THE NEWS had approved the new State Constitution of 1876, which sealed the victory of the Conservatives over the Radical Republicans and provided what was thought to be a satisfactory regulation of railroad abuses in Texas.

Viewing the Tilden-Hayes presidential race, the newspaper cried out in protest against "the great national shame" involved in the Republicans' seating of Rutherford Hayes in the White House; the Democrats were convinced that Tilden had clearly won the victory. But, "for the sake of the peace of the country" THE NEWS counseled acceptance of this "usurpation in legalized form." There was an effort to revive the Federal income tax imposed during the Civil War but repealed in 1871. Like the silver issue, this proposal roused the wrath of the financial interests of the East and revealed the great new crack opening up between the agrarians of the South and West and the urbanized, industrial East. "It was in the interest of 39,000,000 people to have the tax maintained," argued THE NEWS, "but the contrary wishes of 1,000,000 prevailed."

As of old, Mexico furnished live news. In 1876—the year that Santa Anna died in obscurity in Mexico City—Porfirio Diaz was using Brownsville as a base from which to overthrow successfully the administration of President Lerdo. While the paper at Galveston admitted that Diaz "may be a good man and a patriot," it predicted on his triumph that "he will not be able to cope with the forces of dissolution and anarchy which surround him."

But there were lighter sides even to the depression. Grave discussions and baneful prophecies had to move over in the column from time to time. In the midst of the bad times three "women of destiny" entered the State at Galveston. They were Victoria C. Woodhull, her sister Tennessee Claflin and their aged mother. Although the world first knew them as women who had dared to become bankers in Wall Street and to speak from the lecture platform, their connection as character witnesses in the recent Tilton-Beecher trial was of prime interest in Texas.

"Do you believe Henry Ward Beecher is guilty?" asked a reporter for THE NEWS on the trio's arrival from New Orleans.

"I know it from the lips of the parties themselves," Miss Claflin answered.

"Then what would you have done if you had been in Theodore Tilton's place?"

"I would have shot Henry Ward Beecher on sight," replied the charming woman lecturer, "and not have paraded my wife's shame to all the world and made it merely a means of advertising myself as a public lecturer."

☆

The depression "without parallel in the memory of living men" had seemed endless, but it lifted suddenly at the end of the decade, and the sun of prosperity once more shone on the land of the Tejas. With its return, the thoughts of most Texans, including those of THE NEWS, strayed somewhat from the subject of economic and financial reform. Even southward, in the land of "pulque and pronunciamentos," there was a marked change for the better. Diaz confounded THE NEWS by asserting control over the forces of anarchy and dissolution. The work of the Mexican Commander-in-Chief appealed to many North Americans, not the least distinguished of whom was a fellow general, Ulysses S. Grant. In the Spring of 1880 the globe-trotting ex-President, accompanied by General Phil Sheridan and their respective families, made a tour of Mexico by way of Cuba. On landing at Havana General Grant was greeted by an earthquake—"a delicate personal compliment"

(THE NEWS remarked) to Grant's supposed ambition to become an American dictator. But in Mexico the tourists found that the great Diaz could suppress even earthquakes, and their visit went off serenely in a fandango of sightseeing, banquets and fiestas. Sheridan, rather than the less articulate Grant, though, took after-dinner speaking honors: "I can well comprehend [said Sheridan in a typical speech] why Cortez burnt his ships. I would have done the same for the sake of remaining in so lovely a country." But, fortunately, the American generals had not burnt their ship, and soon Grant, Sheridan and party were steaming northward in the Gulf from Vera Cruz on the S.S. *City of Mexico*.

The ex-presidential party came into Galveston harbor on March 24. Reporters and members of the welcoming committee spotted General Grant at a distance "puffing a cigar." At closer range they found him "extremely affable, there being no sign of the reticence and hesitation for which he is famous." The next morning General Grant was escorted by the Mayor of Galveston and other dignitaries on a pedestrian tour of the business district. On Market Street they stopped to inspect the plant of THE NEWS, which at this time boasted of having a circulation "equal to that of all the other daily press of the State combined." The honor of showing the General how some of the new equipment, an address-ing machine, worked fell to the same office boy who had entered the counting room six years earlier, G. B. Dealey, now foreman of the mailing room. The General shook hands with the young man. The latter was impressed by the visitor's resemblance to John Sealy, a leading merchant and financier of Galveston, who was another inveterate cigar smoker.

Grant and Sheridan were guests that night at a public dinner at the Tremont Hotel where John J. Hand, among others, proposed toasts. Grant responded in a heavy, carefully worded address anent the necessity of healing old wounds that had divided the county. But Sheridan again stole oratorical honors. Unlike Grant, this was not Sheridan's first trip to Texas. No one had forgotten military Reconstruction days when Sheridan had been the de facto ruler of the State. Little bitterness remained toward him person-ally as late as 1880, although that night he wiped out any enmity that might still linger. At the end of his talk, which had been filled with sentiments flattering enough for any Texan, Sheridan concluded:

Speaking so kindly of Texas—and I speak from my heart—probably I ought to explain a remark I once made about it. I had just returned to San Antonio from a hard trip to Chihuahua on some Mexican business when I received an order to proceed at once to New Orleans. It was in 1866.

I hired relays and coaches so that I had only to hitch on the wagon and go speedily to get the boat from Galveston. I traveled night and day. It was in August and, need I say, very warm. I arrived here covered with dust, my eyes and ears and throat filled with it. I went to a little hotel in that condition and had just gone up to the register when one of these newspaper men rushed up to me and said, "General, how do you like Texas?"

I was mad and I said, "If I owned Texas and all Hell, I would rent out Texas and live in Hell." Needless to say, that did not represent my true opinion of this magnificent State.

So cordial was the Galveston reception that both Grant and Sheridan accepted invitations to visit Houston and San Antonio as well. They were able to reach the Alamo city by through train, since the old Buffalo Bayou, Brazos & Colorado had been extended shortly before from Columbus. As in Reconstruction, so during the depression, railroad building had gone forward in Texas. By 1880 there were 3300 miles of line. Financial control, however, had been altered by the financial storm and had passed largely into the hands of two men: Jay Gould and Commodore Charles Morgan. Between them they held the greater part of the Texas mileage. Gould was just at the beginning of his long rule over the destinies of the Missouri-Pacific, Missouri, Kansas & Texas, International & Great Northern and other Southwestern lines. Morgan had acquired control of the Houston & Texas Central, the B.B.B. & C. and the through line to New Orleans. Thus he had formed the basis of the "Sunset Route," or at least the eastern half of what, under the subsequent drive of Collis P. Huntington and E. H. Harriman, would become the Southern Pacific Lines, first Southern trans-continental railroad.

Texans generally had been more prosperous during the 1870's

than many realized. Population almost doubled to a total of 1,591,000. Wheat production soared, the cattle industry boomed and cotton, whose doom was thought to have been sounded at Appomattox, reasserted its dominance, invading, after the railroads entered it, even "the great wheat region." From 350,000 bales in 1870, the crop of the State increased to 805,000 bales ten years later, or practically a third of the American production.

THE NEWS reflected this development. The problem of circulating the paper in Houston and of making connections with trains leaving that city became pressing. In 1877 the paper had made in St. Louis a motor car, or dummy engine, which was operated over the Galveston, Houston & Henderson Railroad each morning to carry THE NEWS from Galveston to Houston. But the outfit was unsatisfactory in operation and was not used for any great length of time. Sometime afterward, the newspaper situation in the city of Houston became such that THE NEWS had an opportunity to furnish news to a much larger number of subscribers. Young G. B. Dealey was stationed in Houston at the time as head of the Houston bureau. On his urgent recommendation the heads of the business at Galveston engaged a real special train which left the island city at an early hour and reached Bonner's Point, in the Fifth Ward, about 4 a.m. A force of solicitors and carriers had been engaged and arrangements had been perfected for the delivery of THE NEWS to any part of Houston—business or residential. Meeting the train at Bonner's Point, the carriers distributed the papers over the city before breakfast. This service continued for some years.

The feat of employing an exclusive daily mail train as an incident of publication was commented on widely throughout the country. The claim to be the first to do so was contested by a newspaper in Boston, but it developed that the Boston paper operated its special train only on Sundays, although operation of such a train antedated that of THE NEWS.

And in 1878 THE NEWS installed the first web-perfecting press in the State, a modern, rotary press fed by continuous rolls, or webs, of paper and capable of printing, cutting and folding 12,000 papers an hour. To match the speed of the press, the forms of each

PRESENT HOME OF THE DALLAS NEWS

Erected 1900 and 1914

ORIGINAL BUILDING, THE DALLAS NEWS

Erected 1885

PUBLISHING PLANT AT GALVESTON

Erected 1883

State capitol correspondents at Austin in the early 'Eighties. *Standing, left to right*—Wm. M. O'Leary, who became the first city editor of THE DALLAS NEWS; Wm. A. Bowen; *seated,* W. M. Spence and John E. Thornton, Austin representative of THE NEWS for many years.

page were now stereotyped for the first time. This likewise was an innovation which attracted the attention of curious thousands of Texans. An expert stereotyper was sent down by R. Hoe & Company, makers of both press and equipment, and C. M. Seay, a youngster in the composing room, was assigned to master the new process. Among the "blessings of 1879" was one furnished by THE NEWS itself, the first of its special "Empire State Editions." These once-a-year compendiums of Texas data, although in newspaper form, compared favorably in completeness and influence with the old TEXAS ALMANAC. So great was the success of these "eclectic editions"—more than 150,000 copies of the 1882 edition were sold at a circulation "exceeding anything of the kind ever before reached in the South"—that their appearance on September 1 of each year came to be something of an event. At the demand of many desiring "to make use of the publication in Europe in the interest of immigration," a special issue of the edition of 1879 was translated and reproduced in full in the German language.

THE NEWS intensified its coverage of Texas news as the prosperous 1880's opened. To this end, permanent reportorial and business offices were opened in San Antonio, Dallas, Fort Worth and Waco, in addition to those already maintained at Austin and Houston. The paper now had eight traveling agents under the direction of D. S. Ryan. Among the staff representatives was G. B. Dealey, who, between 1882 and 1884, served in turn at Waco, Dallas, and Houston. To the latter place he brought his bride in 1884. She was Miss Olivia Allen of Lexington, Mo., daughter of a well-known Missouri newspaper publisher.

More than ever was THE NEWS proving its claim to be a State-wide newspaper, as revealed in its circulation, news and advertising figures. But this latest expansion only aggravated the basic difficulty of distribution, particularly since THE NEWS prophecy as to the settlement of "the great wheat region" was fast becoming a fact. The special train to Houston only ameliorated, did not solve, the growing problem. Colonel R. G. Lowe, after serving in

turn as printer, commercial, marine and managing editor, was by
now one of Colonel Belo's "most trusted aids and counsellors."
And it was Colonel Lowe who gave much of his thought to this
question. Soon he would arrive at "the daring and ambitious
scheme" of THE DALLAS MORNING NEWS, the ultimate answer to
the matter of how to secure proper circulation in the northern half
of Texas.

The immediately preceding move came in 1881. The partnership conducting THE NEWS since 1876 was converted into a joint
stock company under a charter from the State. With Colonel
Belo as president, other officers included Colonel R. G. Lowe, vice
president; Thomas W. Dealey, secretary and treasurer; John J.
Hand, D. C. Jenkins and Cornelius Ennis, additional members of
the board of directors. Chief interest in the charter lay in the
provision that A. H. Belo & Company might establish "one or more
newspapers at such places within the State" as the corporation
might desire.

The incorporation of THE NEWS served to crystallize the ideals
which Colonel Belo had acquired from Richardson and which
grew out of his own experience and character. After 1881 Colonel
Belo's poor health, due chiefly to his old wounds from the war, led
him to travel much in search of relief. He retained, however, a
close watch over the development of the institution. The noticeable shift in THE NEWS was toward the ideal of impersonal journalism, pre-eminently exemplified in the English journals of the
day, in which "it is the paper and not the editor or publisher that
the public recognizes."

A great newspaper conducted in the spirit of THE NEWS must
absorb or eliminate individualities [it was now declared as an article
of faith] because it must itself be a distinct personality, a moral and
responsible person.

A great newspaper must be serenely indifferent to personal likes
and dislikes, personal opinions or prejudices inside or outside of its
organization which would interfere with its functions as a faithful
collector and disseminator of news; and as a voice, an intelligence and
a reasoning conscience, to interpret for the reading public the ripest
thought and best judgment of the time touching all questions of
public concern.

A great and rightly inspired newspaper must sink all personality but its own.

As for the character of this "corporate personality" which was soon to launch THE DALLAS MORNING NEWS, the same pronouncement gave this self-portrait:

This is a period when efficient and successful journalism must be the work of a vast ramification of costly agencies and services, held in coordination and maintained in cooperation by a system as highly organized and as vigorously administered as that of a regular army equipped and thoroughly disciplined.

The spirit of the Fifty-Fifth North Carolina Regiment lived again in Texas!

CHAPTER VII

BIRTH OF "THE DALLAS MORNING NEWS"

1885–1886

THE DALLAS MORNING NEWS was born at 4:15 a.m. on Thursday, October 1, 1885. The delivery of this first born of "the Old Lady by the Sea" was in sharp contrast with that of its parent at Galveston, forty-three years earlier. It occurred only after long and careful preparation.

After its incorporation in 1881, THE NEWS began searching actively for a solution of its growing circulation problem in the inland empire of Texas. Colonel Belo was much perturbed by this problem and delegated Colonel Lowe to study all possible solutions. On one of his periodic trips to Dallas, Colonel Lowe met one of the old friends of his youth in Shreveport, William H. Newman, then traffic manager for the Texas & Pacific, the International & Great Northern, and other rail lines in Texas controlled by Jay Gould. He was later to become president of the New York Central Lines. Newman pointed out that THE NEWS for some time had been using a special, daily, leased train to carry its papers as far as Houston to serve subscribers in that city and to make rail connections for points farther inland. He was of the opinion, however, that the rapid development of cities in North Texas called for a more drastic plan.

"What you ought to do," said Newman, "is to ship your papers by wire. Do in a few seconds what it takes our clumsy locomotives hours to perform. That is, establish a duplicate of THE NEWS in North Texas—complete printing plant, staff and all—but connected by means of your own special leased telegraph wires with the main office at Galveston three hundred and fifteen miles to the southeast."

"Ship your papers by wire!" It was a bolder idea than any

vague plans which THE NEWS had in mind in drawing up its
charter. Then nothing more radical in the industry had been
thought of than one or more additional newspapers, held loosely in
common ownership. Joseph Pulitzer of the St. Louis *Post-Dispatch*
had acquired control shortly before of the moribund New York
World and was operating it in that fashion. The matter was put
up to Colonel Belo and a coterie of the management including
Colonel Lowe, Thomas W. Dealey, John J. Hand and Donaldson
C. Jenkins. They seriously pondered the scheme and at last agreed
upon it, the first instance of a "chain" newspaper in the United
States. But where, in all the northern half of the State, should the
duplicate be placed? Newman had assured Colonel Lowe that
one large city was destined to rise there to challenge the supremacy of Galveston. "Personally," the railroad man added, "I believe
that Dallas will be that city."

The corporation heads might adopt a radical idea, but they approached its execution with caution. They moved without haste
to investigate all angles, including the most suitable point of publication. In the meantime THE NEWS evidenced its prosperity by
erecting, in 1883, a three-story new home in Galveston, the first
fire-proof business structure in the Southwest and one of the most
modern newspaper plants at the time in the United States.

At this point young G. B. Dealey began his long connection with
what was to become THE DALLAS MORNING NEWS. Learning of
the proposed expansion, he showed so much interest in it—he
begged, in fact for the job—that executive heads soon assigned
him to make a study of circulation and business prospects in a number of North Texas centers. He cleared his mind, therefore, of all
preconceptions and studied the various rival points within "the
great wheat region." Dallas, eventually, appealed to him as a
logical selection ; he had been impressed by its people and potential
advantages during his brief residence there some months before as
staff correspondent and agent. With 10,358 people, Dallas was
already fifth in rank among Texas cities, according to the Federal

census of 1880. It trailed only Galveston, with its 22,248 inhabitants; San Antonio, with 20,550; Houston with 16,513, and Austin with 11,013. But Waco, Fort Worth and Sherman, all within the coveted area, were prosperous communities of 6,000 to 7,000 people each. It was possible that any of these might outstrip the forty-two-year-old settlement at the junction of the Elm and West Forks of the Trinity River.

Business and civic leaders of Dallas enthusiastically endorsed the proposal, once it was rumored that THE GALVESTON NEWS might place a duplicate of THE NEWS in North Texas. They were not content with the journalistic leadership then afforded by their local newspapers. The historic Dallas *Herald* had fallen on less fortunate days; other papers were weak and struggling. THE GALVESTON NEWS, on the one hand, and St. Louis newspapers, on the other, were types of more metropolitan journals which they wanted. Led by Col. J. T. Trezevant, another friend of Colonel Lowe's from Louisiana, Dallas spokesmen urged the advantages of their city and offered to raise subscriptions to stock in THE NEWS corporation to the extent of $25,000. One other city joined in the bidding; that community raised the ante much higher than the sum promised by Dallas.

"But, in the end, THE NEWS chose Dallas because it suited all purposes better," G. B. Dealey recalled later. And so, on July 22, 1885, the management at Galveston served notice through the columns of THE NEWS that "on the 1st of October, 1885, they will begin publication of a daily paper at Dallas, Texas, the title of which will be THE DALLAS MORNING NEWS." The exact form of the name grew out of the fact that several enterprising gentlemen, learning of the proposed move, had started a new venture under the title of *The Dallas News* a few months earlier; it was indicated that they would surrender the name for a consideration. But Colonel Belo and associates refused the offer, used the other name for their paper, and soon only THE DALLAS MORNING NEWS remained in the field.

☆

Early that summer young Dealey had been sent on to Dallas as business manager. Officials from Galveston were also on the ground almost constantly. Soon the first home of the new paper was under construction, a three-story brick structure built for little more than $10,000 and never planned as a permanent home. It was built by Col. William E. Hughes, prominent Dallas banker and attorney, former cattle king, and one of the most honored citizens of Texas, who leased it to the newcomers to Dallas. It fronted fifty feet on the north side of Commerce Street between Lamar and Austin.

Appropriate as it might be that the offspring of Richardson's paper should be housed between streets named for the Father of Texas and the godfather of THE NEWS, the site was chosen for less poetic reasons. It was notable at the time because it lay almost in the center of the business district. Within a radius of two blocks were to be found most of the banks, stores and jobbing houses of the day—the private bank of Flippen, Adoue & Lobit; Sanger Brothers and E. M. Kahn & Co.; the Keating Implement and Machinery Company, the wholesale houses of R. V. Tompkins, T. L. Marsalis, Schneider & Davis and others. Diagonally across, on the southwest corner of Commerce and Austin, stood the new Opera House; on the same side of Commerce as THE NEWS, on the northwest corner of Austin, was Colonel Hughes' Grand Windsor Hotel. Immediately abutting THE NEWS' building to the east stood the two-story City Hall and central fire station, which extended fifty feet along Commerce and sixty feet northward on Lamar. On the west side of the building, extending to Austin Street, was the steam laundry of Dietz & Leachman. And, less than one hundred feet eastward, the "magnificent" new Merchants' Exchange commanded the northeast corner of Lamar and Commerce.

One of the problems arising during construction was that of lighting the building. Most structures were illuminated then with gas, and the manufacturers of this fuel assumed they would get the contract. But they did not count on the enterprise of the newcomer. The Edison Incandescent Electric Light Company sent T. F. Cronise specially to Dallas on a sales trip. He showed the officials how, by spending a little more money, THE NEWS building could be equipped with Mr. Edison's newest and most spectacular invention, the incandescent lamp. This was a marked advance over the arc electric light, already in use in Dallas. The new system had only recently been placed on the market, and the incandescent lamp had been introduced into Texas to a limited extent, but THE NEWS plant was the first isolated, or independent, one of its kind in the State. The contract called for 100 lamps, to be lighted by a 25-horsepower Westinghouse dynamo. Cronise and his electricians spent weeks installing the wires and lamps, doing a job which today, because of the advance in the electrical industry and building codes, would not pass muster under any building inspector.

In the meantime, John J. Hand as head of the mechanical department journeyed to Chicago and St. Louis, in which markets he bought new equipment for the paper. Several tons of type and chases, stereotyping machinery and an eight-page, web-perfecting Bullock press, capable of printing some 12,000 copies an hour ready for the folding machine, were included. The press was specially designed, Hand noted, "to take in seven columns to the page, in case the business at Dallas should hereafter require a larger paper" than the contemplated six columns. By the time these purchases began arriving, a 15-horsepower Skinner & Wood engine to drive the press, the dynamo, and the boiler were ready for installation by the R. V. Tompkins Machinery Company.

Executive heads from Galveston spent much of their time in Dallas during the late summer and early fall. The stock subscription offered by citizens was accepted, partly to help finance the expansion but more to enlist the interest of residents in the business. Details of news gathering were ironed out. By leased telegraph wires across the 315 miles between Dallas and Galveston, the offspring would tap the elaborate system of special correspondence which the parent had built up over the years. An imaginary line was drawn across the State from Texarkana to Del Rio, generally along the route of the International & Great Northern Railroad. Correspondents north of that line were instructed to file news dispatches directly to Dallas after October 1. The Dallas *Herald* controlled the local franchise of the Western Associated

Press, the predecessor before 1900 of the present Associated Press, but THE NEWS contracted with the rival United Press (no connection, however, of the present organization of that name), and the Baltimore and Ohio Telegraph Company for a daily budget of 7,000 words on national and foreign news.

As the time drew near to put the first issue to press, the staff began to assemble. In proof that the Dallas paper would not be a mere echo of the Galveston edition, the president of the company, Colonel Belo, moved with his family from Galveston to Dallas in 1885. Three years later he bought property on the corner of Ross and Pearl Streets, where he built a residence which was one of "the show places" of Dallas for many years. The editor-in-chief, Donaldson C. Jenkins, also moved to Dallas. William O'Leary, for some time staff correspondent for THE NEWS in Dallas, became the first city editor. W. G. Sterett, a leading newspaperman of Dallas, sold his interest in the *Times* and would soon join the staff of THE NEWS as one of its most famous members. At the head of the business department—or counting room, as the name persisted—was G. B. Dealey. His department comprised twelve men, including the cashier, one advertising solicitor, a collector, a mailing clerk and assistants, a city circulator and assistants. The composing room which set up the first edition comprised thirty-one men. Beside the foreman and his assistants, there were twenty-five compositors, two apprentices, a proofreader and a copy-holder. The stereotyper had two assistants. The pressman, the engineer, their two assistants and a helper were stationed in the pressroom. Pressroom, engine room, and mailing room were all to be found in one ground-floor compartment of the building, which measured only twenty-five by sixty feet.

Throughout the last day of September and past the first hours of the next each member of the organization worked at his appointed post. The machinery had been oiled and tested, but many last-minute adjustments had to be made. Tension increased after midnight. Earlier in the evening hundreds of townspeople had

visited the building; drawn, however, fully as much by the novelty
of the incandescent lamps "with their beautiful soft mellow light,"
as by the shiny new machinery. But some fifty spectators doggedly
waited for the first press run. Then, when the last stick of type had
been set and the last plate sent down from the stereotype room and
adjusted on the press, "the heads of the several departments of the
paper, the members of the editorial staff and the gentlemen of the
business office" filed into the pressroom, the signal was given and
the press began to roll. The circulation at the start was approximately 5,000.

"THE DALLAS MORNING NEWS was born at 4:15 o'clock yesterday morning," the account in the second day's issue stated.
"The event was quiet and calm. There were a few remarks to
show how freely the employees breathed when the first paper came
forth, followed by hundreds of others as fast as the press, a thing
of beauty, could disgorge them. Then until 6 a.m. the paper rolled
in endless stretch from the frame that held it to the press. Every
man stood up to the racket from ground floor to roof until the
finish Thursday morning."

Among the spectators was Pat O'Keefe, bartender, alderman
and friend of Presidents. As the first copy came from the press,
he grabbed it and made for the exist. The keen-eyed guardian of
the press, with Irish in his own blood, had seen that the paper
failed to take the ink properly. "Don't take that," he yelled, "it's
a bad impression." "Never mind," replied Pat, "an Irishman always makes a bad impression at first." The first perfect copy went
to another spectator, General Rudolph Gunner, aide and con-
fidant of the ill-fated Maximilian in Mexico twenty years before,
an exile making his living by selling books, magazines and newspapers from a little shop on Main Street.

The chief task was to get the papers printed on schedule so that
all the early morning trains out of Dallas might carry their quotas.
"If the chief of the business office rolled up his sleeves and took
a hand in the mailing of the packages, what of it?" asked the reporter of the scene. "He meant business and saw to it."

"We never missed a link in our connection," G. B. Dealey was
quoted directly in the same account. "The Santa Fe was to take

our last batch, and we had only twelve minutes more to make it, when the press stopped. There was some kink to be ironed out. 'Can't you let us have just 200 more papers?' I said to the press-man. 'We've got to have our record clear.' Grunting in assent, he started the press and, kink or no kink, the huge machine went rat-tling along until the mail was all up and delivered on schedule." Then, and then only, the account concluded, did "the business manager silently and composedly seek his bed."

☆

The little heralded event of the birth of "chain journalism" was to have consequences beyond Dallas and THE NEWS itself. Charles A. Dana, commenting on the experiment to Colonel Belo in New York, remarked that "it is well worth watching." In England, there was a restless young genius by the name of Alfred Harms-worth, and, in America, there was Senator Hearst's son, William Randolph, both of whom, among others, would carry the implica-tions of the plan to its logical conclusion. As an authoritative his-torian of journalism, James Melvin Lee, commented years later, "to Texas, therefore, belongs the honor of being first in co-opera-tive journalism in America."

The new paper which greeted the citizens of Dallas and North Texas that morning, except for its title and local news, seemed no stranger to subscribers of the old GALVESTON NEWS. In fact, as the Fort Worth *Gazette* pointed out, "its identity with the parent sheet is closely traced in the news, editorial, and general make-up of the paper, which is as high a compliment as the new publication could ask." The Dallas *Herald* described its new rival as a "facsi-mile of its parent stem," and "as neat and newsy as its other half." In extending a welcome, the *Herald* assured its readers that the newcomer "would be a credit to Dallas and to the State press."

It was such a welcome as THE NEWS itself hoped for. In the leading editorial of that first issue—the famous "encyclical" begin-ning "Today, pursuant"—THE NEWS assured readers and rivals that the move came in "no spirit of invasion or rapacity . . . , with no intention of destructive competition."

In establishing a regular daily edition at Dallas, THE NEWS does not conceive that it is introducing itself as a stranger in a strange country [the editorial continued] but it merely proposes to cover more fully a familiar field and to converse more directly with a familiar public. . . .

No promises or boasts were to cloud its course, added the editor:

The supreme obligation of THE NEWS is to serve the public in the office of an honest, diligent and faithful newspaper. While keenly sensible of this obligation, THE NEWS, however, has no promises or boasts of intended performances to make. It is calmly content to be judged by its record in the future as by its record in the past.

The antecedents and traditions of the paper commit it to the cause of reform and progress, but also to an uncompromising conservatism on the fundamental point of law and order as absolutely indispensable, alike, to liberty and security, to all true reform, and to all wholesome progress.

But the same editorial made it clear that THE NEWS did not accept every idea masquerading under the name of reform as possible of realization:

While advocating every practicable form of amelioration where there is a wrong condition, THE NEWS will continue to recognize, as it has recognized, the presence in politics, in public affairs, in society, in industrial and business arrangements, of a certain measure of persistent evils that defy rectification—that in the nature of things, and by the inexorable force of human imperfections, are inevitable.

Where this is the case, the nearest approach to remedy or compensation is to accept the inevitable with philosophic resignation. And, where this is the case, the part of a wise and faithful counselor of the people in journalism is to inculcate such resignation—not to excite vain and vexatious strife for impossibilities.

In matters of real reform, however, THE NEWS served full warning that, "out of honest convictions and insistent fidelity to truth, conscience, justice and the public welfare," it stood now as in the past "ready to prosecute a mission of generous endeavor and peaceful conquest in the domain of political agitation and public discussion."

But whatever may impend [the editorial concluded], whatever the situation, the emergency, the occasion from this time forth, THE

NEWS expects, by virtue of the step this day taken compassing a wider range of circulation, to be more largely than ever a people's university of information, a people's forum of discussion, a people's electric circle of illumination, and in the highest sense of the words, a people's inquisition and censorship.

Despite the enthusiasm which greeted the start of THE NEWS at Dallas, it was obvious that the city, numbering less than 20,000 people, could not support two morning newspapers. Within less than eight weeks, therefore, the inevitable happened, and the newcomer took its second most important step. This was the outright purchase, "lock, stock and barrel," of the old Dallas *Herald*. By this means, a friendly, but nonetheless destructive, rivalry was ended. It also enabled THE NEWS to add the morning franchise in Dallas of the Western Associated Press. Notice of the purchase was published November 30 :

THE NEWS takes pleasure in announcing that, for personal and business reasons of their own, the editors and proprietors of the Dallas *Herald,* Col. P. S. Pfouts, Col. J. F. Elliott and Col. W. L. Hall, have identified themselves with THE NEWS by becoming purchasers of [some of] its capital stock. . . . This involves, of course, the discontinuance of the Dallas *Herald,* but it does not involve any changes in the business status, the business principles or the general policy of THE NEWS.

On the same day the Dallas *Herald* printed its valedictory :

With this issue, the Dallas *Herald* ceases to exist. . . . Since 1849, through peace times, civil war and peace again, this *Herald* has been the faithful reporter for the past thirty years. It first came to Dallas as a weekly weakling on a little ox cart from Paris, Lamar County, with the popular, able and beloved Mark Latimer as proprietor and editor.

In 1874 after a quarter of a century of honorable existence, it blossomed into a daily. . . . It passed into the possession of these its last proprietors in 1879. . . .

And now to further evince the fealty of its proprietors and to extend the fame and fortune of this city and section, they today enter into combination and hearty cooperation with the newcomer in our midst. With it they trust their own fate under the conviction that a harmony of feeling and the general effort in the direction named can better be secured throughout the community than by possible antagonisms that might ensue with two Richmonds in the field.

Thus within two months from its birth THE DALLAS MORNING NEWS received new impetus of material as well as sentimental value. For, to the traditions of achievement and high enterprise inherited from Galveston, there was now added the record of Dallas' own pioneer newspaper. If THE DALLAS MORNING NEWS did not elect, as it might well have done, to number its volumes from the founding of either the *Herald* in 1849 or THE NEWS in 1842, the decision was prophetic of the fact that it would develop an independent character of its own, evolving as the community itself advanced, and tied only to the finest and most enduring traditions in its double inheritance. Yet the present claim of THE DALLAS NEWS to the title of "the oldest business institution in Texas" was guaranteed and made incontrovertible by the fact that its direction was in the hand of the same closely held publishing concern that guided the destinies of the mother paper at Galveston.

CHAPTER VIII

THE TWO FAIRS IMBROGLIO

1886–1888

As if taking a new lease on life because of the establishment of The News in its midst, Dallas entered a period of remarkable growth in the five years after 1885. Choice of the city by the long established journalistic institution focussed attention on the community and led a number of other Texas and out-of-State concerns to move there. The population of 18,000 more than doubled in this period, taxable wealth increased four and one-half times and by the Federal census of 1890 Dallas advanced in size from the fifth to the first city of Texas.

Whether The News "fetched along the boom," or was merely a reflection of it, the new paper from its start gave unquestioned support to the commercial and civic interests of Dallas, supplying an effective, if somewhat bristling, leadership that got results. Business leaders who had sponsored the move were more than gratified. Their judgment was confirmed from an outside source in 1890 when A. Frank Richardson of the Minneapolis *Pioneer-Press* visited the city. Referred to by the *Journalist* of New York as "the best authority in the United States on newspaper circulation," Richardson remarked that he had last seen Dallas a year before The News located there. He had believed at that time that another North Texas community would grow faster.

"But I have concluded now," added the visitor, "that the other town is no longer in the race. Without any attempt at flattery, but merely doing justice where it is merited, let me here observe that, in my opinion, Dallas owes its supremacy and growth to the establishment of The Dallas Morning News. . . . I can conservatively say that the paper is at least 40 per cent in advance of the State today. . . ."

The success of the paper exceeded the hopes of its founders. It rapidly confirmed the estimates made in the surveys by G. B. Dealey and others. By the end of the first year, THE NEWS had attained a circulation three times as great as the old *Herald* had enjoyed in its palmiest days. This was due chiefly to the intensive fight made for circulation throughout the trading area of Dallas. Almost at once a special train on the Texas & Pacific Railway was leased to carry the papers to Fort Worth, for distribution in that city and to insure railway connections out of there. On May 21, 1887, at much heavier expense, a daily train was leased on the Houston & Texas Central from Dallas to McKinney, Sherman and Denison for similar reasons in the distribution of the paper. When THE NEWS started at Dallas in 1885, the St. Louis newspapers had a larger circulation in the tier of North Texas counties than any Dallas or Texas paper. These moves enabled THE NEWS to displace out-of-State rivals. The "Comet," as the high-speed, sixty-mile-an-hour special train was called, constituted a breath-taking exploitation stunt in itself and helped spread the fame of the paper to the farthest reaches of the State. By the end of its first decade, the daily average circulation of THE NEWS at Dallas was 15,000 copies.

No less encouraging was the rise in advertising volume and revenue. Starting publication with an average of only twelve columns of revenue space, THE NEWS by its third birthday was averaging twenty-four columns of advertising. As a result, Sunday issues averaged sixteen pages, while the weekly editions often had to be enlarged from eight to twelve pages. In less than four years "the business at Dallas" forced expansion of the page from six to seven columns. By the time the sixth anniversary rolled around, a second new press had been put in service, a Seymour-Brewer inset machine capable of printing 24,000 copies an hour and equipped for two-color printing. A so-called fire-proof annex behind the original building was erected to house it. The addition was crude and unsatisfactory, as judged by present day standards.

Within the space of a few years, THE DALLAS MORNING NEWS, both in circulation and advertising, was overtowering its parent at Galveston. North Texas skeptics who had feared that the Dallas

Facsimile of the front page, first issue of THE DALLAS MORNING NEWS,
October 1, 1885

Original Bullock perfecting press, used by THE DALLAS NEWS at its beginning in 1885. Around it are seen several who were with the paper at the start. (*Left to right*— T. M. Rinehart, mechanical department superintendent; H. M. Campbell, Sr., foreman of the composing room; A. F. Hess, assistant foreman of the composing room; Arthur Geen, auditor; Wm. G. Sterett, an editor; W. H. Hall, printer; and G. B. Dealey—only survivor of this group—then business manager.

publication would prove a mere echo of the tidewater journal now had the satisfaction of seeing that "the tail is wagging the dog." At the height of the booming '80's, the Dallas paper in one regular Sunday edition carried some eighty-nine columns of advertising. "These are, in truth," commented the editor, "rapid, pushing times." Dallas held the front of the Texas stage.

☆

A host of national and State questions engrossed the editorial attention of THE NEWS at the time it began publishing its duplicate in North Texas. Cleveland was sending his first message to Congress in December, 1885, recommending, among other measures, that the Bland compulsory silver coinage act of 1878 be repealed. While THE NEWS believed that a majority of Democrats were opposed to the monetary views of the President, it expressed the hope that no one would question "the conscientious aims" of Cleveland, and it was frank in its admiration of the forceful style of the message; the paper was impressed, above all, by "its charm of honesty and sincerity."

Closer at hand, THE NEWS was perturbed over the management of the leasing for grazing purposes of millions of acres of State-owned land in West Texas, laying the burden of its criticism chiefly on the State Land Board. There was, also, the ominous strike among dock hands of the Mallory Line at Galveston, called by the Knights of Labor, the new (and in the eyes of THE NEWS) revolutionary working-class organization which seemed to have sprung up overnight throughout the nation. It was almost as inexplicable as this new movement among the growing body of tenants in Texas, the Farmers' Alliance.

Several months later, the power of the Knights of Labor was felt more heavily in Texas as the first great interstate railroad strike spread to the very doorstep of THE NEWS. The paralysis developed from the walkout, early in 1886, of some 3,700 "conspirators" on the Gould lines, following an initial dispute in the shops of the Texas & Pacific Railway at Marshall. Railway facilities of four Southwestern States and the then Indian Territory were affected, resulting in the use of militia units from Dallas for riot duty in Fort Worth and drawing a Congressional committee to Texas to investigate. Under the sponsorship of THE NEWS, members of the Merchants' Exchange met and expressed their sympathy for the great Southwestern railroad king, Jay Gould; the meeting inveighed particularly against "the open and secret, subversive influence of the strikes and boycotts now existing." The dispute was soon lost sight of by the nation at large in the greater public excitement over the Haymarket Riots in Chicago.

THE NEWS had been more than displeased by the spineless attitude which it considered Governor John Ireland had shown toward the Southwestern strike. He should not have hesitated, the paper felt, to have kept the common carriers in operation by the use of armed State troops. Ireland, in fact, had many sins of omission to answer for, including the failure to enforce the State land laws. Only the fortuitous flare up of a threatened war between Texas and Mexico restored him to the newspaper's good favor.

Early in 1886 sentiment had been aroused over the State by the arrest of an El Paso editor, A. K. Cutting, in adjoining Ciúdad Juarez across the Mexican border. While this editor languished in a Chihuahua jail, a naturalized Texan at Eagle Pass, one Francisco Rasures, fell into the hands of Diaz' *rurales* on the Mexican side of the line. A wave of hysterical resentment swept over Texas as THE NEWS and other papers broadcast reports of this second outrage. Street parades and patriotic rallies sprang up in Dallas and in scores of other places, thousands volunteered to fight Mexico again and Governor Ireland, in a message to Secretary of State Bayard at Washington, demanded, "in the name of the State of Texas and its people, that this wrong by Mexico be atoned for and punished." What was more to the liking of an aroused citizenry, Ireland further informed Cleveland's cabinet officer that "if this State and her people must depend upon themselves for protection, the necessary redress can and will be obtained."

In a front-page editorial styled "Provocation Beyond Edurance," THE NEWS approved Ireland's ultimatum to Washington:

Governor Ireland has taken bold steps. If somewhat brusque and irregular, his message to Secretary Bayard is full of genuine Texas spirit. Texas by herself has whipped Mexico, and can do it again with the same sympathetic aid of her American brethren, if necessary.

Not since Bangs and French in 1842 demanded blood atonement had THE NEWS felt so strongly on a Mexican matter. The editorial continued:

Unfortunately the hands of Texas are tied by membership in the Federal Union. Texans love the Union in every regard, except that it subjects them to outrage without defense. They have stood more from Mexican marauders than it is human nature to take quietly. The proper way for the Washington government is to demand . . . complete satisfaction in the several cases now pending . . . or, failing this, to declare war and occupy Mexican territory. This issue has to come, or rather it has come, and disastrous must be any shrinking.

Texans demand nothing less than what Governor Ireland has said to Mr. Bayard, and Texans will be moved as one man in sustaining the State authorities in any practicable and necessary action to force Mexico into measures of redress and justice. No driveling diplomacy at Washington must be allowed.

But driveling diplomacy was permitted, finally, to settle the issue. The war spirit burned fiercest in Texas and press comment throughout the nation was in a light, even ragging spirit, although the New York *Herald* solemnly weighed the consequences of an ill-timed war. More typical was the comment of the St. Louis *Post-Dispatch*, which said that "almost anybody can safely insult the United States, but in insulting the State of Texas, Mexico has waked up the wrong passenger." Diaz, at first, refused to recognize "such an insignificant affair between two disreputable journalists," but the Cleveland Administration stood firm; in the end the Supreme Court of Chihuahua released Cutting by dismissing the case against him.

The State Democratic Convention which met in Galveston in August of 1886 had for its main business the nomination of Sul Ross for Governor and James Stephen Hogg for Attorney General. It gave some of its attention to the Cutting Affair, though, even if the war spirit was ebbing in Texas. "Decisive action in demanding indemnity for past and existing grievances . . . will meet the unequivocal approval of the Democracy of Texas," this body sent word to the President. But by the time Congress assembled in

December, Cleveland could announce that the issue had been resolved. He added a thought, however, which later was to charm
another great Democratic chieftain, William Jennings Bryan; at
least, as Secretary of State, he paid it the tribute of a paraphrase:

Nature has made us irrevocable neighbors [President Cleveland
said of Mexico and the United States], and wisdom and kind feelings
should make us friends.

But fateful as these questions seemed, THE NEWS, from its arrival in Dallas, was first of all concerned with the destiny of its
home city. As the slight business recession of 1886 faded into
memory, Dallas experienced the great unloosing of energies and
growth already noted. THE NEWS sought to keep the boom from
reaching dangerous proportions. Jay Gould in 1886 was telling the
rest of the country that, "although I do not expect to live to see it,
Dallas will have a population in another generation of 250,000
people." Already Dallas enthusiasts (as Bill Nye noted on a visit
in 1891) had formed the habit of "drawing an imaginary radius
of 100 miles around the city," in which magic circle were to be
found enough cotton, sheep, wheat, beeves, acres, buildings and
people to make a king's ransom. The twenty-mile trade area in
the form of a crescent had long been exceeded, and Jefferson had
bowed to her more booming rival.

THE NEWS played its part in encouraging trade and industry,
but all the while it insisted firmly that there were human and even
economic values besides mere size. While the population was over-
flowing in four directions into suburbs served by four steam rapid
transit lines, the paper called for a more comfortable, a more
healthy, and withal a more attractive city to live in. "Dallas
should look to the future," it repeatedly warned. "A city that
grows from a population of 1,700 in 1870 to 37,000 in 1887 would
be liable to the charge of being wild indeed in calculating only for
the present." It was becoming axiomatic, as G. B. Dealey noted,
that no local improvement was ever designed adequately enough.

More and better street paving was pointed to as a first essential,

as the bounds of the old town—measuring only one and one-half
square miles—were obliterated. Citizens were encouraged to
obey the new law requiring sidewalks in front of their property.
Although the city owned one park in South Dallas at old Browder
Springs and T. L. Marsalis provided another in his new suburb of
Oak Cliff, THE NEWS asked that provision be made for much
more common acreage. When Col. J. T. Trezevant returned from
Philadelphia in 1889 to propose that Dallas emulate the great
Fairmont park system by converting Turtle Creek into a chain of
parks and parkways, THE NEWS seconded the motion.

Public health should be made paramount. The germ theory of
disease was itself infecting the mind of the populace, and THE
NEWS called for appointment of a city chemist and got one. The
paper prevailed upon the city health officer to order all sewerless
premises cleaned and disinfected to prevent epidemics, and it published the formula for a cheap disinfectant to wipe out plague
spots. Above all, it tackled the apparently insoluble problem of an
adequate and healthy water supply, a problem that had made and
unmade city administrations since 1872. Browder Springs was
playing out as a source, and the idea of surface reservoirs was
toyed with, although the faction which favored damming the
Trinity River instead almost succeeded in securing this plan at a
cost of $100,000 in 1887. Only the prejudice against water which
had coursed through Fort Worth, thirty-two miles to the west,
defeated it. The prejudice was successfully revived by Alderman
Cochran and others, who (THE NEWS reported) "portrayed quite
a vivid picture, entirely too strong for publication in a religious
paper, of some of the handwriting on the unspeakable walls of
Fort Worth." Then in 1890, THE NEWS was able to print "as
welcome a piece of intelligence as was ever published in this
paper," the bringing in of an artesian well of gusher proportions
on the courthouse grounds. A young geologist then at the University of Texas, who had formerly been a compositor on THE
NEWS at Galveston, Dr. Robert T. Hill, had given as his opinion
that a vast underground stratum of pure water could be tapped in
Dallas. Now, at last, the paper believed, the city had solved its
problem of a water source for all time. THE NEWS drilled and

found a second artesian well on its own property on Commerce Street.

City government should be run on a business basis, the journalistic newcomer argued without end. The corporation of Dallas had been placed on a non-partisan basis in 1890 upon the merger with East Dallas. Overwhelmingly Democratic in State and national elections, the city elected Republicans and Democrats alike to its city council. For this, Dallas was singled out by the old *North American Review* as an example to the nation of a municipal corporation freed from the worst features of partisan politics. THE NEWS supported, therefore, the new charter adopted with the merger, which insured a small governing body free from party control. In addition, THE NEWS listed as one of the most valuable civic assets "an increased air of refinement and artistic elegance" which should be striven for over the city. "Let us have a more cultivated taste in architecture, in the arrangement of lawns, fountains, parks, in the selection of rare flowers, shrubs and vines," it said.

☆

These various concerns of the paper came to a head in its part in the creation of the State Fair of Texas. The task was one of the first to which the paper set its hand.

As a result of continued discussions and agitation in the paper, a fair association was formed early in 1886, with J. B. Simpson as president. "The movement is a strong one and is another forcible evidence of the ability of Dallas to organize and carry out a great undertaking," said THE NEWS in February. "There is a feeling that a grand opportunity is presented by the commercial center of the State to gather into one enclosure the varied and magnificent showings that can be made by Texas. The best energy and wisdom of Dallas have been enlisted in the plan."

Scarcely had the preliminaries been started, though, than the directorate split in two. The point of dissension proved to be the site chosen by a majority of the sponsors for the fair grounds, some forty acres in East Dallas near the crossing of Main Street with the

Texas & Pacific Railway, and officially styled the Dallas State Fair. Representatives of the farm implement dealers seceded from the board in protest, incorporated a second enterprise and bought another tract of ground along the right-of-way of the Houston & Texas Central Railroad in North Dallas (now Central Avenue) near the proposed extension of McKinney Avenue, and opposite what is now the grounds of the North Dallas High School. Headed by C. A. Keating and with the backing of leading spirits in the Knights of Labor and the Farmers' Alliance, the rival fair announced it would hold its exposition at the same time as the "East Dallas" show.

"The ground selected by the old association is the worst kind of a hog wallow," complained C. A. Keating. "That is why the implement and machinery interests almost to a man refused to show their goods there."

Then began a battle of words that waxed into appeals to the city council, to court injunctions and to exhortations from numerous individuals within and without Dallas that the factions should compose their differences. THE NEWS was shocked by this outbreak of petty jealousy and bickering founded on nothing more substantial than rival real estate interests. Promptly affirming that it would not take sides in the unreasonable schism, the paper deplored "the turn affairs have taken and respectfully expresses the opinion that every means should be adopted by the people of Dallas to secure a united effort for a State Fair."

There was never a time in the history of Dallas when unity of action among her people was more imperative [THE NEWS added on April 27]. The spectacle which this community is now making of itself in the eyes of the State is not flattering. The battle for civic supremacy is not over yet by long odds. The present untimely and suicidal controversy should be brought to an immediate close.

Despite the refusal of THE NEWS to take sides, or rather because of it, the paper soon became a target in the crossfire. In July, C. A. Keating called on the management of THE NEWS to espouse the cause of the North Dallas fair. When G. B. Dealey assured him that under no circumstances would the paper swerve from its set course, the implement dealer angrily announced that he would

"unload" all five shares of A. H. Belo & Company stock which he
had bought at the start of THE DALLAS NEWS, offering to sell
them for fifty cents on the dollar. He then inserted an advertisement in the paper offering the stock for sale on the ground that
the owner was "not satisfied with the course pursued by this paper
toward certain interests of Dallas." THE NEWS obligingly called
attention editorially to the bargain offer of its stock and added:

THE NEWS is desirous of aiding the Keating Implement and
Machinery Company in finding a customer for this stock. This is a
small piece of chagrin growing out of "the two fairs imbroglio," to
which THE NEWS is perfectly indifferent.

But the time was as good as any, directors of the newspaper
decided, to settle a larger issue, once and for all:

A point has been reached, however, where THE NEWS management
deems it necessary to say that it is master of its own business and will
submit to no dictation at the hands of anyone. There is little sentiment about THE NEWS, and certainly THE NEWS is nobody's toy.
THE NEWS is here in a legitimate business capacity and THE NEWS
is here to stay.

This fact the Keating Implement and Machinery Company may
rest assured of, for THE NEWS will be doing business in Dallas long
after the Keating Implement and Machinery Company and all connected with it are dead and forgotten. Meantime, the heavy "block"
thus rushed on the market is not likely to "bear" the stock of the A. H.
Belo & Company incorporation to any considerable extent. THE
NEWS will endeavor to keep cool, even with the thermometer touching 98 degrees in the shade, and the implement company hot with it
at the same time.

Meanwhile preparations for the simultaneous opening of the
two fairs continued throughout the summer, and THE NEWS was
reconciled, temporarily at least, to the prospect. Former Governor
O. M. Roberts, "the Old Alcalde," came in his capacity as professor of law in the University of Texas to open, with fine impartiality, both expositions. The Texas State Fair in North Dallas
opened its gates on October 25. A fair-sized crowd entered by way
of the newly macadamized extension of McKinney Avenue, or in
special trains which operated from the downtown depot of the

Houston & Texas Central on Marilla Street at Austin. The war dances of the Modoc Indians, the celebrated exhibition mare, Lady De Jernette, and the Roman chariot races between "a lady and a gentleman, each drawn by eight horses to the chariot," were attractions widely commented on.

The rival Dallas State Fair opened its gates the next day in East Dallas. Mule-drawn street cars on the Main Street line and special trains of the Texas & Pacific Railway operating from the downtown depot on Pacific Avenue at Lamar Street, conveyed slightly larger crowds to it. Speaking here, Governor Roberts again ignored the local schism by emphasizing the need for a deep-water port at Galveston—some three hundred safe miles away. A troop of Comanche Indians, spirited horse races, and music by the Presidential Band from Mexico City were its starred attractions. As chief executive of the city, Major John Henry Brown welcomed the fifty-six musicians from Mexico in Spanish, a linguistic feat never equalled by any subsequent mayor of Dallas.

Contrary to almost everyone's expectations, both fairs proved successful. The rivalry, in fact, accounted in part for this outcome, in the opinion of a staff correspondent for the New Orleans *Times-Democrat,* who termed the double-headed exposition "in many respects the most remarkable event seen in the Southwest."

"The rivalry throws the managers on their mettle," he added, "and hence they spent $200,000 before the gates opened. The associations have offered no less than $60,000 as premiums or purses. The railways, as a mark of special favor to their pet city, put their fares to almost nothing. As a consequence, the attendance the first day was 20,000, and the second, 27,000 and yesterday no less than 38,000 passed through the gates. It is doubtful if even some of our world's fairs ever had more on one day."

☆

At the close of the two fairs, THE NEWS was first to congratulate the backers of each. Their pluck rewarded, their judgment complimented by satisfactory returns at the cash boxes, the organ-

izers were labelled benefactors of Dallas and Texas. THE NEWS
was more convinced than ever, though, that "differences, estrange-
ments and misunderstandings must be obliterated." Early in 1887
the two fairs were consolidated into the Texas State Fair and
Dallas Exposition Association. Control now was placed in hands
not identified with the previous squabble, James Moroney being
named president of the united organization. Both old tracts were
sold for town lots and a new site farther east along the Texas &
Pacific right-of-way was bought—the same site used for fifty years
by the State Fair of Texas, and which, with some additional land
acreage, also served as the site of the Texas Centennial Exposition
of 1936.

This victory for a united city was sealed in the second State Fair,
held in October of 1887. Governor Sul Ross, noted Indian fighter
and rescuer of Cynthia Ann Parker, officiated at the opening.
Here, in addition to a wider display of the produce of Texas farms
and ranches, of the products of manufacturers and distributors,
an even more elaborate entertainment program was provided.
Horses races, bicycle races, and other events exerted their appeals;
but the greatest popular interest undoubtedly lay in what was
"nothing more nor less than a street railway run by electric power,"
which, THE NEWS reported, had been installed for actual operation within the fair grounds.

By 1888, the State Fair of Texas was fixed on a surer financial
basis. Always privately supported, the association distributed its
debt burden among a larger number of citizens at the insistence of
THE NEWS. J. S. Armstrong was serving as president at the time.
This was a wise step, the paper held, for too long had it been "a
positive shame and downright reproach" for an entire city to impose on six or seven men who had taken the main risk in this non-
profit enterprise; all the more so since "everybody gets the benefit
of the fair and since the fair is already a Texas institution and a
fixture for all time." Something of outside recognition of the
pluck, self-sacrifice, and community spirit of Dallas which made
the fair possible was given during the exposition of that year by
Henry Grady. The noted Georgia editor and spokesman of the

New South arrived from Atlanta to address 10,000 gathered to hear him on Georgia Day. It was one of Grady's last speeches and takes rank as one of his best. It has been widely reprinted.

"I salute the first city of the grandest State of the greatest government on earth," began Grady. "In paying earnest compliment to this thriving city and this generous multitude, I need not cumber speech with argument or statistics. . . ."

CHAPTER IX

"THIS AGE OF CHANGE"

1885–1890

LIFE IN the young metropolis of Dallas in the 'Nineties was a rip-snorting affair, somewhat gaudy, often violent, but always filled with the hearty humors and virtues of frontier existence. The destiny of the town had been seized by youthful hands. It was a time, when, with the imminent passing of the frontier, urban life was becoming ever more glamorous in the eyes of the more restless of Americans. As the swarm of newcomers outgrew the old village boundaries, the adolescent city presented a scene of contrast, change and exuberance.

Automatically, THE NEWS caught and reflected much of the outlines, the features, even the flesh tints of that lusty life. The ideals, tastes and manners of North Texans of half a century ago indelibly traced themselves in the pages of the newspaper. If THE NEWS saw Dallas in 1886 as "now floating upon a tide of legitimate prosperity uncrippled by the Red Man and border ruffian, . . ., free from all the embarrassments to which newly settled communities are subjected," it felt no cause to apologize for, or to condemn, a number of customs and interests which a later generation might frown upon.

The crusade of THE NEWS for strict observance of law and order antedated its arrival in Dallas by many years. Nor was the crusade abated. The paper gloried in the fact that it was the official organ of only one group in Texas, the association of sheriffs. Its daily "Sheriffs' Department" column, fed by more than 200 local correspondents, proved a valuable bureau of crime notification and detection. But the newspaper refused to suppress crime news in its efforts to suppress crime itself. As a result THE NEWS fed its readers a fairly stout diet of violence; nor were such items

122

confined to distant places. A typical example may be found in the
front page news story on February 20, 1886, which was headlined:

AND YET ANOTHER HORROR
TO SHOCK THE VIRTUOUS
PEOPLE OF DALLAS

After reciting the specific facts of the crime in a subhead, the
headline writer added, in equally bold type, "What Next?" Along-
side "Choice Cable Cullings," "Washington Whispers," "Waco-
isms Winged By Wire" or "Lispings From Laredo," the reader
was more than likely to have his attention arrested by "Murder
Most Diabolical" or "Lynchers After John Doe." Thirteen out of
twenty news stories on the front page of one issue might deal with
violence, ranging from "A Mad Dog's Fearful Work" to "A
Woman Killer Hanged." Diagrammatic illustrations of the scene
of the crime, including the well known X-where-the-body-lay, were
brought to a high state of perfection in this period.

THE NEWS, at last, felt called upon to defend its frankness. It
is not to draw lessons and morals that crime news is ordinarily
given, the paper explained, but because it is news. Even on moral
grounds, nothing is gained by suppressing the knowledge of evil,
it contended. And paralleling the thought expressed by Charles
A. Dana, the editor added, "the greatest of religious teachers never
ceased to point His lessons with illustrations from the morbid anat-
omy of human nature." But, beyond these considerations, the
paper judged it an evidence of social progress that the idea of
suppressing crime news was giving way to the healthier concept
which recognized that evil exists in human society and that through
such recognition crime itself might be lessened. THE NEWS concluded its argument by saying:

Tricks of evasion, concealment and illusion only aggravate the
power of bandit elements of evil prowling under the cloaks of mystery
furnished them in the name of decency. Virtue can grow to no sturdi-
ness out of a soil of organized ignorance. To be healthy, vigorous and
stable, it must be rooted in knowledge, enlightenment and comprehensive culture.

☆

But crime after all occupied only a small part of the attention of readers. Sports were much more absorbing. The sports editor of THE NEWS had a fearful responsibility and must possess an appreciation broad enough to range successfully from the fine points of chess and billiards to those of the prize ring and the cocking main. Football was still something of an exotic, confined chiefly to Eastern colleges, and a golf course was talked of mainly by the few sons of St. Andrew who had settled in Dallas as representatives of Scottish investment houses. THE NEWS' account of the Yale-Princeton football game of 1885 was covered in one short paragraph, which ended with the simple, scoreless statement that "Yale won." Baseball, on the other hand, was fast becoming the national game. Long a popular sandlot sport in Texas, the game was put on a professional basis in 1888 with the first season of the Texas League. T. L. Marsalis and associates backed the financing of the Dallas Tigers, whose first ball grounds were located near the St. George Street station of the elevated steam railway to Marsalis' suburb of Oak Cliff. Marsalis, one of the most important of early day civic leaders in Dallas, had laid off the suburb with improvements totalling $500,000 in 1887.

Already ahead of other States in many things, Texas has been behind all the Northern States at least in the matter of outdoor sports [commented THE NEWS]. The prize ring—the protest against effeminacy or dudeism—has found small favor in Texas, but as a compromise between the two extremes, the game of baseball has been entered into on a large scale and promises to be the most interesting feature of the season's pastimes.

The status of prize fighting in Texas, as a matter of fact, had remained doubtful until the Legislature in 1889 seemed to legalize exhibition matches by means of a high license law. Interest in the sport reached a new high in Dallas the next year when Jake Kilrain, fresh from his defeat by John L. Sullivan in the bare-knuckle fight that had scandalized Mississippi, brought his "troupe of fistic entertainers" to the Dallas Opera House. During a sparring match open to local challengers, a Dallas carpenter stepped on the stage to go several rounds with Louis Baznia, one of Kilrain's understudies. The carpenter received a knockout blow and, after attempts to revive him proved futile, was pronounced dead. Interest shifted the next day to the justice court of John Henry Brown, who by now had moved from the mayoralty to the county judiciary. Justice Brown pondered long over the evidence in the sensational trial but concluded by freeing the defendant, since, the court was convinced, Baznia's unfortunate act was "utterly devoid of the quality of murder."

Horse racing held its old supremacy throughout these years. The consolidation of the two fairs at Dallas had enabled "the finest race course in the South" to be built on the new grounds. Other animals besides horses were sometimes pitted against each other. A dog fight never failed to attract a crowd. In THE NEWS of February 27, 1887, appeared this account:

> Last night old Turner Hall was packed from pit to dome by the sporting elite of Dallas and Fort Worth, the occasion being the bull-dog fight between John Heffron's Spot and Charles Neimeyer's Rowdy. . . .
> Both brutes were in excellent trim. The standard rules and regulations having been read, the dogs [which have] physiognomies that would do credit to a New York alderman, were introduced and irritation effected by pulling their tails. The next minute they were locked in one another's throats. . . . Time being called for the third round, Rowdy declined to move and Spot was declared the winner.

Dallas and Texas held national honors in one sport—cock fighting. In the Glen Lea, Sunny Side, and other local pits were fought week-long tournaments which attracted game cock breeders and entries from all parts of the country. Interest extended even to the White House itself, for President Cleveland, from the days when he had been sheriff of Buffalo, patronized "this kingly sport of ancient and noble lineage." More than 100 breeders entered more than 500 game birds of various strains in the great Dallas tournament of 1886 which, THE NEWS observed, "firmly established Texan supremacy in the cocking world."

"The most brilliant event of the tournament," in which $2,500 changed sides in the result, was a four-round go between Shawl-neck, a Dallas Redquill with a ragged gill, and Spooner, the champion of St. Louis, a dark ginger-red bird with a high comb. They weighed in even at 4:15. In the first round both birds jumped to the scratch, the dark one showing the better judgment, the Red-quill going low. On the turn they came together, hung and were separated. In the second round, St. Louis made the dash but went wild, and the dark cock lanced for the first blood of the great main. In the third round the birds jumped to a hang. St. Louis came up groggy in the fourth, and at the first shock lay down to its punish-ment. The Dallas champion shattered his steel at the second blow, ending the battle in three minutes and six seconds.

Betting on horse races, dog fights, and cocking mains did not exhaust all the gambling proclivities of the community. Perhaps the most popular form of chance was furnished by lotteries which then, as before, used advertising space in THE NEWS and other Texas papers. The *Beneficencia Pública* of Mexico, which main-tained a State agent at Houston, enjoyed a large following. The most popular in Texas was the Louisiana State Lottery, presided over by General P. T. G. Beauregard, a hero of the Confederacy, and backed by the State of Louisiana. Banks and bankers in-vested steadily in Louisiana lottery tickets.

In Dallas proper, gambling halls ran on what Colonel W. G. Sterett termed "a wide open basis." Although technically against State law, they operated because popular sentiment at the time went little further than to demand that games be fairly conducted. An early reform wave forced separation of gambling devices from saloons, so that devotees of the goddess of chance were forced, in some instances, to walk up a flight of stairs to pursue their hobby. As late as 1890, according to reports in THE NEWS, there were five faro banks, one keno board and several other "palaces of chance" within two blocks of the Grand Windsor Hotel. In the same period, crap shooting came almost to dominate the halls. A reporter for THE NEWS analyzed the popularity of dice, citing the terminology, the novelty and "the small amount of capital re-quired to admit one," as reasons for the prevalence of the game. The newspaperman had one suggestion to make, however:

If craps is to be recognized as one of the legitimate games of chance, then some stringent measures should be adopted to bar boys from the game. Any night of the week, but particularly on Saturday, a casual observer can see that from one-third to one-half of the crap shooters are boys ranging from fifteen to nineteen years of age.

Even more widespread was the interest in the theater, a field of amusement that poached, in its best forms, on the preserves of art itself. At the so-called lower end of the scale were numerous variety houses that flourished on Main as well as Camp Streets and included The Black Elephant in the Central Avenue section of the Negro district. This was credited by THE NEWS with being "the hardest den in Texas." But the legitimate theater, represented in the winter seasons at the Opera House, the summer season of light opera in the Oak Cliff pavilion and in the advance guard of vaudeville to be heard and seen on the stage at Mayer's Garden on Elm Street, drew even larger gate receipts and attracted a fashionable patronage from all parts of North Texas.

One of THE NEWS' own staunchest traditions called for the support of worthy theatricals—subject, of course, to equally sound canons of reviewing. The Dallas Opera House, under the guidance of Henry Greenwall of Galveston, Dallas and New Orleans, was fed by a continuous stream of the best attractions produced in the country. As the endless caravan of artists, entertainers and spectacles came through Dallas in the heyday of the Road, from Emma Abbott and her company in the new Gilbert and Sullivan success, "The Mikado," to Booth in "Hamlet" or Bernhardt in "La Tosca," THE NEWS pitilessly winnowed the chaff from the wheat. In this THE NEWS both at Galveston and Dallas had the support of Greenwall, who began his managerial career in Galveston in 1867 as lessee of Willard Richardson's Galveston Opera House, more popularly known as the Tremont Opera House, from its opening in 1871. Pointing out that the season of 1885 was the most successful in Texas since that year, Greenwall warned the theatrical trade journal, the New York Mirror, that while Texas was one of the best fields for good attractions, "we have no use for ham-fatters . . . and poor shows must keep out of this State." Despite Greenwall's protestations, THE NEWS did not always agree with the czar's judgments and was frank to say so. The first dramatic review of THE DALLAS MORNING NEWS concerned the performance of "Fortune's Fool," by the Rial-Bigger troupe, on October 2, 1885.

Of literary merit, the piece does not possess much. The incidents have been rehearsed often on the mellow drama stage and suggestions of the Phoenix and of the Creole in Article 47 are apparent in the development of the plot. . . . In justice it should be said that the troupe is deserving of a better play and this they no doubt will have this evening.

When THE NEWS was not amused by a performance or a player, its comment was sometimes considered harsh if not down-right rude by the less critical in the community. When the famous Jersey Lily, on her second American tour, finally overcame a fear of Southwestern train robbers to play in "A Wife's Peril" in Dallas, THE NEWS appraised her after the performance as "one of the most thoroughly developed theatrical charlatans that ever pre-sumed to tread the stage." Thoroughly developed, most of the audience might agree, but there were some who thought the paper was too severe on a good friend of the Prince of Wales:

As an actress Mrs. Langtry does not rank very high. Her personal charm seems to be the secret of her popularity. . . . She certainly has a magnificent physique of the tall, queenly type, and an exceedingly attractive face. Mrs. Langtry's bust is a model. . . . Her support, like the play, is light. Such a play in the hands of such a troupe un-relieved by Mrs. Langtry, who at best gives it only her moral support, would be intolerable.

Much of the same opinion prevailed in the mind of THE NEWS' reviewer when Bernhardt made her first entry into Texas in 1892. But where Lillie Langtry failed to dispel the prejudice, the French-woman triumphed. One personal interview with the now aging player was enough to bring the critic into camp. The spell of en-chantment did not dull critical faculties entirely, however:

La Tosca offers Mme. Bernhardt splendid opportunities for the display of her brilliant art. Eminently Sardouian in construction, it is not burdened with the poetry of drama, but it abounds in theat-rical effects. It is a tribute to her genius that she invests the character of Floria with an interest that is not merely theatrical but essentially and irresistibly human. That such a role, rendered in a foreign tongue, can be made absorbingly interesting to an American audience is a tribute to Mme. Bernhardt's powers.

The mill run of attractions during those years got its proportionate attention. McIntyre and Heath's minstrels, Bartley Campbell's "The White Slave," with its imperishable line: "Rags are royal raiments when worn for virtue's sake"; Clara Morris in the "Lady of Lyons"; James O'Neill, "probably the most versatile actor on the American stage," in "The Count of Monte Cristo"; Salvini in "Don Cesar de Bazan"; Joe Jefferson; Frederick Warde; Mrs. Bowers; Lawrence Barrett, in "Julius Cæsar"—the names and titles recall a golden age.

But the great enthusiasm was reserved for Edwin Booth on his first performance of "Hamlet" in Dallas. This event occurred on February 24, 1887, and THE NEWS, Dallas, and North Texas held back no stint of praise. The Opera House was sold out a week in advance. With tickets selling for $15 each, the box office shattered all previous records. A throng arrived by railroad train, carriage, street car and on foot on the night of the performance; hotels reported more than 1,000 out-of-town guests. It was a gala social function as well, and the society editor of THE NEWS mingled in the crowd to describe the dresses of the women and to list the more notable guests from surrounding cities and towns.

The master mind that last night enthralled the intellectual element of Dallas and surrounding cities was greeted with a cordiality both spontaneous and graceful [THE NEWS reported.] The world wide reputation of Mr. Booth of being the most satisfactory interpreter of the character of "the melancholy Dane" was fully borne out.

The first thing that most everybody does on turning attention to Hamlet is to sue out a writ de enquirendo and pass on the sanity of that individual. They do this because their fathers before them have done it. Some decide that he is stark mad, others that he is only half and half, and others that his madness is only feigned. There is no end of testimony to support each of these conclusions, but Mr. Booth has never bothered his head with any of these theories.

Mr. Booth went to the text, and he there learned how to rehabilitate the character with the mind of Shakespeare. He took it as a microcosm, not as a one part piece, and he has made an authentic restoration. He has removed Hamlet from the purely metaphysical sphere and given him a place in the province of human affection, passion, virtues and weaknesses. In doing so he has not only brushed away many absurd theories of literary polemics but he has given us a Lord Hamlet as a man among men, vexed by many things he cannot understand and surrounded by circumstances he could not control. . . . There are a few great men on the stage and Booth is one of them.

☆

Beyond the dramatic stage, neither THE NEWS nor the majority of its readers ventured far into the domain of the fine arts. Concerts of a professional calibre were few and far between. The Boston Symphony Orchestral Club in January of 1892 gave one of the first. THE NEWS' review of the program, devoted chiefly to the works of Haydn, Brahms and Bach, was largely negative—"The wind instruments were not overblown, the strings were not rasped and the pulsatile instruments were legitimately employed." Nor did the paper give much attention to current literature. Although it encouraged the women of Dallas in their efforts to assemble at least the nucleus of a public library, its own comments on current books were confined to one or two short notices on the Sunday editorial page, together with summaries of the contents of the more literary of monthly magazines. When Wilkie Collins died in 1889, THE NEWS printed a front-page editorial voicing the opinion that, by the Englishman's death, "the world loses the recognized greatest writer of fiction of the century." Interestingly enough, THE NEWS at the moment was publishing serially "The Blind Love," said to be one of Collins' masterpieces.

With increasing wealth, social life was becoming more formal in terms of the standards of older communities. In October of 1885 the newly formed Idlewild Club gave its first reception and ball in the Merchant's Exchange. The ballroom "was lighted with several clusters of the Edison incandescent electric lights supplied by the dynamo in THE NEWS' Building in the adjoining block." The society editor wrote that the club "has made a superb beginning as the leading social institution of our city."

Intellectual and esthetic interests, especially for the women, also became more fashionable. The Shakespeare Club and the Standard Club were formed about this time. A group of young ladies began the study of art with a certain Professor Lenz. The first showing of art, held in his classroom in the summer of 1887, became memorable because of one of the professor's own oil paintings, "View of Dallas From Oak Cliff." The society editor reported "a perfect crush of spectators" because, "never before has Dallas had an opportunity of calling such a painting her own." Civic leaders became impressed and added that fall a fine arts department to the State Fair of Texas.

But one fine art remained in masculine control—architecture. A State association had been formed in the early stages of the boom. Many of these men were citizens of the world either by birth or training, and they insisted upon the pioneer's privilege of speaking out in public if the tastes of their clients offended them. The clients might be public officials or wealthy private citizens building new homes. Among the more outspoken was James Wahrenberger of San Antonio, president of the State Association of Architects when it met in Dallas in 1890. He attacked the custom of demanding competitive designs for public buildings, a practice even then being carried out by Dallas County officials in the proposed new courthouse. And, while speaking of this, he spoke more broadly:

It appears absurd to me that in this age of steam cars, electricity, etc., courthouses, post offices and other public buildings should be of such antique architectural styles as to remind one of the dark days of the Inquisition and the carrier pigeon. . . .

Of that hideous nightmare, the so-called modern, Queen Anne residence, perhaps the least said the better. Also of the peculiar misapplications of the misunderstood Byzantine and Moresque forms, in which some of the younger brethren of the profession seem to take special delight to show their ignorance of architecture and esthetics —which in a great degree may account for the depraved taste displayed in much of our modern architecture.

If the women of Dallas paid little attention to the designs of public buildings, they carried out well such civic and cultural commissions as were assigned them. Nor was THE NEWS one to argue complacently that woman should confine her extra-household energies to cultural activities, interspersed, of course, with church, charitable and social diversions. "The modern woman," with her tendency toward emancipation, excited the admiration rather than the frown of the paper. Although woman, in what THE NEWS referred to as "this age of change, upheaval and domestic infelicity," seemed to be smashing old conventions, the newspaper called for ever greater iconoclasm. Particularly, the newspaper defended higher education for women, ruling out of court the argument that collegiate study overtaxed the physical health of young women. This was made the occasion for an editorial lecture against "pernicious fashions" which were, in fact, undermining the health of such students.

Little girls are dressed for show and not allowed to run and play in a natural manner necessary to health. Then a little later they are put in the vice-like grip of an apparatus for compressing the vital organs, and in dresses and cloaks which do not allow the elbows to be raised above the waist. . . . People should cease torturing and deforming their offspring!

What was more, THE NEWS refused to subscribe to the objections raised in Dallas when gymnasium classes for women teachers and girl pupils were introduced in the public schools in 1893. Defending the innovation, the newspaper said that "one thing that commends the course is its evident adherence to grace and truth. . . . It is becoming proper for woman to acknowledge that she is a biped and that she has 'legs' instead of 'limbs'."

☆

In the spiritual field, THE NEWS of the 1890's scrupulously maintained a purely secular character. Although it lightly referred to its own editorials as encyclicals, and staff members could write as well as speak of "the great religious paper," THE NEWS did not presume to encroach on the creeds and theologies of the day. It acknowledged religion as "one of the great sublimating influences of society" and respected the faith of Jew, Catholic and Protestant alike. But, out of this respect, it opposed any and all attempts to mix religion and partisan politics. As a result, the newspaper drew the fire of certain zealots in a contest which combined moral fervor with partisan politics.

This was the great State-wide campaign of 1887 in which prohibition leaders, backed by many religious leaders, sought to outlaw the liquor traffic on moral and political grounds. The result of years of agitation on the part of those dissatisfied with the non-political temperance movement, State prohibition finally became an issue within the Democratic party. Early in 1886, months before the Democratic State Convention met in San Antonio, "the Hotspur of the Texas Prohibitionists," Dr. J. B. Cranfill, then editor of the Gatesville *Advance,* informed THE NEWS that unless the convention provided for the submission of a prohibition amendment to the people, he and his followers were prepared to resort to separate political action. This, in the eyes of THE NEWS, was an unthinkable demand, and when the convention that summer merely straddled the issue by refusing to pledge the party against submission, the paper was indignant. Convinced that prohibition was "a fallacy, a delusion, a denial of personal liberty and, where not a practical abortion, a galling tyranny," the newspaper scolded the politicians for not having forced the issue :

Instead of placing prohibitionists on the defensive, the Democratic party platform recognizes the right of a prohibitionist to be a Democrat—a recognition, in the platform, of heresy! This is a warning to the Democrats that they cannot keep running on a party name for an eternity without taking issue squarely with the anti-Democratic tendencies. Only Democrats should be permitted shelter under the Democratic umbrella.

As 1886 drew to a close, politicians realized, however, that "thousands of good people" had been attracted to the banner of prohibition. Even Congressman Roger Q. Mills, bitterly opposed to all regulation measures from local option to national prohibition, weakened to the extent of saying that it was possible for a man to be "both a Prohibitionist and a Democrat." John H. Reagan, recently elevated from the House to the United States Senate, openly espoused the State-wide prohibition cause. As a result, the Legislature submitted the question in the form of a

proposal for a constitutional amendment by the people in August
of 1887. The campaign was in full swing by early spring. Democrats opposed promptly enrolled themselves under the banner of
"the True Blues" of Texas Democracy. They held their first rally
in Dallas on May 5, where plans were laid to oppose "the tidal
wave of intolerance which, beginning in New England, has already engulfed Kansas and Iowa and now threatens to overflow
into Texas." Barnett Gibbs of Dallas presided and Roger Q. Mills,
D. C. Giddings, and George Clark of Waco were among the
speakers. Attorney General Hogg was unable to be present but
wrote of his opposition to the amendment because of "its utter
impracticality and of the prolific evils that would certainly flow
from its adoption."

But prohibitionists made a surprisingly effective campaign. One
of their heaviest guns in the tier of black land counties in the
northern half of Texas was young Joseph Weldon Bailey, recently
arrived in Gainesville from Mississippi. Reagan's prestige was
enormous, dating from his service as Postmaster General of the
Confederacy. Charges and counter charges grew bitterer as the
summer wore on, and record-breaking crowds were listening to
speakers on both sides. It was a strange kind of political contest
in Texas, with Protestant ministers on the stump and anti-prohibitionists fighting zeal with zeal; one could not admit it openly, but
the outcome was becoming doubtful. THE NEWS brought its
heaviest editorial arguments into play, blasting away daily at the
proposal, while its news columns were crowded with reports of the
contest. In the midst of the fight, THE NEWS scored certain tactics of the Rev. G. W. Briggs, editor of the *Texas Christian Advocate* at Galveston, and the Rev. S. A. Hayden, editor of the *Texas
Baptist and Herald* at Waco, rushed to the defense of his fellow-
religious journalist. For a time the exchange of compliments between THE NEWS and these reverend editors threatened to crowd
out the campaign itself into the back pages.

Then, at a critical period toward the end of July, the "True
Blues" held their second State-wide rally at Fort Worth. It was
attended by a trainload of anti-prohibitionists from Dallas. Mills,
Hogg and others brought the crowd cheering to its feet, but it was

reserved for Francis R. Lubbock, Governor of Texas in the days of
the Confederacy, to produce the great sensation of the campaign
—a last-minute move that became obvious as Lubbock started, "I
once followed a leader of armies and the head of a nation. I
followed him to prison, and, when the doors were opened, I crossed
the Atlantic with him. In war and in peace, in public and private
life, he was always the same statesman and gentleman, than whom
this country has produced no greater. Let's see what Jefferson
Davis says about prohibition :"

I have heretofore declined to answer any of the many inquiries
made for my opinion on the Constitutional amendment now pending in Texas [Lubbock read from a letter from President Davis sent
seven days before from Beauvoir, Miss.] My reason for not replying
was an unwillingness to enter into a controversy in which my friends
in Texas stood arrayed against each other. In departing from
the rule heretofore observed, I trust that it will not be an unwarrant-
able intrusion.

Jefferson Davis' letter then placed him on the side of the anti-
prohibitionists :

Reared in the creed of Democracy, my faith in its tenets has grown
with its growth, and I adhere to the maxim that "the world is governed too much." . . . Drunkenness has become less frequent within
the last twenty years. The refining influences of education and Christianity may be credited with this result. Why not allow these hand-
maidens of virtue and morality to continue unembarrassed in their
civilizing work?

"The wildest Indian that ever scalped an enemy on Clear Fork
never uttered such notes of triumph as rose in the air," THE NEWS
correspondent reported from Fort Worth, in detailing the scene
which followed the reading of the letter. And, with it, was read
the death sentence of the prohibition movement of 1887 in Texas.
Even Reagan, in a public letter to his old chief in the Confederate
Cabinet, admitted as much two days before the election.

"We believed we could carry it against the saloon keepers, professional politicians and a number of good men like our friend
Governor Lubbock," Reagan wrote Davis, "but the power of your
great name is now being paraded against the Prohibitionists."

Defeat of the amendment was confirmed at the polls on August 5
by a vote of almost two-to-one; thus was buried the issue of
State-wide prohibition until long after Davis, Lubbock and Reagan
were dust in their graves.

The attacks on THE NEWS from certain moral crusaders had
increased as the campaign drew to a close. Now the paper was
used as a target in the post-mortem discussions. J. C. Bigger, a
former Republican officeholder, was quoted as saying "it is a
peculiar coincidence" that THE NEWS inaugurated its costly special train to Denison and Sherman just before the campaign
opened. Anheuser Busch of St. Louis and other brewers were credited with having "bought" THE NEWS, a charge of corruption
which several clerical advocates of prohibition enlarged upon.
THE NEWS noted in sorrow that some members of the clergy,
having gone upon the hustings, had "not hesitated to resort to
abuse, misrepresentation, vituperation, angry and provocative language and the low arts of the demagogue."

Weeks after the decision at the polls, Hayden in his Baptist
journal continued to urge a boycott of THE NEWS by the church
people of Texas. In this he had the support of a part of the secular
press. As one weekly expressed its opinion, "the two papers at
Dallas and Galveston are a baneful influence upon the country in
the direction of a lack of respect for religion and good morals. . . .
The time has come when our people should give an emphatic condemnation to this course and vicious attack upon the Christian
ministry."

THE NEWS reproduced the editorial from the *Caldwell News*
and replied:

This is one of the foul eruptions marking the sequel of a moral
pestilence bred by the prohibition campaign. It is one of the strongest
practical arguments against agitations of this nature that they bring
forth agitators inflamed with bigotry and intolerance and riotous with
the very drunkenness of malignity.

Why this concerted scheme to brand and proscribe THE NEWS as
an enemy of morality and religion? It is because THE NEWS met the

rising virulence of the prohibition contest with a sincere plea for temperance in all things. . . .

THE NEWS is quite willing to remit to its readers the case of this lordly band of conspirators and calumniators, with perfect confidence that justice will be awarded them, tempered with a degree of forbearance and mercy befitting an educated, intelligent, virtuous and altogether civilized body of citizens.

But the would-be boycotters were not moved by the same strain of mercy and forbearance. In October of 1887, the General Baptist Convention of Texas met in Dallas. At a special, called session of some 200 delegates, a resolution was offered, the heart of which read:

We regard THE NEWS as dangerous to the morals and good order of society and recommend to our friends everywhere to shun it as they would the *Police Gazette* or any other impure literature.

Not all the delegates, nor even a majority, would agree to this extreme proposal. Dr. J. B. Cranfill, it was reported, "made a strong speech against the adoption as unwise and impolitic, benefiting THE NEWS as an advertisement more than it would be hurt." The Rev. R. T. Hanks, pastor of the First Baptist Church of Dallas, moved that the resolution be tabled. His motion prevailed at last, but not until it was agreed that Major W. E. Penn, a lay evangelist, might substitute a prayer instead. Whereupon Major Penn "fervently and feelingly prayed for THE NEWS and all its editorial staff, petitioning that they might be directed into right paths, might conduct the journal in a way to do good, and that they might all be saved finally in Heaven."

Editor-in-chief Jenkins and his staff at Dallas were outraged by the compromise. Even to the prayer, THE NEWS the next morning demanded the right of final word:

Although the result was a virtual repudiation of the calumnies against THE NEWS invented and disseminated by the editor of the *Texas Baptist* and *Herald* and kindred spirits in malignant, unchristian and unscrupulous enterprise, the delegates did themselves and their church credit by rejecting the resolution.

Major Penn might very consistently have supplemented his prayer for THE NEWS and all its editorial staff with a prayer for the riddance of his church from such pestiferous excrescences.

CHAPTER X

THE FARMERS' REVOLT
1885–1890

WHILE DALLAS and other cities of Texas were "floating upon a tide of legitimate prosperity," the ranchmen and farmers of the State failed to enjoy the same measure of material advancement. The lag in rural wealth was lost sight of for a time in the dust of speculative hope raised by the opening of the two last frontiers of the Southwest, West Texas and Oklahoma. But, as the 'Eighties drew to a close, the plight of the agrarians became acute enough to force political action at Austin. There, through pressure from the new Populist party but under the championship of James Stephen Hogg, the farmers of Texas drove through a legislative program headed by anti-trust laws and the Texas Railroad Commission. THE NEWS considered both of these remedies to be dangerously radical and inimical to the progress of Texas. Out of this concern over "the communistic forces" exalted to power with Hogg grew THE NEWS' prolonged struggle with "the Tyler Statesman," a contest a passionate words that recalled, in bitterness, much of the earlier quarrel between the newspaper and General Sam Houston.

☆

THE NEWS discovered, in a sense, the last frontier of Texas, the great empire of the Panhandle. The revelation that this rich ranching country was admirably adapted to agriculture came out of the fight which the paper was making against the management of State-owned lands at the time THE DALLAS MORNING NEWS was born. In October of 1885 the paper was "importuned to let up on the subject"; it refused, holding fast to its contention that

138

"in the last six years the State has sold 8,000,000 acres of school lands for about $8,000,000, which are now worth probably $40,000,000." It was also concerned over the charge that some ranchers and large cattle companies were using a large acreage of State lands without paying any rentals.

In the last two and one-half years [THE NEWS added] the State has demanded pay for the use of over 20,000,000 acres of school lands occupied and used to enrich persons and companies defying the whole power of the government. No attempt was ever made to obtain the true value of the lands that have been sold and no attempt to force users of the land to pay for their use. Under the circumstances THE NEWS must be permitted to judge when to let up.

Early in 1886 the newspaper deputed its own "commissioner," John E. Thornton, capitol correspondent at Austin, to make a first-hand investigation of the Panhandle, where the old line cattle baron was prepared to make a last stand against the encroaching farmer. It made the decision after "the stockmen of the Panhandle, and particularly Col. Charles Goodnight," complained that "they have been misrepresented and abused by the officers of the State and the leading newspapers." Thornton spent weeks traveling over the great, table-like plateau, surveying the prospect of the country, interviewing the cattlemen and visiting with the few farmers who had been bold enough to invade this domain hostile to the man with hoe or wheat binder. His findings were specific and against the cattlemen. The report was published serially in THE NEWS:

From what appears in the following [the editor prefaced the series], it will be found that there has been no material error in the assumptions of the State officials and of the press in their discussions of the land question.

Individuals may have been misrepresented . . . but the bare facts are that the great majority of stockmen had no leases and did enclose the lands. If the State authority was right, the inclosures should have been removed. By failing to remove them the rent is lost to the State, and in fact the right of inclosure is conceded. It has entailed the loss of the legal rent on millions of acres at four cents an acre. . . . One most important conclusion is that the schools in the selection of lands have been fearfully and wonderfully cheated.

Later, Thornton testified as a central witness in the investigation of the public land problem by the Legislature and aided materially in arriving at reformations finally worked out in the system. But, more lasting in effect than the abolition of the State Land Board, was the impetus which the findings gave to the opening of the lands for farming purposes. Colonel Goodnight had found scarcely any white men in the Staked Plains area when he set up his cattle principality in the Palo Duro Canyon ten years earlier. As late as 1875, there had been only a small settlement of Mexicans, who were believed to be mainly a "fence" for stolen horses and goods which Indians foraging farther east in Texas and Oklahoma brought them in trade. With understandable pride, Colonel Goodnight recounted that the cattlemen had stamped out this banditry; he was equally confident that the Panhandle would remain forever as a fief of the livestock industry. "We did not, and do not now, believe the land capable of sustaining farmers," the noted ranchman informed Thornton. But the latter insisted on hearing the other side. He talked with those less interested in beef, who had eyed the land and even broken it up for crop purposes. The country itself aroused his enthusiasm. His descriptions and analyses were such as to convince THE NEWS that the Panhandle-Plains country was destined to become the future granary of the State, a wheat region far greater and more lucrative than North Texas had formerly been considered. Thus the newspaper started a westward trek of colonists, with binders and reapers, toward a newer, and more alluring, Eldorado.

The Panhandle is well adapted to the production of wheat and oats [THE NEWS concluded] and should produce $250,000,000 worth of grain instead of $15,000,000 worth of beef.

It is only a question of time, of course, when the farmer will possess the country. Granting that it is true that it will become a great wheat producing region, every interest of trade and production may be promoted by a wise and liberal policy [which shall foster] great cities built in the center of population in the producing region. Yet ignorance and jealousy would dedicate the Panhandle to the cowboys and coyotes for generations.

☆

But the populating of West Texas received a harsh check shortly afterwards. An unprecedented drought, which lasted twenty-one months, caused an outward flow of settlers, particularly from the counties lying just east and south of the Panhandle-Plains country. THE NEWS at first failed to grasp the size of this calamity. But early in January, 1887, the county judges of the twenty-one counties hit hardest assembled at Albany in Shackleford County and issued a true picture of the situation. Declaring that "in each of these counties there has been a partial, and in many parts an absolute and complete failure of all crops," the county judges confirmed the existence of great want and suffering and announced that 30,000 men, women and children required financial help for five or six months, or until the next crop could be produced.

The Legislature at Austin responded quickly with an appropriation of $100,000 for food and emergency relief. THE NEWS sent a staff correspondent to accompany the Legislative committee entrusted with the administering of direct relief. An appeal was dispatched also to Washington, where Congress voted $10,000 for seed loans. Cleveland, with rare courage, or insensate stubbornness, depending upon the political philosophy of the commentator, vetoed this Federal aid for Texans. THE NEWS swallowed hard, then commended the President. The paper consoled Texas Democrats with the thought that "they should look with peculiar pride and satisfaction upon an executive act indicating that the official head of the Democratic party of the country is disposed to assist a principle which they have so long cherished: the redemption of the National government from the vice of paternalistic officiousness and worse than paternalistic prodigality. . . ."

What the Federal government refused to do, though, should be done by Texans. This thought was accepted all the more readily after the great humanitarian and founder of the Red Cross, Clara Barton, came to Texas to study conditions for herself in the distressed area. Moving eastward to Dallas, she underscored the report previously issued by the county judges. In a statement to THE NEWS, she emphasized the need for financial assistance for new seed. "At the same time," the paper explained, "she rests in the belief that Texas can and will take care of her own. In this she reflects the views of THE NEWS."

Almost no rain had fallen during the period [Miss Barton said to the great masses of Texans in the older agricultural sections]. Two planted crops have perished on the ground and the seed wheat sown last Fall gave no sign of life.

The dust was rolling over the great wind-swept fields . . . and literally a heaven of brass looked down on an earth of iron. Here were twenty to forty counties of a size commensurate with Texan dimensions, occupied by new settlers making their first efforts in the pioneer work of developing home life in an untried country, soil and climate.

THE NEWS undertook the task of raising a seed fund by public subscription, opening its columns daily for the listing of donors. Heading the list was the name of Clara Barton, who sent $20 out of her own purse to Colonel A. H. Belo, president of THE NEWS. In this way, thousands of dollars were raised and placed at the disposal of the distressed. In a remarkably short time the settlers in the new country were on their feet and the emergency relief no longer was needed.

☆

During these same years Southern California and later the nearby Indian and Oklahoma Territories, became powerful magnets attracting thousands of restless Texans. They, also, became formidable rivals to Texas in drawing settlers from older parts of the United States. Since 1876 the State had been forbidden by its Constitution to set up immigration agencies and bureaus, but, under the urgence of THE NEWS, many local communities, private citizens, and the railroad companies met in a State convention in Dallas in December of 1887 to create a private agency of this character.

THE NEWS considered it fairly simple to prove that "the boom has burst" in San Diego, and many "A Returned Exoduster" was allowed to tell his fellow Texans in the news columns how insubstantial mere climate and scenery might be in California. "The

Oklahoma Craze" was more difficult to cope with, once the lands were announced ready for opening. The pressure on the Federal government to release these choice holdings of the Indian Nations had been increasing. In 1888 Kansas City commercial interests held a meeting of representatives from all Southwestern States to petition Washington. The only Texans to show any marked interest were the cattlemen; they strongly opposed the move, chiefly because (as THE NEWS explained) they desired Oklahoma lands to remain "the place where they have been maturing their steers since the western range has become impoverished."

But, when the pressure to open Oklahoma finally triumphed, thousands of Texas farmers, particularly in the northernmost tier of counties abutting the boundary line, were swept into this latest land frenzy. One of Benjamin Harrison's first executive acts on entering the Presidency in 1889 was the setting of 12 noon, April 22 of that year, as the moment when the land rush might begin. THE NEWS now admitted that "the rush to Oklahoma could no longer be delayed." In fact, boomers were already within the area and could hardly be ejected. The paper was glad to note, however, that, as a result of a treaty executed with the Indians by the outgoing Cleveland, "the new administration is able to pursue without legal question a policy which will conform to the demands of Southwestern progress with respect to the Oklahoma Territory."

The rush itself in the spring of 1889 proved one of the more exciting mass movements in the history of American colonization. The 30,000 to 40,000 families camping around the edge of "the beautiful land" for days and weeks, held back only by United States soldiers, caused it to be one of the largest single land rushes. It was memorable for other reasons as well. Because of the late date in history, it enjoyed the benefit of modern news-reporting methods, so that less adventurous contemporaries might stay at home and receive from hour to hour a comprehensive, colorful and fairly exact picture of what was happening. Moving in the most diverse and contrasting modes of transport—the covered wagon racing against the excursion train, the stage coach and the fleet saddle horse out-distancing the bicyclist and the foot traveler

—the Oklahoma boomers recapitulated in twelve short hours the long story of Anglo-Saxon settlement in America during three centuries of expansion.

Some 150 special and staff correspondents of the country's leading newspapers were in the thick of the rush, their coverage of the event being planned in advance with the thoroughness of battle plans. In co-operation with the railroad and telegraph companies, they were able to relay what was happening in almost every part of the twenty million acres of land almost instantaneously to the readers of the nation. The rapidity with which the job was done constituted its most striking feature. Oklahoma City, for example, was no more than a lone station building on the line of the Santa Fe railroad on the morning of April 22. Fifteen minutes after the first train arrived, fifty acres of a new city had been divided into streets and town lots and small white stakes selling for five cents apiece dotted the prairie. By nightfall, the new city had fifteen thousand inhabitants, with a mayor, aldermen and other representatives of a duly elected civil government; a full-fledged daily newspaper, set up in a tent on a press brought in on the first train, had issued its first edition to tell the story of the city's birth. Similar scenes were unfolded at Guthrie. The rest of America stood by marveling; it was as novel as if Columbus were to discover America to the accompaniment of a full battery of sound cameras, field radio stations and, possibly, a television set.

THE NEWS had its own correspondents on the ground, both in advance and accompanying the first contingent of boomers, who left Texas from Gainesville on the Santa Fe train in the dark hours of the morning of April 22. Among these was Nanita R. H. Daisy, a talented and somewhat audacious newspaperwoman, who had thrown up her job in Dallas to become THE NEWS' first staff correspondent in Oklahoma. The paper at Dallas boasted of being first to arrive at all points along the Santa Fe; its sale that day in the coveted territory exceeded 12,000 copies. "THE NEWS is here to get into all places where people go," its correspondent telegraphed, "and on this account it got to Oklahoma first."

Dated from Oklahoma City on April 22, 1889, the first staff special story from "the beautiful land" read in part:

It is done.

Oklahoma Territory has been opened to settlement, and contrary to expectation, it has been accomplished without bloodshed. The excitement has been intense. For the most part good humor prevailed throughout. . . . It was a wild struggle and a scramble for the promised land in which nearly everybody was armed, but the reports of guns and pistols was unheard except when some rejoicing boomer announced his pre-emption of a claim by firing into the air as the stake was driven into the ground.

But neither the Oklahoma Craze, nor the opening of cheap lands in West Texas, could allay the growing unrest of the farmers as the last decade of the century opened. After 1885, the old Grange movement had experienced a new birth in the Farmers' Alliance, Texas-born, which soon spread over much of rural America. By 1887, this organization was tackling the problem of low farm income through the establishment of farmer-owned hog, cotton, grain and cattle exchanges. Dallas business interests raised a $10,000 bonus and donated a block of land in the business district at Jefferson, Market and Wood Streets, on which national headquarters for the Alliance was erected.

The farmer's organizations waxed as his prosperity waned. THE NEWS took cognizance of this new agrarian distress and was honestly alarmed. It saw that "there is an increased activity in the cities, which may well be described as congestion, while the country is left to take care of itself and is rapidly going to the dogs." The outlook was so serious that THE NEWS came to believe "the phenomenal development of manufacturing and mining industries in the South is scarcely a matter of congratulation on the part of the people as a whole, since development and expansion in one direction is purchased at the expense of contraction in the others."

What, then, was the way out?

"The subject of diversity of crops has become rather hackneyed," THE NEWS answered in 1889. "Yet it is one that cannot be safely ignored." Continuing, the paper said:

The same crops are being raised in the same way as twenty and thirty years ago. Cotton is the great stumbling block in the way of the Southern farmer. The cotton blight is as potent today as ever.

It is cotton, always cotton, even in the face of repeated demonstrations that there is no money in it for the producer. [As for townspeople], what good does it do to build up immense manufacturing centers, if the consumers are too poor to buy the goods produced?

THE NEWS had other solutions to offer in addition to diversification. From 1888 onward it urged improvement of country roads, the better to enable farmers to get their products to market. The State Constitution should be amended, it urged, to permit the issuance of bonds for such a highway system. And, in April of 1890, THE NEWS finally succeeded in convening the first State Good Roads meeting in Dallas, out of which grew the powerful County Judges Association. As before, the paper also inveighed against the iniquitous tariff which, despite the best intentions of Cleveland, Mills and other Democratic chieftains, remained a Chinese wall.

The majority of Texas farmers, on the other hand, were not satisfied with these more orthodox solutions. Increasingly after 1886, were they turning to political saviors. In South Carolina, Ben Tillman was rising to power, while in Texas Jim Hogg, John H. Reagan, A. W. Terrell, and others were becoming convinced that they were destined to lead the farmer out of the wilderness. And, increasingly, was the animus of the agrarians turned against the rail transport companies and the growing combinations of business and industry, which were charged with taking too large a part of the money return from the production and consumption of goods.

One reason why THE NEWS particularly resented the passage of the Texas anti-trust code of 1889 was the fact that stockmen's and farmers' co-operatives were exempted from its provisions. This proved to the paper that the laws were a "monstrous progeny emerging from the long drift and widely scattered spawn of predatory politics and class legislation." Sawing against the grain of more popular economic thought of the day, THE NEWS even went so far as to defend the trustification of industry and commerce:

Such combinations arise naturally and after a sort irresistibly in the line of economic evolution under pressure and stimulus from constant progress in mechanical improvements and the larger facilities of production and consumption.

Nor can it be truly said that the concerns which have thus arisen have been inimical in policy or detrimental in effect to the interests of the community as viewed from the standpoint of the average consumer. . . . A policy designed to destroy the fruits and stifle industry is a policy which, beginning with confiscation, would complete the work of intolerance and tyranny by placing people in general on a dead level in a desolate communism of poverty and disability.

The advanced agrarians in the Legislature seemed to respond to these criticisms by seeking to impose more drastic restraints on large combinations of capital. Particularly in the session of 1889 was the proposal to create a State railroad commission for the control of rates and services advanced at Austin. It will be recalled that for decades before THE NEWS planted its banner at Dallas it had ever been the champion of the steam carriers. From its earliest days it had fostered railroad construction, in the fixed belief that the economic life of Texas was dependent upon rail transportation. The paper did not propose, therefore, to stand by idly and see these pioneer factors of civilization "crippled or destroyed." The Federal Interstate Commerce Act passed by Reagan and others at Washington had seemed restrictive and vicious enough in the eyes of THE NEWS; this proposed Texas regulatory body must be shown up in all its monstrous colors. Thus the paper required no ulterior persuasion to train its gunfire on the Brown Railroad Bill of 1889, finally defeated in the Texas Senate. Yet, in the political turmoil soon to follow, THE NEWS would be charged from the stump with having sold its editorial and news columns to the great railroad octopus.

☆

During 1890 a premonitory business recession spread from the farms and ranches into the suburbs, if not into the business centers proper, of Texas cities. It was a year of financial distress, and the urban land boom in the Southwest felt its first rude shock. The accompanying ground swell of political revolt would shake even the centers of the cities.

But, even before the quake struck that summer with Hogg's campaign for the governorship, Texans were sharply reminded of the growing cleavage between rural and urban populations; this was shown in the first returns from the Federal census of that year. In February, THE NEWS commented on the fact that the urban population of the State had grown to 691,000, or an increase of 120 per cent since 1880. At the same time the State as a whole had grown only 27 per cent. "At this rate," the paper pointed out, "another decade will close with urban and rural population about equal." It analyzed the prospect further:

Land values are appreciating, tenants are growing in numbers relatively more rapidly than farm owners, and city population is increasing over all other classes. Here are facts which suggest interesting political as well as social problems for the statesmen of Texas to solve. If rural interests are to rule the dominant party, which of the rural classes—renters or farm owners—will rule the rural faction? This and various like questions will interest the conservative farmer and the Democratic statesman.

One Democratic statesman, Jim Hogg, was already interested in this and like questions. A native of Rusk, derived from robust, hard-hitting and intelligent pioneer stock, Hogg had led the life of an itinerant printer in Texas before taking up the study and practice of law at Tyler. Possessed of a large frame and early disposed toward corpulency, he appeared as an unusually big man in any gathering. At base he had the outlook of his inheritance—the aristocratic views and interests of the slave-owning, planter class of the Old South, once removed to Texas. But more on the surface of his heart and mind, due, doubtless, in large part to the hard times in Texas in which his boyhood was spent, Hogg early became a champion of the underdog. Shrewd, skillful in the art and language of the backwoods political husting, and a born leader, he possessed the qualities for an effective commoner in American public life. As Attorney General of Texas from 1886 to 1890, he indicated the reform policies and tendencies that might be expected of him as Governor. In announcing for the latter office, he placed foremost a demand that the Constitution of Texas be amended to authorize a Texas railroad commission. THE NEWS at once accepted the gauge of battle on this issue, and the fight was on. Not only did the paper charge that such a commission would prove "an insidious form of communism," but its chief backer was also said to be nothing more than a demagogue. In this view it had the almost complete backing of the mercantile interests of Dallas and other cities. In April Jay Gould, on a periodic inspection trip to Dallas, confirmed the worst fears of business interests by saying, "I do not think there will be much railroad building in Texas this year. Capital has grown timid for certain reasons, and you have got to give it time to recuperate."

As usual, the political campaign seemed slow in warming up; but once started, it gained rapid momentum. Hogg spoke first in Rusk on April 19. If THE NEWS had characterized his exercise of the office of Attorney General as "a finer exhibition of the autocratic truculence than the brief but eventful rule of Sancho Panza over Barataria," it was no more complimentary of this opening address. The speech was, THE NEWS believed, "in Mr. Hogg's line of political agitation and popular appeal, a masterpiece of ingenious elaboration." The Conservatives in the Democratic party experienced some difficulty in getting a worthy antagonist to Hogg. Their hopes centered for a time on the now aging Throckmorton, but poor health forced this Civil War figure to decline. They turned next to George Clark of Waco, still known as the Warwick of 1886 because of his successful management of Governor Sul Ross' first campaign. But, when Clark finally excused himself, Gustave Cooke of Houston was persuaded to lead the opposition to Hogg and the railroad commission.

Hogg in the meantime shelled the woods. Nor did he forget what he termed "the journalistic double-ender of the GALVESTON-DALLAS NEWS." To criticisms from the paper, he retorted with equally frank epithets. Some of his partisans were freer of tongue and less charitable, devoting much of their time on the stump to circulation of rumors designed to destroy the reputation and character of the journal. The crux of the counter-assault came in the closing moments of the campaign when it was charged that the

major railroads of Texas had bought the editorial influence of
THE NEWS for $1,200 to fight the Brown Railroad Bill of the
previous year.

THE NEWS on August 7, 1890, replied at length to "this conspiracy of falsification and detraction." All the known facts upon
which such a rumor might be based were bared in print before its
readers. Curiously enough, the story emanated from Tyler, Hogg's
city of residence at the time he entered politics. At the core of the
matter was a letter written by the receiver for the International &
Great Northern Railroad, a document which reflected gravely
upon the integrity of the newspaper.

☆

Here it should be recalled that the International & Great Northern was a part of Jay Gould's Southwestern railway system. As
such, it had been a party to the Texas Traffic Association, an
inter-railroad pool dissolved by Hogg during his term as Attorney
General. The traffic pool for a time had also apportioned the advertising of its member railroads among the newspapers of the
State. Soon after the pool disbanded, the I. & G. N. was declared
bankrupt in a district court at Tyler. T. R. Bonner, a banker of
Tyler, was appointed receiver and took office in February of 1889.
A young attorney of Longview, T. M. Campbell, later to be Governor of Texas, was appointed the master in chancery. In November of the same year, Receiver Bonner authorized the payment of
a bill from the GALVESTON-DALLAS NEWS for ten months of advertising, which totalled $1,200. But, at the same time, Bonner
wrote a letter to the auditor of the railroad which, after coming
under the gaze of the master in chancery, finally found its way into
the hands of Hogg's partisans—"to be used," Bonner later testified
before an investigating committee of the Legislature, "for political
purposes." How damaging it might be to the anti-Hogg cause was
seen when THE NEWS on August 7, 1890, reproduced it in full.
For Bonner, on November 23 of the year before, had written to the
auditor:

Returning the papers attached to your letter of the 22nd instant, I have approved the claim of THE GALVESTON NEWS for $1200, but before returning it I wish you would confer with Mr. Galbraith [chief traffic officer] in regard to it, as I think THE GALVESTON NEWS has made an error of $120.

My understanding of this whole contract is that our proportion of a general sum agreed to be paid to THE GALVESTON NEWS for service rendered during and before the last session of the Legislature amounted to $1,440. But in order to take from the transaction the appearance of bargain and sale for influence, it was agreed that the sums might be liquidated in monthly payments under the head of advertisements, the insertion of our columns being a part of the general consideration. . . .

Colonel R. G. Lowe, vice president and general manager of THE NEWS, indignantly denied at Galveston the import of this letter in the same issue of the paper. A letter from the publishing executive to Bonner, reprinted in the same issue, declared:

A copy of your letter [to the auditor] has been forwarded to our Mr. Jenkins, editor-in-chief of THE NEWS, who will make such use of it as, in his judgment, seems proper and correct.

The general tenor of your letter to Auditor Maury is so at variance with the facts in the case, and so totally unsupported by any semblance of truth in so far as it relates to money paid THE NEWS for services rendered before and during the last session of the Legislature, that we cannot yet realize why such a letter should ever have been penned by you.

Colonel Lowe went on to state that the contract for advertising between THE NEWS and the I. & G. N. railroad had existed for ten years. "Why," added Colonel Lowe, "your 'understanding' should have been so clouded when you came into the road as one of the receivers is difficult for us to understand." He then declared:

We desire to state specifically to you that no understanding was ever had with any railroad man or any railroad manager touching the services of THE NEWS for other than purely legitimate advertising; so much advertising space for so many dollars per annum. There is nothing [more] whatsoever in these contracts than in any [other contract] with a private individual. All are placed upon an equal footing by THE NEWS, and its advertising space is held at so much per annum without any other consideration whatsoever being guaranteed or understood.

Forced into open print at this moment by THE NEWS' own election to air the whole matter, the charge was widely discussed in both the weekly and daily press of the State. The Fort Worth *Gazette,* "appreciating the gravity of the charge" against its contemporary, immediately instructed its correspondents at Tyler, Dallas and Longview to make full investigation. With his hand called by Colonel Lowe, Receiver Bonner now completely disavowed the implication of his own letter.

"I had heard rumors in regard to the railroads having paid THE GALVESTON NEWS for services rendered," Bonner told representatives of the *Gazette* and other papers on July 4, "and it occurred to me that these contracts might be to cover up the appearance of bargain and sale for influence in that matter.

"But investigation gave me no proof upon the subject, and hence I approved the vouchers for $1,200 as above related. . . . The fact is, my understanding was based upon such rumors as are sometimes used against large daily papers on account of their advocacy of particular matters."

More impressively, perhaps, Receiver Bonner further repudiated his original charge by pointing out that THE NEWS for years had paid the International & Great Northern Railroad, operators of the Galveston, Houston & Henderson Railroad, $500 a month for THE NEWS' special daily train between Galveston and Houston. The payment, in turn, by the railroad of $120 a month for three display ads each month, was a matter of record; the files of the paper itself bore testimony to the running of the advertisements.

But, while the *Gazette* and most other contemporaries of THE NEWS were convinced by the denial from the paper, by Bonner's recantation of rumors started by himself, and by their independent investigations, the Hogg partisans refused to suspend coinage of political capital out of the matter. They were aided by Master in Chancery Campbell, who, on July 29, scarcely two weeks before the State Democratic Convention met to decide between Hogg and Cooke, filed a special report in the Seventh District Court at Tyler, branding the payment of the $1,200 bill to THE NEWS as improper. In his conclusion Campbell said:

Therefore, in reference to this disbursement, said master in chancery, after a careful examination of the statutes classifying claims in matters of receivership, fails to find a class under which it could legitimately be paid. It is, therefore, held to have been an improper disbursement, wholly unauthorized by law or the order of the court.

Such was the status of the charge against THE NEWS as the Democratic hosts assembled in State convention at San Antonio. The Hogg forces triumphed quickly and made short shrift of any and all opposition. Along with the nomination of "the Tyler Statesmen" for Governor and young Charles A. Culberson of Dallas for Attorney General, the convention ensured the adoption of the railroad commission amendment in the coming November election by declaring it a matter of party loyalty to vote for the change in the Constitution. The radical agrarian wing, its leaders in the main, like Hogg, members of the younger generation which had come of voting age since the Civil War, were now to taste the full fruits of their victory.

CHAPTER XI

POLITICS AND PANIC

1890–1893

SCARCELY HAD the chant of affectionate hog calls died away at the San Antonio convention which nominated Hogg for Governor than the attention of THE NEWS and Texans shifted for a moment to national affairs. The money stringency of the fall of 1890, as noted, did little more than slow down the real estate boom in the towns and cities, but the politically triumphant agrarians were more unhappy. Numerous subscribers on farms and ranches insisted on knowing why the depression in agriculture was so severe. The paper obliged by analyzing the causes "political, financial and natural."

THE NEWS attributed most of the blame to the tariff—"that monument to the genius of dishonest politics and the stupidity of the American voter." But an immediate factor was said to be the lack of "a greater and more elastic volume of sound and solvent currency which, under existing conditions, can most readily be furnished by the free and unlimited coinage of silver, as well as by the sub-treasury system." Many a reader, particularly the politicos, were to make note of that editorial statement, for it proved to be the last good word which THE NEWS would have for the white metal.

The Republican administration of Benjamin Harrison was at midstream, and the Democrats were urging the nation to change horses, at least in so far as Congress was concerned. The McKinley Tariff Act of 1890 was the chief issue in the Congressional elections of the same year. Roger Q. Mills, Democratic leader in the lower house at Washington, represented Texas' most notable contribution to the tariff reform movement. He spoke throughout the

154

Middle West during the campaign. When the Democratic landslide piled up in November, he received much praise. Henry
George, in Texas on a lecture tour, informed THE NEWS that no
one did more than Mills to win the victory.

The inauguration of Governor Hogg in January of 1891 revived
the fears of THE NEWS and the Conservatives generally over
purely Texas affairs. Especially were they aroused by what they
considered Hogg's almost indecent haste in forcing a bill through
the Legislature to create the Texas Railroad Commission. The
same Legislature also enacted a law prohibiting foreigners from
owning or holding land in Texas—another example of "radical
communism" which caused THE NEWS to redouble its fight on
Hogg's economic creed.

But the Conservatives were not without some weight in the same
Legislature. Chiefly, they forced appointment of an investigating
committee to examine into the history and circumstances surrounding the receivership of the International & Great Northern Railroad—a move which the Hogg partisans charged was designed
solely to embarrass the Governor. The investigators began their
work in June. For more than a month they sat as a court of inquiry
at Tyler and elsewhere, moving on to Galveston, where for several
days they probed into the matter of the $1,200 advertising bill of
THE GALVESTON NEWS. Master in Chancery Campbell, it will be
recalled, had filed his criticism of this payment on the eve of the
gubernatorial election of 1890. At that time Receiver Bonner had
filed affidavits from THE NEWS with the court, repudiating the
charge of "bargain for sale and influence," but the court, now
under fire itself, had elected to approve Campbell's condemnation.
At Galveston Colonel Lowe took the stand before the inquisitors
and repeated the denials offered the year before. He introduced
the books of the publishing company to prove that space had been
sold to the railroad companies on exactly the same terms as to all
non-railroad advertisers. J. Waldo, formerly head of the Texas
Traffic Association, also testified that no understandings or under-

handed agreements were involved in the contracts with THE NEWS.

The investigation ramified through the long story of the receivership, including the attempted intervention by Hogg while Attorney General—an intervention denied on appeal to the Supreme Court of Texas. George Clark and General Felix D. Robertson of Waco acted as counsel for the committee in the role of unofficial prosecutors. Many of Hogg's closest political allies were called to testify. By August, the committee of six members reached its conclusions. A majority of four exonerated the judge of the State court of the charge of official misconduct; the other two members were less certain the court should be held blameless, judging from the language of their dissent. But all six were united in recommending that Texas laws be changed to provide greater safeguards of the rights of the owners of railroads and other properties which might be declared bankrupt in the future. The friends of THE NEWS were also satisfied that its honor and reputation had been cleared of any possible taint by the same proceedings.

On the creation of the Texas Railroad Commission, Hogg persuaded United States Senator John H. Reagan to become its first chairman. The Legislature had adjourned, and Hogg was free, therefore, to appoint Reagan's successor at Washington. He was besieged by the friends of various candidates, mostly those who thought that Roger Q. Mills should be accorded this honor of a temporary appointment. But "the Big Governor" passed over old land marks such as Mills, A. W. Terrell, S. B. Maxey and other veterans of the party. He named, instead, his close friend from childhood, Horace Chilton of Tyler. This act incensed the Conservatives, and when Lieutenant Governor Pendleton, a supporter of Mills' candidacy, quoted Hogg as having said that he made the choice because "his close personal friend, Horace Chilton, was not embarrassed by a Confederate record," the older generation of Texans were aghast.

THE NEWS that year attacked the alien land law as the worst evil of the Hogg-dominated Legislature. Designed originally to force railroad companies and ranch syndicates to dispose of excess land holdings, presumably to small farmers, the bill, as it finally emerged, struck at the greater part of the farm mortgage business in Texas. English and Scottish investment houses, most of them with headquarters in Dallas, had poured millions of dollars worth of foreign capital into land mortgages in the State. The new law prohibited them from foreclosing on Texas land in the event of default. The paper campaigned for months to arouse public sentiment. Despite a mounting tide of adverse opinion to the law, the Governor refused to call the Legislature into special session to repeal it. Meanwhile, a test case was brought in court at Dallas by a Scottish company. The lawsuit was passed on finally by the Supreme Court of Texas in December when Chief Justice Stayton, supported by his associates, declared the law to be void—but due solely to an error in the caption of the bill. While victory was won on a technicality, the Conservatives of the State breathed easier.

"The fearful financial strain imposed upon the State will quickly be relieved by the decision," Colonel J. B. Simpson said in Dallas. "The unparalleled distress in all the industrial centers of Texas since the bill went into effect testifies to the fact that this measure was one of the supreme follies of the day. I know of no one act by the Legislature since the war which has been the means of wrecking the fortunes of so many men." To which F. N. Oliver, also of Dallas, added that "gratitude is due THE NEWS for its tireless work as the friend of all professions of the people in showing up the cause and effects of the most hurtful law yet placed upon the Texas statute books."

As 1892 appeared on the calendar, THE NEWS refused to entertain the idea that Texans would return Jim Hogg to the governorship. "Unless all signs fail, there is going to be a thundering campaign in Texas this year," the paper predicted in February, "a war to the knife, and the knife to the hilt, is only a mild way to express it."

Certainly no crisis in the affairs of Texas ever called to the heart and conscience of the State's good citizenship with a livelier occasion for concern [THE NEWS added editorially]. The testimony of this crisis is not to be mistaken. It tells the good citizenship of Texas that the administration which came in as a menace developed into a calamity. It tells them a State so fair in natural features and so vast in natural possessions as Texas is surely worth delivery from the blight of such misrule, and that if they prove recreant to the work of delivery, the curse of a lost commonwealth will lie everlastingly upon their memories and their souls.

Partisans lost no time preparing for the war. While chieftains of the Hogg wing of the Democracy met at Tyler to plan their strategy, anti-administration leaders met in Dallas on February 2, where it was decided that George Clark, "the Little Giant" of the Texas bar, should be their standard bearer. Clark in his announcement cleared away all doubt as to where he stood. The railroad commission, he said, was not of itself an issue. But, since it was here to stay, there were at least certain "living issues" in the commission law. Among amendments that should be made was a provision for the election, rather than the appointment, of commissioners, and the liberalizing of procedure to permit railroad companies to appeal decisions to the courts. Existing limitation upon the right of court appeal smelled, he declared, "of rank communism and is the spawn of a midnight conclave foisted on the statute books under the lash of an intolerant executive."

Just as the campaign began to gather force, the Legislature met in special session to elect a permanent successor to Senator Reagan. It also cured the defect in the alien land law. As re-enacted, the measure no longer interfered with the farm mortgage business of Texas. As for the election of Senator, Horace Chilton made a bid for the long term but was opposed by Roger Q. Mills. Chilton also had to carry the burden of a haunting phrase—"not embarrassed by a Confederate record." As a result, Hogg's close friend withdrew on March 21, and Mills was chosen the next day almost unanimously. THE NEWS, in the meantime, was sounding the tocsin, "Turn Texas Loose." In supporting Clark and in urging Texans to strike off the fetters of abused power, to purge the commonwealth "of a deadly blood poison of political folly," the paper stepped on the toes of Reagan himself, by now the "noblest Roman of them all," in the political parlance of the day. The chairman of the Texas Railroad Commission took pen in hand, therefore, in March to answer the critic of his chief in the Governor's Mansion :

THE NEWS at Galveston and the one at Dallas have persistently lied on me and slandered me ever since it entered on the present campaign for the corporations and against the people [said the former Postmaster General of the Confederacy.]

By misrepresenting the condition of Texas and the conduct of her public officers for the purpose of securing political support of corporations and monopolies over the people, the two NEWSES have been and are now inflicting serious injury on the material interests and on the character of Texas and her people. I know of nothing which equals their mendacity and rotten corruption except their brazen hypocrisy.

Hogg's temper against THE NEWS rose as the fight progressed. Leaving direct attacks for a time to Reagan and his lieutenants, he was goaded finally into open verbal retaliation, particularly when THE NEWS poked fun at some of the Governor's tricks on the platform.

"I have been charged by a press with slang and indecent language," Hogg said in Clarksville in May. "I am speaking of one that never fails to do me an injustice when it can . . . the double-ender put out at Galveston and at Dallas."

The people have no confidence in it [Hogg continued]. When it has been publicly branded as it deserves by men whose character is beyond reproach, by men of honor and high standing in this state, it is not necessary for me to say anything. . . . I hope the day is coming when the people of Texas can have at least one newspaper published every morning that can tell the truth.

Running fire as this duel was between Hogg and THE NEWS, the contest after all lay between Hogg and Clark. Interest in the preconvention campaign reached its climax in the debate between the principals at Cameron on May 3. There Hogg and Clark spoke before 10,000 people brought from various parts of the State by special trains. THE NEWS had a corps of shorthand reporters, staff correspondents and telegraphers on hand in the open field ; as a result, the debate was reported in full in the news columns the next morning—a feat which its rivals and even its political enemies applauded. Free of bias and editorializing as the news columns continued, THE NEWS editorially increased its appeal for Hogg's defeat as the campaign drew to a close, with county conventions naming delegations to the State convention of the party. Then, just before the nominating convention opened, the paper rested its case with this somewhat previous, funeral-like oration:

Mr. Hogg might have been a capital executive, but he dropped the reins in plying the lash. . . . He is a failure, splendid in attempt, mournful in effect, pitiable in contempt and a costly example to his country unless his career shall amply warn other men and other times against the dangers of premature reformers. Let him slip down the easy way of his last decline to forgiveness and forgetfulness.

☆

The State Democratic Convention of 1892, which normally would have settled the Hogg-Clark contest, convened in Houston on August 16. But, twenty-four hours before, it was obvious that all the elements of "a thundering campaign" still hung in explosive suspense. Rival and contesting delegations from scores of county conventions, each claiming to hold credentials from the true Democracy of their precincts, foreshadowed this. Midnight moves to align the Houston police force and the Harris County sheriff's department indicated that bloodshed was not an impossibility.

The festivities were held in the Houston street-car barns, only assembly place large enough to hold the cohorts. Both factions put standing room at a premium as the meeting assembled under an armed truce. A few moments later bedlam broke loose as the opposing factions sought simultaneously to organize the convention. From opposite ends of the platform both sought to elect officers amidst a confusing scramble of yelling delegates. Order was found possible at last only by a surprise motion that the gathering temporarily adjourn. But, when the Clark men returned a little later, they found their opponents had taken control of the building and were patrolling all entrances. The Conservatives then moved to another hall, and by nightfall two conventions, each claiming to be the spokesmen of the Democratic Party of Texas, were completing their work of nominating two slates of candidates and two platforms. It was the most serious split in the historic party since Sam Houston ran for Governor as an independent in 1859.

THE NEWS welcomed the result which carried the Hogg-Clark contest beyond the conventions, placing the final decision directly in the hands of the voters at the polls in the November general elections. "Logic and decency have equally been vindicated by this final alignment," the paper said. It saw the issue now placed before the voter as one of "Democratic conservatism versus the more or less revolutionary impulses of communism, pointing to the final subversion of the whole fabric of constitutional liberty." And, for nine more weeks, Texas was subjected to a political campaign more emotional than even that which had preceded the Houston convention. Licking their chops over this schism in the ranks of the dominant party, Texas Republicans abandoned their own slate of candidates and announced support of George Clark.

THE NEWS threw itself into this post-convention fight with gusto. Running its eyes over the State, it professed to see "empty factories, stagnated industries, shrunken cities, empty railroad trains, hungry cottages, terrified upbuilders"—all because of "the curse of Hoggism." From the State comptroller's records it recited that fifty-one counties had reported a shrinkage of $2,000,000 in taxable values during the course of the Hogg regime. Occupation taxes had slumped in many important lines of business—cotton buyers, bankers, dentists, gas and electric light companies, livery stables, lawyers, shipbrokers and others. But, at the same time, "whiskey and beer sellers, billiard halls, flying jennies, shooting galleries and money lenders" paid in larger taxes to the State. This situation led THE NEWS to admit wryly that the people of Texas were at least having "more fun, if less business."

To this campaign of business fright the Hogg partisans replied with angrier denunciations of THE NEWS and its allies. The newspaper matched insult with insult, finally stating that if the people of Texas had to choose between "passing under the regime of Diaz or remaining under the regime of Hogg," there was much to be said in favor of the Mexican alternative. The campaign whirled to a finish in a storm of charges and oratory. Fittingly enough, the Clark men rested their appeal in Dallas, with a torch-light procession on the night of October 26. There, 25,000 enthusiastic followers of "the Little Giant" joined in the street demonstration. THE NEWS took fresh hope from a last-minute slip made by Hogg; in one of his speeches bejewelled with a jest at the expense of the prohibitionists, it was thought that he might have made one of those fatal mistakes which can turn a close election. For the jibe had been interpreted to include the women, as well as men, who were in the ranks of the reform movement. Thus it was heartening to the paper to hear Dr. J. B. Cranfill say, "I would not vote for Governor Hogg if he was the only candidate in the race. . . . His well-known speech, the language of which cannot be printed for even chaste-minded men to read, not only exceeded the bounds of the most strained political ethics, but was a reflection on the queenly prohibition women of Texas . . . [an affront] that the advocates of prohibition can never forget."

In its final appeal THE NEWS reviewed its exchange of words with Hogg. Emphasizing that, while it knew "a professional prevaricator when it sees one," and while such campaigns "develop this species of degenerate humanity," the newspaper had not been concerned "about Mr. Hogg as a person."

It is in his public career as a personification that he rises to the dignity of evil significance, [THE NEWS concluded] a significance that commands from millions of intelligent people the homage of respectful abhorrence.

THE NEWS has seen in him a baleful personifying of all that is worst in the despotism and voracity of machine politics, all that is worst in professional agitation of class prejudices, class hatreds, class cupidities, to the final peril of all classes and to the mortal peril of free institutions.

THE NEWS opposes his rule as a deadly menace to these precious interests and urges all good citizens to join in their might in a patriotic effort to rid the State of such a pernicious and execrable presence.

But it was the judgment of the voters, by a fair sized majority, that Hogg should have another lease of power at Austin. A few weeks later fate provided a mournful obbligato, for THE NEWS was forced to record the death in New York of Jay Gould.

While Texans were absorbed in their great internal fight of 1892, the national Democratic party, under the leadership of Grover Cleveland, had been marching to complete victory.

After 1890, THE NEWS veered more and more to the right on the currency question. When the Democrats organized the House of Representatives in 1891, THE NEWS was chagrined to note that Roger Q. Mills, "recognized champion of tariff reform," was defeated by a coalition of Southern and Western free-silver men. By placing silver above tariff reform, the Texas paper argued, the party had taken "the first step toward political bankruptcy." The dominant Hogg faction was itself committed to the white metal. But, when it came in 1892 to the selection of the Texas delegation to the national convention, the Hogg men gave the right-of-way to supporters of Cleveland. For all factions, free silver fanatics as well as gold bugs, were convinced that without Cleveland the party could not hope to win the presidency and thereby consolidate itself in Congress. Although the Hogg Car Barn Convention at Houston reiterated its creed of free and unlimited coinage of silver at the ratio of 16 to 1—in open contradiction to Cleveland's well-known views—Cleveland in November received, along with Hogg, the usual Democratic majority in Texas.

The adherents of the single, gold standard were greatly heartened by Cleveland's victory. Eight years before he had unsuccessfully called for the repeal of the Bland Silver Purchasing Act. While the Republican Administration in 1890 had gone further in the remonetization of silver in the passage of the Sherman Act, the gold-standard men of the country knew that in a crisis they could depend upon Cleveland. The crisis was not long in arriving.

As the months dragged on between Cleveland's election and his second inaugural in 1893, the alarm of the hard money adherents increased. The agricultural regions—Texas in particular—entered the year on a gently rising tide of higher prices for farm products. THE NEWS on January 1 estimated that the value of all Texas products had increased $50,000,000 within the past six months. But the financial centers of the country were becoming uneasy over the inflation, which they held to be a result of the government's continued purchase of silver. Money as a medium of exchange was itself getting cheaper when measured in terms of the gold coins of England and the Continent. There was no escape from the fact that the United States was drifting gradually from a gold basis.

"The gold is going out of the country at a lively rate," THE NEWS warned on February 14. "This is precisely what had been predicted to occur sooner or later under the operations of the Sherman Act."

The guardians of finance in New York became vocal. Already stock exchange prices, at first oscillating erratically, were slumping. The free gold of the country flowed ever more steadily across the Atlantic, and the government's treasury reserve of the metal sank lower and lower. George C. Williams, president of the New York Clearing House Association, issued a decree on February 15 that the compulsory purchase of silver must be stopped, that the Treasury must at once sell $50,000,000 in bonds to build up its gold reserve, "if salvation is to be found." THE NEWS shared the apprehensions and advice of Eastern financiers. It went further, however, to urge the creation of "some lasting remedy, one that will restore confidence in the stability of the American currency system."

Our panics and disturbances in money circles [said THE NEWS a few weeks before the Panic of 1893 unleashed itself] could not occur if there were not something radically wrong in our system. Great Britain, Germany and France have no periodical treasury frights such as we have. . . .

THE NEWS went on to say that what the then existing situation suggested was "the creation of a great central financial institution embodying the best features of the Bank of England, the Imperial Bank of Germany and the Bank of France." But the outgoing Harrison Administration hesitated to act on any of these counsels. The financial and stock market situation continued to drift dangerously. In the week preceding Cleveland's second inaugural, a near panic developed in New York as enormous drains of currency were made from the West and South. Entering the Presidency on March 4 under these circumstances, Cleveland acted boldly and dramatically to restore the morale of the country. In his inaugural address he gave first attention to "our present embarrassing monetary situation." Manifestly, he declared, "there is nothing more vital to our supremacy as a nation . . . than a sound and stable currency. Its exposure to degradation should at once arouse to activity the most enlightened statesmanship . . . and produce prudent and effective remedial legislation." But, with Congress absent from Washington, what could be done? Cleveland electrified the country by announcing that he was ready to use the vast powers of the Presidency in the event of a money crisis. "None of the powers with which the executive branch of the Government is vested will be withheld," Cleveland told a shivering nation, "when their exercise is deemed necessary to maintain the national credit or to avert financial distress."

THE NEWS was ecstatic in admiration:

The expectations of those who have learned to appreciate most highly Mr. Cleveland's distinguishing traits as a citizen, political leader and public man, will not be disappointed by the tenor of his inaugural . . . [with its] high and sustained pitch of incisive candor and directness of expression.

From beginning to end there is no wavering of tone—not a syllable or accent to suggest hesitation on the line of the great commission put upon the new president and his political comrades by the American people: the commission to save the country, and especially the honest toil of the country, from the curse of a degraded and profligate currency . . . and to rescue politics and legislation from a fearful brood of predatory communism. . . .

The immediate effect of Cleveland's inaugural address was to halt the drain of gold from the country and of currency from New York. In the rebound of confidence, Washington could forget the financial situation for a moment while the subject of patronage took the center of the stage. Texans did not expect much, although the one large plum asked for by a united Congressional delegation —the appointment of Congressman Kilgore as minister to Mexico—was denied. This was in accordance, THE NEWS explained, with "the rule at Washington that no Texan shall ever be appointed minister to Mexico." It was noised about, shortly afterward, that Cleveland desired to honor his close personal friend and journalistic supporter, Colonel A. H. Belo, with the appointment as minister to the Austro-Hungarian Empire. Members of the Texas delegation refused to give this plan their unanimous endorsement. THE NEWS quickly relieved the embarrassment of all concerned:

Scrupulous to maintain its deliberately adopted course of unbiased, non-partisan and impersonal journalism, THE NEWS has hitherto silently declined to take notice of such gossip. . . .

THE NEWS takes occasion to say, however, by authority, that the foregoing rumors are without foundation in fact. Colonel Belo has never applied nor contemplated applying to Mr. Cleveland for appointment, and is not an aspirant for any public position whatsoever.

The time had come for THE NEWS to make clear to the public its long observed policy of keeping members of its official family out of all entangling political alliances. The responsible head, Colonel Belo, had been importuned shortly before by "a distinguished Democratic leader of Texas" to intercede with President Cleveland in the matter of a certain appointment. Colonel Belo's reply, written on December 24, 1892, declared:

In my responsible identity with the course of THE NEWS as an advocate of the principle of civil service reform laid down in the platform on which Mr. Tilden was elected in 1876 and reaffirmed in the platform on which Mr. Cleveland was elected in 1892; and as a journal maturely committed alike by profession and practice to independence and frankness in the discussion of public men and public affairs, THE NEWS might have occasion to criticize the incoming administration with reference to some feature or incident of its policy.

This it could hardly do with decency if I, as its responsible head, had urged solicitations to the President for office, or had become indebted to him for the favor of appointments made upon my recommendation.

☆

By the middle of April, the financial situation was again uppermost in the news dispatches from Washington. During the week ending April 14, a second gold raid occurred, and financial agencies reported that free gold in the Federal treasury had slumped to a mere $2,000,000. Rumors raced through the money market that the new Secretary of the Treasury, John Carlisle, had suspended redemption of silver certificates with gold and had prohibited the future issuance of gold certificates. Bears used the rumors to smash stock market prices in New York and London. Within seven more days the free gold was entirely exhausted, and the government was now forced to dip into its sacred $100,000,000 hoard of the metal to sustain gold redemption payments.

Cleveland met with his Cabinet on April 21 for a day-long session on the condition of the Treasury, and Colonel W. G. Sterett, now Washington correspondent for THE NEWS, telegraphed that "the Democrats are solicitous about the crisis, but say that if it comes, or a panic should sweep the country, the Republican party will be entirely to blame for it." The President, however, was more than solicitous. On April 23, Cleveland called newspaper correspondents to the White House, where he denied point-blank that he or anyone in the administration contemplated even the temporary suspension of gold.

Of course [added the President] perplexities and difficulties have grown out of the unfortunate financial policy which we found in vogue and embarrassments confronting us at every turn, but with cheerful confidence among the people and a patriotic disposition to cooperate, threatened dangers will be averted, pending a legislative return to a better and sounder financial plan.

Thus led by the President, press and business leadership throughout the nation sought to buoy public opinion. Colonel Sterett shot reassurances daily from Washington to Texas. Even if the government did not have its hand on it, he wrote, there was more gold in the country than in any other except France. Secretary Carlisle estimated the total American stock to be $750,000,000. Colonel Sterett further reminded readers of THE NEWS that "there is general prosperity throughout the land." This combined attack on hysteria seemed for a time to succeed; the dollar improved against leading European currencies, and President Cleveland felt free enough to journey to Chicago, where he opened the Columbian Exposition on May 1.

But, almost at the instant when Cleveland pressed the electric button to swing back the gates of the great Chicago World's Fair, a more shocking current passed through Wall Street. It was the failure of a cordage company, news of which set off a general stock market slaughter of security values. A week later, on Monday, May 8, THE NEWS carried a summary of this "Week of Panic," a subhead of which declared "Nothing Like It Since the Crash of 1873."

The events of the past week [the same summary continued] will pass into Wall Street history as "the industrial panic." The time of extreme stress, the full force of it falling on the industrial stocks, lasted over three days. It reached its most acute stage on Friday morning when, for nearly two hours, it seemed as if the whole Street would go down in a crash of bankruptcy similar to 1873.

And now, despite all that Cleveland and business leaders might do or say, the money stringency spread fan-like from New York, moving with inevitable, paralyzing effect across the continent until by the fourth week in June it had halted trade in places as far distant as San Francisco. But, thus far, most bank depositors had kept their heads, so that banking institutions were able to function fairly normally. Then, on June 26, Gladstone arose in the House of Commons to announce that the British Government had ordered the immediate closing of Indian mints to the free coinage of silver. The cabled report of that action set off detonations in the silver-producing areas of America. Four days later Cleveland took the last resort, calling Congress into extraordinary session on August 7 to repeal the Sherman Silver Purchasing Act. Meanwhile, banks in widely separated parts of the country were engulfed in the panic of terrified depositors. On July 18, six banks in Kansas City closed their doors, while the crash of three savings banks in Denver caused "such a scene as was never witnessed in all the West," with depositors besieging the eleven clearing house banks in the silver capital. The Panic of 1893 had arrived.

THE NEWS hurried to endorse Cleveland's proposal, insisting that as the first step out of the crisis "the government must stop buying silver." In the meantime as Congressmen journeyed toward Washington, THE NEWS and Texans in general had time to take stock of the effect of the panic in Texas. Picking themselves up from the shock, they were able to congratulate all concerned that the State had escape at least the money panic, with its concomitants of moratoria, clearing house certificates, etc. Texas banks were largely responsible for their weathering of the crisis, THE NEWS commented on August 7. For years they had done business "on a cash basis," and the contraction of 1890 had largely cleared city banks of "the fictitious paper . . . of acreage and lot speculators." The triumph over bank hysteria was due chiefly, however, to "the people of Texas who, in the present excitement, have not become panic-stricken and made runs on their banks." But the real cost of the crash was yet to be computed in Texas.

CHAPTER XII

SOUND MONEY AND SOUNDER MORALS

1893–1896

IF NEITHER Dallas nor Texas was hit as hard by the Panic of '93 as the more industrialized sections of the country, they were not to escape a part in the long, hard pull necessary to reach recovery. THE NEWS, facing the lean years, pulled in its belt a notch or two, spat on its hands and set to work willingly to do its share toward rehabilitation.

Three months after Cleveland called a special session in 1893, Congress repealed the Sherman Silver Purchasing Act. So far, however, from curing the depression, this deflationary move deepened the crisis. THE NEWS, at first, had been inclined to dismiss the unhappy turn in economic affairs as a bank depositors' panic. The paper pointed to the fact that not one bank in Texas had withheld payment of a single deposit. Nonetheless, the paper proposed there should be some "system of government guaranteeism" of deposits in the future. With such guaranty and with repeal of the silver act, THE NEWS looked for an early lifting of the economic clouds.

While "here and there are temporary inconveniences in certain classes on account of the hard times," THE NEWS said in September, "there is nowhere in this great State any army of the unemployed to paint hunger and foreshadow trouble." The very phrases admitted, however, that elsewhere a grave unemployment problem existed. Soon Texas itself was being overrun by "idle mechanics" and other victims of the economic jam, most of whom had taken to the steel highways of the nation. Already "the idle laborers of Chicago and New York" were demanding bread—"and even beer,"—demands which THE NEWS said should be denied, lest the country find itself in due course "rocked and riven by irresistible revolution." When Governor Hogg announced in October that he would pardon all unemployed workmen arrested as vagrants for riding Texas freight trains, THE NEWS expressed alarm. "Charity and sympathy are all right," said the paper, "but this dramatic display in august office of sickly sentimentalism and of demagogism coddling anarchy is apt to cost the people of Texas much more than some readers may conceive."

☆

New Year's Day, 1894, was saluted by anything but a cheerful American people. R. G. Dun & Company summarized the expiring year as "the worst in fifty," closing as it did with the prices of many products at the lowest level ever known, and "with millions of workers seeking in vain for work and with charity laboring to keep back suffering and starvation in all our cities—a dismal record, indeed, a collapse of industry and business almost without precedent." By now the newspaper was convinced that it was more than "a bank depositors' panic." But if THE NEWS, as the mercantile agency, could find little comfort in the national outlook, there was at least the encouragement of a change pending in the State administration.

Early in the new year, Democratic chieftains moved to heal the two-year-old-rift that had grown out of the Houston State Convention. A State-wide harmony meeting was held in Dallas in January. There Governor Hogg eliminated the basic issue of Hoggism with a characteristic flourish, announcing that he was through with public life forever. The growth of the Populist party was more threatening than before; and, as Hogg phrased it, reconciliation was necessary if Democrats were to "march on united to success in fraternal good feeling, with all sores of the past healed forever." Further to seal the pact of peace, Hogg personally visited THE NEWS building where he was received by the entire working staff and a special copy of the paper struck off in red ink in his honor.

It may seem strange to many to read of Governor Hogg being a guest of THE NEWS [the paper reported the next morning] but it must be remembered that the Governor is an old newspaperman himself and is full of that fraternal feeling which makes all newspapermen akin. . . . After shaking hands with different members of the staff, the Governor's party were escorted to the composing room to see the wonderful Mergenthaler typesetting machines [then just installed by THE NEWS at Dallas].

"This is the first time I ever saw one of these things," commented the Governor as he sat before the keyboard and touched off the inevitable SHRDLU. "When I was a boy setting type I used to dream of machines that would some day knock me out of a job. By gatlin! it was like a nightmare to me and made me perfectly miserable; and here they are!"

Hogg chose to make his tour through THE NEWS instructive to others as well. As he prepared to leave he drew a lesson for the Democracy of Texas. "Just to see that office all at work illustrates the necessity for harmony," he said to a reporter. "If the printers should bolt, the other departments could not issue the paper. If the presses should break, all the printers in Dallas couldn't print the paper. . . . The Democracy is just a great engine of human liberty, and the life of the Republic itself depends upon every piece of machinery being in its place and responding in unison to every revolution of the driving wheel."

☆

The truce between THE NEWS and Hogg died quickly, however. Revival of hostilities came over "Coxey's mad march," the nationwide protest by the unemployed, which terrified the conservatives of the country. As the jobless converged on Washington to demand a public works program, THE NEWS branded them "an insane band of malcontents" who would have had plenty of jobs "if the government, through manipulation by graceless demagogues, had not trained them to expect somebody else to provide opportunities for them." Texas was to have its own reflection of the mass movement. The Desert Contingent, composed mainly of marchers from California and other Pacific-Southwestern States, began moving eastward across Texas on freight trains. As the transcontinental system most seriously affected, the Southern Pacific Railroad appealed to Texas authorities, only to be informed by Hogg that no State law existed making it a crime to "bum" a ride on a freight train.

Governor Hogg has virtually proclaimed a state of communism in Texas [THE NEWS declared in white heat.] His declaration in effect that there is no law for the protection of freight trains against the trespass of tramps is an invitation to able-bodied wayfarers forcibly to seize and ride on any train that suits their convenience.

The railroad company acted in the matter. Toward the end of March it caught more than 700 marchers on board one of its eastbound freight trains as it moved across the State from El Paso. Hauling these uninvited guests seventy miles eastward, the railroad company switched cars and human cargo onto a siding at a particularly deserted place, unhooked the engine and left the men to their fate. When word of their plight reached Governor Hogg, he ordered the railroad to return to their rescue. The company refused, whereupon the chief executive became angry. The men had been brought into Texas by this octopus, he reasoned, and by gatlins! they would be hauled out by the same agency. Thus he wired Julius Kruttschnitt, then general manager at Houston, serving notice that "this State will not submit to such wholesale murder of human beings on her soil without testing the company's life and every right claimed by it under Texas law." In the face of this ultimatum, the company promptly complied, sending a train to convey them across the State on their way to Washington.

It is fatiguing to have to try by the test of reason and by a right standard of fitness to occasion and to office [commented THE NEWS wearily] Governor Hogg's periodical eruptions of paroxysmal rodomontade . . . these apparently irrepressible outbreaks of a disorderly mind and a convulsive temper.

Not all the unrest in the summer of 1894 was confined to trespassers on the railroads. Strikes, riots and lockouts in the industrial sections of the country and among the employees of the railroad companies themselves in the Middle West testified to the strain imposed on the existing order by the economic crisis. Nowhere was the struggle between organized labor and capital more sharply dramatized than in Chicago, where the great Pullman strike reached its climax. There, on July 7, President Cleveland at last acted, following up Federal court injunctions against the strikers with the dispatch of Federal troops, sent into Illinois over the protest of Governor Altgeld. These vigorous executive acts met, of course, the full approval of THE NEWS. Less than two weeks later the Texas Volunteer Guard concluded its annual encampment at Austin. Hogg as commander-in-chief received a gold watch from officers and men on the concluding day. And there, in an offhand address, the Governor of Texas scored Cleveland's action as "a fatal bow at State's rights" and announced that he had wired "headquarters" that he would not tolerate Federal troops in Texas for similar strike-breaking activities. "I would be there to stop them," Hogg blustered. He concluded with a direful prophecy of revolution in the United States and proposed that in such event, the Republic of Texas should be restored:

Go home, gentlemen, and learn your lesson of obedience to the laws and to your superiors well, for the day is close at hand when your mettle will be tried. I do not know how soon it will come or how it will end, but this strike is but the preliminary of terrible times in this country. The conflict is bound to come unless a change is made, and those fourteen story buildings in Chicago will be bespattered with blood, brains, hair, hide, livers and lights, and the horrors of the French Revolution will be repeated two fold.

When the row comes and if disintegration should come, I am in favor of Texas standing on the Constitution of 1836 and going it alone as a republic again. I am for Texas first, the United States second and civilization at large next. . . .

Now THE NEWS shattered the last vestige of its truce with Hogg. Picking up the speech almost by accident, the paper gave the widest and fullest circulation to this "unspeakably shocking address." The Dallas Commercial Club, followed by like organizations throughout the State, felt called upon to hold special meetings to repudiate the sentiments of the Governor. Not only would Texas "never withdraw from our great sisterhood of States," but (the Commercial Club vociferated) "such communistic talk and

The Dallas News special daily train, "The Comet," which began operation over the Houston & Texas Central Railroad from Dallas to Denison in 1887. On the platform of the first car is G. B. Dealey, then business manager of the newspaper

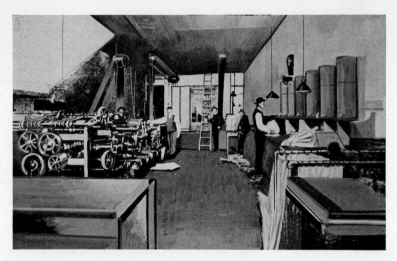

Combined press room and circulation department of THE DALLAS NEWS
at its start in 1885. The power room was immediately to the rear. This
room measured 25 by 60 feet.

Advertising, bookkeeping and general business office of THE DALLAS NEWS
in 1887

prophecies are certain to do incalculable harm to the financial and industrial interests of the State." As for THE NEWS:

If this is not an eruption of seditiousness and incendiarism in spirit and proclivity, then language and conception are beggared for a definition. . . . As for the people of Texas [as proven by] this last exhibit of their governor . . . they have been guilty of him and he has duly brought on their punishment in shame and confusion. The sooner this State rids itself of this costly incubus, the better for both its credit and its peace.

True to his promise, Hogg eliminated himself from political office in 1894. The Democratic State Convention which met in Dallas in August to name his successor appeared to vindicate THE NEWS in its long struggle with the "Tyler Statesman." The chief candidates were Chairman John H. Reagan of the railroad commission and the young Attorney General from Dallas, Charles A. Culberson. Due to the skill of Colonel E. M. House as campaign manager, Culberson held the edge on his elder rival. But Culberson's nomination was assured when the convention adopted the party platform in favor of sound money, as opposed to free silver. Reagan at once withdrew, announcing that he would not consider accepting a nomination on a gold standard platform. Culberson, at heart a free silverite, was less conscientious; as a result the convention nominated him by acclamation. The party hosts further rebuked Hogg and approved the position of THE NEWS by endorsing the Cleveland national administration. The paper was jubilant:

THE NEWS has not wavered for eight years. . . . It has been a fight for honest money, equal rights, law and order. . . . The vindication of the cause for which THE NEWS has so long and so inflexibly contended is approximately accomplished. The Democracy of Texas has declared for Cleveland and sound money. It has endorsed emphatically the policy of the President in suppressing the Chicago insurrectionists.

The campaign plays and diatribes with which politicians of an unwholesome and happily obsolescent sort have sought to discredit the press have fallen flat and cold. THE NEWS expected the Democracy of Texas to fall in line with its labors and aspirations, because it has been moved by patriotic purposes that must always win in the end.

That Culberson as a candidate promptly repudiated the sound money plank did not greatly worry THE NEWS at the moment. In its relief over the prospect of an early release from Hogg, this detail could be overlooked—all the more so, since the paper did not believe that free silver would ever again be a national issue. The gubernatorial succession, in fact, allowed the journal to relax somewhat its overweening concern over matters purely political.

Dallas was slowly recuperating from the worst effects of the panic as 1894 wore on. The Oriental Hotel, halted by the crash, had been carried to completion by new backers, chief of whom was Adolphus Busch of St. Louis. The end of the year saw a slight increase in building permits, a marked increase in postal receipts and an even more noticeable revival in wholesale and retail distribution. Much of the credit for this showing, THE NEWS believed, should go to the Commercial Club, which had proven that "it is a good sound nucleus upon which all the enterprising citizens of Dallas may readily unite . . . to secure astonishing results."

Most emphatically did THE NEWS back the Commercial Club's three-point program: the construction of a system of all-weather county roads, the creation of the Dallas Terminal Railway and Union Depot Company to facilitate entry of additional rail lines into the city and the vigorous prosecution of the plan to navigate the Trinity River. This last project had been revived with a great show of public spirit on May 24, 1893, when the steamboat Harvey arrived from the Gulf. That red-letter day, marked by an issuance of THE NEWS in red ink, had induced thousands of enthusiastic North Texans to gather on the banks of the stream and on the streets of Dallas to greet a new era in transportation. Since the arrival of the first railroads early in the 1870's, the navigation project had slumbered. It was revived chiefly because, with the passage of national and State regulatory laws, the railroads were no longer free to grant Dallas shippers such preferentials on freight rates as both parties might desire. With water competition, it was felt, Dallas distributors and manufacturers would be able to compete more effectively with trade centers enjoying water shipping facilities. The Trinity River Navigation Company was organized, one lock-and-dam was built at McCommas' Bluff, and it was even proposed that an effort be made to enlist the financial assistance of the Federal government. THE NEWS also revived its agitation for an improved water supply, resulting in the construction in 1896 of a dam on the Elm Fork of the Trinity River at Record's Crossing.

Throughout the panic years, public sentiment in both Dallas and Texas began to veer toward more Puritan standards on several moral questions. Organized religion was strengthening its influence on city councils and State legislatures. The third annual convention of the Texas Equal Rights Association met in Dallas in 1895, and Colonel Andrew Jackson Houston, son of General Sam Houston, was persuaded by his wife, the secretary of the group, to lend his patronage. There was a growing sentiment against race track betting, "a somewhat fanatical furore for moralizing the race track" which THE NEWS felt inclined to hold justifiable. The paper, in fact, was itself veering somewhat to the right in the matter of public morals. It was specially concerned over the growing ease and prolixity of divorce in Dallas. While the newspaper believed "no good woman should be required" by the laws either of society or of the land to continue living with a brute or a drunkard, it held that in more than half of the cases the courts should refuse to grant divorces, due to the utterly trivial causes cited for them. "Something should be done," THE NEWS continued, "to discourage a large class of loose litigants in their eagerness and efforts to change mates with every change of the moon."

As early as 1893, the forces of righteousness had struck at the toleration of prize fighting in Dallas. An ordinance was offered to the City Council to bar boxing matches in September of that year. One alderman asked what kind of families would care to move to Dallas to educate their children "while they are confronted by sparring matches and variety theaters?" Alderman Pat O'Keefe was almost ready to concur; the prize fights staged in Dallas, he said, were frauds "perpetrated by men who can't tell a pair of gloves from a set of harness." But the mayor pro-tem, Dr. Arch Cochran, insisted that the proposed ordinance would be in accord with neither "the laws of Christianity nor humanity;" and General A. P. Wozencraft, the city attorney, ruled that there was no State law authorizing the city to bar boxing. The ordinance, as a result, was tabled. On the question of segregating "fallen women" or "soiled doves," as THE NEWS was fond of styling them, the City Council acted in the same year. Here the city attorney again questioned the powers of the municipal corporation. But, while holding that the city had no authority to license or to locate disorderly houses, he explained that "if the police board desire, they can instruct the chief of police to diligently watch and prosecute all violations in all portions of the city except a certain portion." Alderman O'Keefe consented to have the plan tried out in his ward, and Dr. Cochran approved the measure with the observation that "as true men, we should protect virtue by regulating vice." Queen Victoria, he added, "has said that they were a necessary evil. The poor wretches are somebody's darlings."

THE NEWS by 1894 came to recognize editorially that efforts should be intensified to discourage vice, particularly the vice of gambling "in growing cities teeming with speculative and adventurous people eager to disregard or to escape the restraints of the statutory rules of justice and good order." Every city "pays the full face of the account for its schools of vice," continued the editorial writer. "They are poor investment save for a few favorites of shameful laxity or discriminations in the laws or enforcement."

Despite these obvious straws in the wind of popular opinion, it was little thought as 1895 got under way that the new administration of Governor Culberson would be identified primarily with a question of public morals. "Retrenchment and reform," the fruits of all depressions, was the slogan in the State capital. THE NEWS, like most other taxpayers, was hopeful that now and finally the fee system for payment of county and State officers would be reformed—and possibly abolished. This hope existed in spite of the fact that John E. Thornton, THE NEWS' correspondent at Austin, reported that a "strong lobby in favor of its retention will spend the winter here." The new Attorney General, M. M. Crane of Cleburne, displayed an alarming tendency to follow in Hogg's crusading tracks; he soon brought suits under the anti-trust laws against the Standard Oil combine and sought the arrest of John D. Rockefeller and H. M. Flagler as fugitives from Texas justice. These gentlemen, THE NEWS asserted, were being hounded by the State of Texas "for reducing the price of oil," a prosecution which was neither "applauded nor encouraged by the people, who prefer cheaper oil." In the next two years petroleum would be found in Texas near Corsicana but not in sufficiently large pools to give birth to a boom.

There was not much on the national horizon at the opening of 1895 to alarm the editorial pilot of THE NEWS. In March, Cuba began to command small but repeated amounts of space; this latest revolt, it was soon conceded, "is of a more formidable character than the Spanish authorities admit." In the spring, the Supreme Court at Washington, by a five-to-four decision, nullified the income tax rider to the Wilson tariff law. "Readers of THE NEWS can understand," the journal declared, "that this paper notes the decision with no ordinary satisfaction." But suddenly the Caribbean area flared into public attention, although it was in Venezuela rather than in Cuba that the trouble started. There the British lion made roaring gestures over a boundary matter not unrelated to the collection of a foreign debt. Then President Cleveland popped the whip of American foreign policy, sending a brusque ultimatum to Great Britain; the American eagle screeched, and war, for a day, seem inevitable. But in this fire-eating gesture Cleveland failed to command the approval of Colonel Belo's paper:

If the conservative and wholesome influences of the age and country are set to work, there will be no war between England and the United States. But if this matter be left wholly to blind hot-heads and unscrupulous agitators who have not the courage to declare for peace, the result may be too disastrous and horrible for contemplation. So far as THE NEWS is concerned, it is opposed to war. Considering all the facts in the Venezuelan controversy, THE NEWS finds no adequate cause for proceedings or utterances on either side looking to the contingency of war.

Cuba, the Supreme Court decision, and Venezuela were all soon submerged, however, in a more local, if not more momentous, agitation. In June of 1895, Eastern sports writers were first to announce that the long-hoped-for fight between James Joseph Corbett and Robert Fitzsimmons for the championship of the world would be held, without fail, in Dallas in October. This positive commitment was made by Dan A. Stuart, representing himself and other Dallas sportsmen. He appeared in New York with certified checks totalling $41,000 and assured principals and backers that no Texas law could be invoked to halt the fight.

But immediately a wave of protest undulated across Texas. Daily the pending battle between "Lanky Bob and Pompadour Jim" grew in public and private conversation. From Austin THE NEWS' correspondent reported that an avalanche of objections had been received from ministers and Christian Endeavorers. When informal legal opinions were gathered to the effect that the anti-prize fight law of 1891 was fatally defective, it was suggested to Governor Culberson that a special session of the Legislature be called to cure the defect. This, at first, was considered impractical; there was no assurance that the lawmakers would act favorably, and, in addition, as John E. Thornton reported, "some members of the Twenty-fourth Legislature believe that, in this time of financial distress, the taxpayers do not feel able to expend several thousand dollars to prevent an athletic exhibition, even if they had a cinch on the special session preventing it."

Dan Stuart, in the meantime, returned to Dallas to receive a conquering hero's welcome. Not only would the fight attract extra thousands of visitors to the annual State Fair, scheduled for the same time, but Stuart also reported that the horse races that year would attract the cream of the racing fraternity. Railroads were planning excursion trains from as far distant areas as New England and California. The lines serving Dallas set to work constructing miles of new railroad side tracks on which to house a city of Pullman cars. A wooden, octagonal auditorium seating 53,000 people began to rise to the sound of saws and hammers, and Dallas looked forward to its most prosperous fall season. But, under the leadership of the Rev. A. P. Morrison, pastor of the Tabernacle Methodist Church, a militant counter-movement arose in Dallas itself. Pressure was brought to bear on local and State authorities. Soon the Attorney General from Austin ruled that the fight would contravene State law, and he instructed law enforcement officers of Dallas County to act accordingly.

In July, business leaders met to consider the situation. George Clark and Colonel W. L. Crawford of the Dallas Bar, the latter attorney for THE NEWS, gave legal opinions to the group which disagreed with the views of the Attorney General. Colonel J. T. Trezevant, J. S. Armstrong, E. M. Kahn, Frank Doremus, managing editor of THE NEWS, and others present resolutely endorsed the fight. The Rev. W. C. Young, presiding elder for twenty years in the Methodist Episcopal Church, South, gave his opinion to THE NEWS that, "as to the moral features of the prize fight, I confess that there are twenty worse things going on in this town about which we have been making no fuss." Meanwhile Dallas business men saw to it that the anti-prize fight law of 1891 was subjected to court test. J. M. Hurt, presiding judge of the Criminal Court of Appeals, heard the case in Dallas and ruled finally in September that the old law was null and void.

Thus, with only a few weeks left before the fight, opponents realized their last chance lay with the Governor. If the moral forces had protested before, now they demanded in loud and piercing tones that a special session of the Legislature be called. "Better that the exchequer of the State were emptied a hundred times than that this foul indignity and outrage should be perpetrated," declared the *Texas Christian Advocate* (which by this time was being published in Dallas). "We regret," the same paper continued, "to see our State turned over for a month to the blackguards and gamblers of America." As a result, Culberson late in September issued a call for the legislators to convene October 1 "to denounce prize fights and kindred practices in clear and unambiguous terms," so that "this affront to the moral sense and enlightened progress of Texas may be averted." Meeting on schedule, the Legislature acted at once to dispossess Dallas of its iniquitous attraction, and Culberson was able to ride safely upon the crest of popular approval as "the young Christian governor." THE NEWS, editorially, had taken no definite stand on the issue. But, in its concluding comment, the paper assumed much the same position as Presiding Elder Young, pointing out that "affairs of a similar character, though between less celebrated competitors, have for years been a commonplace occurrence in Texas without causing sensational paroxysms of concern either in executive, legislative or judicial circles."

☆

But, even as the moral fervor of Texans reached these new heights, THE NEWS' attention was recalled to a subject on which it felt much stronger emotion—the older and more economic issue of free silver.

In the middle of June, 1895, William Jennings Bryan, still representing the Lincoln district in Congress—and even then termed "the idol of the 16-to-1 silverites" by THE NEWS—made his first incursion into Texas. Two thousand enthusiastic citizens greeted him at his first stop in Fort Worth. An even larger host met him at the station in Dallas. So resurgent was the free silver spirit that, following a conference of its adherents in Fort Worth, the sound money men felt obliged to stage a counted-demonstration in Waco. There George Clark counseled his fellow Democrats "not to fear to be called gold bugs." Perhaps, THE NEWS now realized, the question might be an issue again in national politics. But, "whenever the issue is squarely defined," the paper believed there should be no fear over the outcome.

The presidential year of 1896 defined the issue squarely. As early as February, "General" Jacob S. Coxey, visiting Dallas, reminded any who might have forgotten that the money question was still uppermost. Bryan was soon announcing that in the event of the capture of the Democracy by the gold standard men, he would bolt the ticket. To which THE NEWS replied that "Mr. Bryan and all his school of free silver Democrats should not stand on the order of bolting, but should manfully bolt at once." It was inconceivable that Cleveland would be repudiated by his own party at the approaching national convention. The Democratic Party of Texas on the other hand (it was realized early in the spring), might easily go over to the silver forces. Commenting that "bolting does not necessarily involve dishonor," THE NEWS informed the sound money conferees in Dallas in April that "the crisis has come. The stalwart Texas Democrats of the financial school of Cleveland and Carlisle should meet it as becomes men who believe principle too sacred to be compromised."

Former Governor Hogg re-entered the political arena in May to make a single speech at Mexia. In urging the renomination of Culberson, he also roundly defended the free coinage of silver. "None but Mr. Hogg," commented THE NEWS, "could be expected to compile such a mass of bold fallacies, arbitrary assertions and crazy statistics." Hogg was now in private life—serving as attorney for, of all possible corporations, the Southern Pacific Railroad—but his great contemporary, Ben Tillman, was still Governor of South Carolina. The latter made a quick raid into Texas, denouncing THE NEWS at Dallas for saying he was not a Democrat and calling upon all Texas members of the party to be ready to bolt the Chicago convention in the event the gold bugs won. Culberson also was emphasizing the cause of free silver. THE NEWS believed the time had come to jump on this platform bolter with both feet, only to have the State's chief executive hurl back in its face numerous editorial pronouncements by THE NEWS itself in favor of the white metal during the 'Seventies and early 'Eighties. "Your course is inconsistent, contradictory and indefensible," Culberson wrote to The NEWS. "All you have said denunciatory of the advocates of the restoration of silver coinage is answered by the following editorials in your paper. . . ." He then cited chapter and verse from the files of the newspaper.

To which THE NEWS replied:

The governor is welcome to the admission that in some things THE NEWS has not been implacably consistent. But on this point THE NEWS has no old chestnut to crack about consistency being the bugbear of fools and about wise men sometimes changing their minds, fools never.

Governor Culberson to the contrary, however, conditions are quite different from what they were at the time THE NEWS stood up qualifiedly for silver and against a presumed prosecution in certain quarters of a scheme to work a contraction of the currency on a gold basis. . . .

The outcome of the Chicago convention became clear though, and both THE NEWS and the sound money, rump delegation from Texas admitted defeat in advance. Neither Bryan nor Tillman but THE NEWS would be forced to bolt, if any should resort to that extremity. The paper was convinced that the Democratic ticket, headed by Bryan and bottomed on free silver, could not even hope to win in November. All the more so in view of the work of the Republicans in St. Louis where, at the whip of Mark Hanna, that party pledged itself to the single gold standard. William McKinley, it felt, would be the next President. In the bitterness of disappointment over the stand taken by the Democratic National Convention, THE NEWS could see nothing but "annihilation of the Democratic party as it now exists":

There seems to be no room for doubt that the Democracy has reached the turning point in its career and is no longer a party having for its creed the living principles which made it strong and masterful in other days. It has turned its back on Jefferson, Jackson, Benton, and Cleveland and proclaims as its faith theories of government which have been rejected by civilization.

Viewing the conditions now presented, the annihilation of the Democratic party as it now exists seems to be almost inevitable. However, committed to a policy which means the devastation of the commercial fabric of the nation and the substitution of dishonor for financial integrity, the Democracy would have no salutary mission to fulfill, and the sooner its deluded and misguided ranks were routed and riven by the overwhelming forces of honest finance, the better for the weal and prosperity of the country.

Nor were these idle words from THE NEWS. Along with a few other conservative Southern papers in Charleston, New Orleans and Louisville, including Colonel Watterson's *Courier-Journal,* THE NEWS of Galveston and Dallas walked out of the political house of their fathers and supported McKinley for President. It was a hopeless fight, of course, so far as the electoral vote of Texas was concerned. But, when the campaign closed, the ballots in and counted, and "the nightmare over," it was seen that Dallas County, at least, had gone for sound money and William Mc-Kinley.

The sun of a new day is now shining in our face [THE NEWS exulted]. It is very clear that the election of McKinley is due to the earnest support he received from the sound money Democrats of the nation.

CHAPTER XIII

NEW WORLD VISION
1896–1898

IT WOULD seem that after its long fight for sound finance had been crowned by the victory of Mark Hanna's cohorts, THE NEWS might have been spared further concern over matters far from home. But destiny itself—some called it manifest—willed otherwise. So, its thoughts, along with those of 70,000,000 other Americans, soared far beyond the sphere of State politics, beyond even that of the nation, to distant isles and seas; and they came to rest at last in a new concept of America's part in world affairs.

THE NEWS, it will be recalled, had been both displeased and repelled by the outburst of the war spirit in the Venezuelan boundary dispute with Great Britain. President Cleveland, early in 1896, reported success in its peaceful arbitration. The paper now professed to see that "Mr. Cleveland at heart and in conscience is for peace;" his previous utterances had been "wildly interpreted by the demagogues and fire-eaters of the country." It could not forego the pleasure of adding that "the recent display of jingoism was the most untimely and ridiculous exhibition of brag that numskulls have ever been permitted to make on American soil."

But the fire-eaters, particularly an aggressive wing of the press and a faction in Congress, were only willing to shift their aim; if not England, then some other "enemy" must be found. Meanwhile, the Cubans were doggedly pursuing their revolt from Spain. Cuban *juntas* bloomed at strategic points from Galveston to Washington and New York, and public sentiment shifted toward the side of the struggling patriots. In February and March, Congress passed concurrent resolutions in favor of recognizing the belligerent rights of the Cubans—an embarrassingly war-like gesture, which Cleveland refused to put into effect. When the International

186

Arbitration Congress met in Washington in the spring, THE NEWS noted ironically that American lawmakers were conspicuously absent from the gathering; they were "too much absorbed in cultivating and pandering to the brutal war spirit of the country . . . to waste half an hour at a meeting of the advocates of law and peace, of civilization and humanity." In this fashion, the Cuban problem had simmered along in the heat of the Bryan-McKinley contest, to be revived in earnest only after the settlement of that domestic issue. How fortunate a thing it would have been, THE NEWS sighed regretfully in November, "if jingoism could have been sunk into oblivion along with the silver craze at the recent election! Then we would have been well rid of the really serious obstacle to the general prosperity so anxiously desired by the country."

Perversely enough, though, there were some Texans who disagreed with THE NEWS even in this instance. In Dallas itself a Cuban Aid Association was formed at a mass meeting on December 13, 1897. It was presided over, most fittingly, by a son of the Hero of San Jacinto, Colonel Andrew Jackson Houston. A letter was read from Luis Peñes, head of the Cuban *junta* at Galveston. Senator Roger Q. Mills offered a resolution urging Congress to direct President Cleveland "to take possession of the Island of Cuba and . . . to hold same until the people of Cuba can organize a government deriving its powers from the consent of the governed." "Of course," Senator Mills explained just before the mass meeting adopted it, "this means war with Spain." To which THE NEWS responded with "the sincere hope that Congress will not take Senator Mills seriously. In Texas there is much sympathy for the Cuban patriots, but the people believe that Davy Crockett's maxim—'be sure you're right, then go ahead'—applies to the United States in this emergency with much force."

Throughout 1897, the drive for American intervention in Cuba grew in Congress, in the press and in certain pulpits. One of Cleveland's final acts, the refusal to annex the Hawaiian Islands, although pleasing to THE NEWS, roused caustic criticism in Congress. He was also criticized in the Capitol for his alleged disregard of the cause of the Cuban patriots. When March 4 of that year rolled around and Cleveland stepped aside in favor of McKinley, THE NEWS went on record that history would reveal "no public career more deeply marked with steadfast devotion to duty, with more lofty patriotism and more exalted character" than that of Cleveland's. While admitting that "he retires from office today with a cloud of factious contumely, partisan malignity and promiscuous misconception hovering about him," THE NEWS added that "the time will come when . . . the country will weigh impartially the great services of Grover Cleveland and hold him in grateful remembrance."

It was also a time in which the New York *World,* Hearst's New York *Journal* and certain like-minded papers redoubled their campaigns to arouse American resentment toward Spain for her cruelties in suppressing the Cuban revolt. The part played by this section of the American press in bringing about the final clash of arms has been appraised fully. But it should be recalled that another large and ordinarily influential section of the press was just as determined to resist jingoism. THE NEWS, which was among the more consistent advocates of peace, recognized the increasing influence which "the horrible pen pictures of devastation and distress sent out from Cuba by the correspondents of the jingoistic press" might have. It hoped, however, that the net result would be "to turn the hearts of the American people away from war as a means of settling differences." This may be looked upon as somewhat naive, particularly in view of the fact that THE NEWS increased the volume of syndicated Sunday feature material of this kind in its own pages. While the editorial page hammered away for American neutrality, the sufferings of the *Concentrados* (as pictured by syndicates controlled by the New York *World* and W. R. Hearst) were being unfolded in the columns of THE NEWS, along with articles such as "Are the Spanish a Decadent Race?"

Throughout Texas the war spirit grew. Filibustering got under way on a large scale, with youngsters, and even some old-time Rangers and Indian fighters, slipping away to join the rebels. The drive for sympathy and funds made such progress that THE NEWS during the summer warned Texans against violation of the Federal neutrality laws. But the new President appeared as the great champion of peace. McKinley declared in his first message to Congress in December that "forcible annexation, by our code . . . would be criminal aggression." THE NEWS was happy to note that the message was "devoid of the jingoism which the war element in the President's party hoped for;" that the new executive was "strictly adhering to the conservative policy toward the Cuban problem" which had been laid down by Cleveland.

As the year 1898 swung into line, the pressure on Congress from the jingo press, and the pressure on McKinley from the jingoes in Congress became more telling. Soon the battleship *Maine* was steaming into the mine-studded harbor of Havana on what was diplomatically termed a social visit. Then, on a fatal day in February, the battleship was blown up with an appalling loss of life. This "unspeakable horror" caused even THE NEWS to weaken in its stand and to admit that if the ship were destroyed by Spanish design, "war would be almost inevitable." So far, however, the paper continued, "appearances indicate that the affair was wholly accidental . . . and until the result of a far reaching investigation is known, the people must suspend judgment."

Most Americans were not in a mood to suspend judgment. Typical of the public meetings held to declare for war was that in the Dallas city hall auditorium on the night of February 27, when indignant patriots jammed all available space in the building. Only one of the twelve speakers favored a peaceful solution. By this time five column headlines—a revolutionary display for THE NEWS— were being brought into play almost daily to recount the crisis confronting the nation; the circulation of the newspaper began to mount almost hourly. D. Prescott Toomey, a young artist on the staff, now produced the first war cartoon in the paper, a representation of Spain's cringing attitude before a screeching American eagle. The front page, the rear page, all the columns, in fact, except those on the editorial page, by now had gone over to the war party. The editorials still urged that it was "time to keep cool," while the caution and reluctance of McKinley, Speaker Thomas B. Reed and others in power to accede to the war demands of press and Congressional opponents drew the warmest commendation of the journal. One Texan in particular, Joseph Weldon Bailey, was most insistent on warlike measures; his influence was effective because of his leadership of the Democratic minority in the House. Bailey, Senator Morgan of Alabama and other Democratic spokesmen were uppermost in the mind of THE NEWS when it said that "bellicose Congressmen are simply betraying the trust which the people have confided to them" in urging American participation in the quarrel between Cuba and Spain.

The committee investigating the destruction of the *Maine* reported on March 23. Its conclusion was that the explosion occurred on the outside of the vessel. Colonel Sterett wired from Washington that even Speaker Reed was now convinced that "war is inevitable." On his own responsibility, Colonel Sterett added that "it is nauseating to think that Senators and members of Congress have been brought to this pass by pushing yellow journals." As late as April 1, THE NEWS believed "there is still hope for peace." In an editorial titled "Stand By the President" it lauded McKinley for his "splendid self-possession, fine moral strength and sound judgment in the grave perplexities confronting the government." When, ten days later, the President delivered his equivocal request for authority to use the armed forces of the nation —the signal for action by Congress which, in fact, made war inevitable—THE NEWS interpreted it merely as a request for "the transfer of all responsibility to him, leaving him unhampered in dealing with the problem as he and his ministers elect."

Believing that peace is yet possible [continued the newspaper] THE NEWS is willing for the President to undertake the delicate trust which he invites, to the end that no peace measures may be overcome by the spirit of martial passion now so strong in Congress.

But Congress was not equally willing. Through the breach opened by McKinley himself in his message, the war spirit roared

C. LOMBARDI
[1906–1919]

MRS. A. H. BELO, SR.
[1907–1913]

Presidents of THE NEWS

ALFRED H. BELO, JR.
[1899–1906]

JOHN F. LUBBEN
[1881–1938]

J. Q. DEALEY
[1929–1937]

WALTER A. DEALEY
[1912–1934]

E. B. DORAN
[1895–1938]

TOM FINTY, JR.
[1897–1929]

D. PRESCOTT TOOMEY
[1893–1918]

WILLIAM G. STERETT
[1885–1924]

through to triumph. In less than a week a joint resolution instructing the President to intervene in Cuba passed both houses, diplomatic relations between Spain and the United States snapped, and Governor Culberson was mustering in the first of 4,000 troops allotted to the State under the President's call for 125,000 volunteers. And THE NEWS, having for three years opposed the bloody expedition to Cuba, bowed to the *fait accompli*.

As was to be expected when the Cuban question was transferred from diplomatic circles to the American Congress and the Spanish Cortes [THE NEWS declared on April 23], the very worst has happened, and after thirty-three years the nation is again at war.

Henceforth the merits of the Cuban question are not open for discussion. In the presence of a hostile foe, every consideration of public safety demands that the people respond to the call of national duty and strengthen the hands of the constituted authorities. . . . And, if some are disposed to feel that somebody has blundered, let them remember that the first hostile shot is a call to duty, and that irrelevant partisan wrangles and spiteful recriminations are execrable and pernicious while an enemy is in the front. . . .

The war itself, fought to a finish in less than four months, appeared to contemporary Americans as one of the turning points in world history. Dewey's bold stroke at Manila, quickly followed by the destruction of Cervera's fleet at Santiago de Cuba, proved the final dissolution of Spain's five-century-old colonial dominion. Not only Cuba and Puerto Rico in the west, but the Philippine Islands in the Far East as well, now fell into the grip of the Yankee. But the reduction of Spain to colonial impotence was only a minor result. The most obvious fact appeared to be the emergence of the United States as a world power, a force henceforth that must be reckoned with in the chancelleries of Europe and Asia, particularly in the problems of the approaching century in the Far East. More important, perhaps, was the change in the psychology of the American people. Intoxicated by victories that set the blood tingling in their veins, a people who had drawn the sword out of vague emotions of sentiment and idealism found themselves overnight with

new attitudes and new purposes. Gone, at last, was any trace of
the spirit of disunion which had existed since the Civil War. The
nation was suffused with a new sense of power and prestige. And
THE NEWS fell a complete victim to this new spirit. A more complete reversal was never registered in the history of the institution,
not excepting its about-face on "the financial question."

For, with war an actuality, the editorial page went over to the
war party to make it unanimous. No expense was spared to get the
widest and most complete news coverage possible. Hearst's own
special daily cable service was added to the full reports of the Associated Press, followed shortly by the inclusion of the New York
Herald's elaborate foreign service. At the same time *Leslie's* pic-
torial service was added. Reproduced in line drawings in the pages
of THE NEWS, these pictures heightened the mental images of
readers as the new heroes and the naval and military victories were
laid before them in five and six column layouts. Extra editions
became the order of the day. The publishers boasted that THE
NEWS at Dallas and at Galveston then received the most costly
war news service of any newspapers in the South. War preparations in Texas raced on, and THE NEWS covered activities nearby, including the dramatic assembling of Roosevelt's Rough
Riders at San Antonio. As a result the circulation of THE NEWS
at Dallas increased more than fifty per cent in one seven-day
period. The yearly averages reveal reader response during the
war years:

1895	17,286
1896	18,682
1897	18,173
1898	26,061

Dewey's victory at Manila was the occasion for announcement
of THE NEWS' conversion editorially to Manifest Destiny. "The
fact is that this victory flashes up in the Far East as a signal witness
that the United States is breaking away from an arbitrary and
stereotyped acceptance of Washingtonian precepts and traditions
of international isolation," the paper declared May 5, "and is rush-
ing into a new epoch of expansion and exploration bristling with

vast problems of foreign antagonisms and foreign coalitions." The
paper then accepted the prospect that the country would soon have
the Philippines, Cuba and Puerto Rico within its hands. "Having
wrenched these territories and populations from the cruel and
despotic grip of Spain, it would be monstrous ignominy for this
country to withdraw from them her redeeming tutelage and to
abandon them to the peril of other alien tyranny or to the horror
and desolation of intestine war or civil anarchy."

The United States, furthermore, must now slough off those older
concepts and be prepared "to take its rightful place among the
mightiest, firmly and forever, in the society and at the council
board of nations." But this prospect was not altogether pleasing to
certain other members of the society of nations, as the course of the
war itself disclosed. Notably there was a coolness in the press and
people of Germany toward America's coming of military age.
Compensating for the coolness of the Central European powers,
however, was a growing warmth of feeling displayed by England
toward the United States. The British, fired by the imperialistic
advances of their American cousins, soon evidenced their sympathy; Joseph Chamberlain, the leading English imperialist,
made his bid in a speech at Manchester for the establishment and
maintenance of "bonds of permanent unity with our kinsmen
across the Atlantic." And THE NEWS urged acceptance of Great
Britain "as our moral coadjutor and, if need be, our active ally in
an easily conceivable emergency."

THE NEWS, moreover, declared for "the development of a
formidable navy," explaining its reversal of attitude as the result
of a better understanding of human nature and of radically
changed conditions. The navy was now necessary in view of the
fact that Hawaii had been annexed in the midst of the war, that
growing commerce of the United States called for the construction
of the Nicaraguan Canal and that America would have to be able
to carry out her part in the proposed Anglo-American alliance.

If we go 2,000 miles to annex Hawaii [THE NEWS continued] we
might as well travel a little further and annex the Philippines and
perhaps insist upon a piece of China. . . . The policy of our government may be the forerunner, through imperative forces and resulting

situations, of a wider humanity than was ever dreamed of in the
minds of those emotionally, though creditably, enlisted in behalf of
downtrodden, cruelly bled Cuba . . . the regenerating factor in the
situation of which the war is but "the dramatic prologue" to the
infusion of the American spirit into the world's great moral and commercial arteries. . . . The very contemplation of the problems to
grow out of the war suggests vast and thrilling changes in our whole
national fabric.

This grandiose program was not accepted unanimously. Cleveland, now in retirement at Princeton, had not changed his mind,
and Minority Leader Bailey, with an inconsistency as charming as
that of THE NEWS itself, began to sound warnings against America's tasting any of the fruits of the war which he had called for.
And there was always Bryan with his touching affinity for lost
causes. In the middle of June, just before joining a regiment of
Nebraska Volunteers as a lieutenant-colonel, the Commoner ad-
jured his countrymen that "if a contest undertaken for the sake of
humanity degenerates into a war of conquest, we shall find it difficult to meet the charge of having added hypocrisy to greed." All
of which THE NEWS rebutted, insisting that "of logical necessity
it must be a war of effective and profitable conquest." Deliberately
to eliminate conquest from the war "would invest it with the most
revolting attributes of a farce, a blunder and a crime . . . nothing
less than perfidy to the inhabitants of Cuba, Puerto Rico and the
Philippines."

THE NEWS was ready to present a definite program to its readers
on world affairs when the dove of peace made her startled appearance on July 26, 1898. Scarcely had the end of the war been sig-
nalized, though, before the new issue of colonial expansion drew
itself across the path of Texas and national politics. The State
Democratic Convention met in Galveston early in August. Two
months before THE NEWS had advised "Bryan, Bailey and the
remnant of the once victorious Democratic party which submits
to their leadership," to step aside. With their croakings against
expansion, they were proving themselves "stumbling blocks in the

pathway of political regeneration and national progress." At Galveston Hogg, Reagan, Chilton, Crane and other leaders were on
hand to espouse the cause of Imperialism. Bailey, seconded by
Congressman R. L. Henry, arrived to make a futile effort to pledge
the Texas Democracy against expansion. When the issue was settled a few months later in the treaty with Spain, whereby the
Philippines as well as Puerto Rico became American territory,
THE NEWS said:

The cry of Imperialism and the opposition of a very respectable
minority of the country [it must be remembered that Cleveland
belonged in that minority] should now cease. . . . All lovers of
liberty, all believers in militant democracy, look with satisfaction
upon the enlargement of the national boundaries of this country. . . .
It is the mission of the United States to demonstrate to the world that
republicanism provides the best government for the alien and the
illiterate, no less than for the intellectual and the powerful men of a
dominant race.

CHAPTER XIV

FAREWELL TO POLITICS

1898–1900

WHILE THE Spanish-American War was recasting the American spirit and altering the world outlook, subtle but far-reaching changes were taking place within THE NEWS as an institution. The "corporate personality" itself was slowly altering, due chiefly to important changes in personnel and to a shifting of emphases in the aims of the paper. As the turn of the century approached, the somewhat new character of the paper became more obvious.

For more than ten years this non-partisan newspaper had been absorbed, editorially, at least, in a series of agitations that were fully as political as they were economic. But, beginning about 1897, the guiding heads of the institution came to realize that the prosperity so long delayed was not to be found in political nostrums. Gradually but none the less surely THE NEWS turned from political harangue to the sponsorship of concrete measures for the improvement of life among the people—whether on farms and ranches or in towns and cities.

There was little agricultural well-being in Texas in 1897. THE NEWS now became convinced that the time had come to do something tangible about the plight of the agrarians. It started, therefore, an intensive and practicable campaign to raise farm incomes. Characteristically enough, this basic plan was the essence of conservatism; the way out, the paper was convinced, lay first of all in crop diversification. The decision was made chiefly by Colonel R. G. Lowe at Galveston, who had been impressed with the advocacy of this program by Julius Runge, one of the best known and most successful cotton factors of the day. But if the plea for farmers to throw off the chains of the single crop sounded commonplace and even hackneyed at the start, the vigor and journalistic snap with which THE NEWS campaigned soon gave the slogan new life. It was a crusade, this work of education, and one which THE NEWS was certain would be far "more profitable than the discussion of politics." It was further convinced that "in the diversification of crops, the raising of fine stock and the increase of attention to the poultry yard and the dairy farm will come a greater degree of prosperity to Texas than in any other direction that could be followed."

Cash premiums were posted by the newspaper in the fall of 1897 for the best articles by farmers on how to diversify. These prize winning articles were published both in the daily issues and in THE SEMI-WEEKLY NEWS issued from Dallas and Galveston. Then in the fall of 1898, another list of cash prizes was posted for articles based on actual experience with crop diversification—for precise farm data on total acres planted, acres to specific crops, yield per acre and gross and net yields for each crop. With cotton selling at 4 7/16 cents a pound, middling, at Dallas at the moment of announcement, this second contest created even wider interest. The management considered the matter so important that Colonel William G. Sterett, Washington correspondent for the preceding ten years and the star of the editorial staff, was recalled to Texas to conduct field surveys and otherwise direct the campaign. This shrewd journalist's observations of farm life at first hand, notably his dissection of the growing farm tenant problem in Texas, contributed largely toward interesting the banker and business man— then, as always, key factors in the cotton culture of the South.

By the season of 1899, THE NEWS and Texas were reaping tangible rewards from the crop diversification campaign. The price of cotton itself had been bettered, largely through general circumstances, it is true, but the cash income from this crop was decidedly larger than usual on account of the wider acceptance of THE NEWS' suggestion to "live at home" by raising more food and feedstuff. There were still some kinks to be ironed out in the agricultural situation. Undoubtedly, much of the value of the increase in truck and fruit growing was being lost, due to poor marketing facilities, and THE NEWS urged Texas farmers to establish and join co-operative shipping and selling organizations. Co-operative marketing of cotton was not necessary, the paper implied; but in 1899 THE NEWS began urging the erection of State-owned ware-houses, where the farmer might store and borrow against his cot-ton. In this way, it was argued, the glutting of the market in the first few months of the fall season might be avoided, with a con-sequently higher level of prices—it was presumed—to the grower through a more orderly marketing of the crop. There was, also, a new menace which had crept across the border from Mexico, the boll weevil; and, in 1900, THE NEWS aided in calling the first State convention to devise means of combating this pest. As early as 1899, THE NEWS began to get its own immediate reward, at least in the form of commendation and good will. A typical state-ment was that by Colonel Aaron Coffee of McKinney, Collin County, who wrote on May 4:

This great State was never so aroused to the importance of diversifi-cation until you enlisted the co-operation of the farmers in your wise step to abandon the suicidal plan of the one crop system. . . . The cry of diversification, instigated solely through your great enterprise and liberality, has brought about in this neck of the woods a pros-perity so great and permanent as to make our tillers of the soil the most independent of all classes.

THE NEWS for its part was gratified that "its efforts in behalf of the farmers of Texas are meeting with great success."

At the risk of becoming tiresome [THE NEWS continued], this paper has hammered away on crop diversification. That is, it has systematically and intelligently kept the subject before the people. The matter has always had due attention in THE NEWS' columns, but only incidentally and as the space and opportunity permitted. . . .
Seeing the deplorable straits to which the farmer was reduced by cheap cotton, knowing his traditional tendency to continue in ruts and to fight it out against the heaviest odds, THE NEWS deliberately and methodically set to work to turn his attention to something be-sides cotton, and to raise his foodstuffs at home. . . . The scales are dropping from the eyes of the Texas farmers and they are getting to

understand the urgent necessity in their own interest of devoting more study and time to material matters and less to jack o'lantern promises and plausibilities of professional vote-anglers.

Hard on the heels of this agrarian relief campaign, THE NEWS in 1899 launched a second crusade of more immediate concern to the citizens of Dallas and other urban settlements. Here the hand of a younger member of the official family, G. B. Dealey, was more directly responsible. Still known officially as the manager of the business at Dallas, he was already a veteran, inasmuch as he had reached his "majority" of twenty-one years of continuous service with the company, and he was becoming more and more an important part of the council that decided basic policies of the institution. Having both inherited and acquired an essentially humanitarian outlook on life and on the function of a modern newspaper in that life, his success in the purely hard-boiled business management of the Dallas paper had won for him, at the same time, the utmost respect of the older heads of the business. Particularly, as Colonel Belo passed the meridian of sixty years and poor health required him to withdraw more and more from active participation, the head of the corporation came to rely heavily upon the Dallas manager in so far as affairs at the Dallas end were concerned.

The great tragedy of the Spanish-American War had been the shockingly high death rate of American soldiers in camps from typhoid and yellow fevers. Perhaps the greatest benefit from the war lay in the ensuing wider public recognition of the connection between insanitary living conditions and germ disease. Thus, at G. B. Dealey's instigation, THE NEWS sponsored the organization in May, 1899, of the Cleaner Dallas League. This small, non-partisan organization of private citizens was to have an incalculable influence, not only in Dallas but also throughout the entire Southwest. For, not only was it instrumental in securing immediate, local objectives; from it likewise sprang the larger idea of communal beautification, city planning and the reorganization of municipal government itself to provide a more efficient urban existence.

The Cleaner Dallas League was organized by precincts and wards, with a central executive committee headed by Sam P. Cochran. Other executive committeemen included such representative civic leaders as Alex Sanger, T. F. McInnis, W. J. Moroney, B. M. Burgher, G. B. Dealey, R. D. Berry and George W. Jalonick. The first step was taken by employees of THE NEWS itself, who pitched in among themselves to purchase the first trash cans for the business district. There was practically no paving on streets, and sidewalks were largely wooden planks when they existed at all. The League now called for the cleaning of all streets, the sprinkling of thoroughfares during the hot, dusty months, for cleaner premises and better sanitary sewer connections throughout the city. Soon citizens were gaining respectful attention at the City Hall, where elected officials readily passed more stringent sanitary and health laws, bought sprinkling equipment and incinerators, and added a sanitary inspector and three assistants to work with the city health officer. The municipal government, also, waged war against undrained pools where mosquitoes, now recognized as the source at least of malarial infection, were heretofore allowed to breed. "In short," THE NEWS declared, "we want not only a greater Dallas, but what is more important, a cleaner Dallas."

Unavoidably linked with the cleaner Dallas crusade was the question of a more adequate city water supply. In 1896, the Turtle Creek storage reservoir had been supplemented by the damming of the Elm Fork of the Trinity River at Record's Crossing. But three years later this was found to be woefully inadequate and there was not enough water to lay the dust of the streets without inconveniencing the householder. Without water, the efforts of the Cleaner Dallas League might as well be halted.

If Dallas is to remain a city and continue to grow [declared THE NEWS on September 8, 1899] this water problem, dust, filth or health problem, whatever one may prefer to call it, must be solved, and in the right way. It presents a difficult task, but wise men with hard heads can meet it. It is an old trouble for which temporary or superficial expedients will not do. It is a work upon which the brains and

energy of Dallas should be brought together, for upon its accomplishment the progress and the life of the city depend.

But the water supply problem, in turn, was inevitably linked
with the broader question of an efficient and economical city government. The league and its backers turned with greater earnest-
ness to the matter of reorganizing the city government. This
seemed to be all the more urgent since the arrival of Federal census
figures that year, when the worst fears of the rank and file of the
citizenry were confirmed—Dallas had not, since the panic years,
grown at a rate to please the Commercial Club. In the race of
Texas cities for physical growth during the 'Nineties, San Antonio
had forged into the first place, formerly held by Dallas, while
Houston, growing at the astonishing rate of sixty-one per cent, had
increased its population to secure second place. Dallas in 1900
numbered only 42,639 people within its city limits, a figure which
entitled it to only third honors in the contest. What was more
alarming, the rate of population increase in the ten year period
had been only twelve percent, lower than that of all its competitors,
including Galveston and Fort Worth.

As early as 1897 THE NEWS had decried the breakdown of a
united Dallas spirit, in so far as the functioning of the city government was concerned. "THE NEWS has always contended that a
city should be regarded as a single community of people," it said
at that time, "all interested in a common, patriotic purpose and
not as a nest of rival wards and ward politicians with trading quarters at the City Hall." The same editorial had called for the election of aldermen by the city as a whole. Under the impetus of the
Cleaner Dallas League and the Commercial Club, the charter was
overhauled by the State Legislature in 1899 and far-reaching reforms introduced shortly afterwards. Under the new charter, the
number of wards was reduced to eight, with only four aldermen
allotted to serve two wards each. Four aldermen-at-large were
then added to the governing body. More important, a non-salaried
board of commissioners was superimposed, comprising the mayor
and two citizens appointed by the Governor. Full power in the
management of police and fire departments, in the granting of
franchises and in regulating the rates and services of public util-

ities, were vested with this board, while its supervisory powers over all public expenditures were extensive.

And, in 1899, the water supply problem was tackled at last in earnest in the laying of the foundation of what was to become the present-day system. The old 1883 report of Engineers Sooy Smith and C. B. Davis, long since shelved, was exhumed and Davis again employed to bring it up to date. The city now adopted his original proposal for a series of impounding reservoirs on the north and east sides of the city, along streams tributary to the Trinity River. These, it was believed, would be freer of pollution than other tributaries, or the river itself. By 1901, the first of this series was completed, that on Bachman's Branch. Although Bachman's Lake has been outgrown and abandoned as a water supply these thirty years, first in favor of White Rock Lake and later of Lake Dallas, it is interesting to note that the city's modern central pumping plant and purification station is located on the shore of this same early day source.

As the 'Nineties drew to a close, THE NEWS gave more attention to fostering the cultural as well as the physical development of its home city. After the dark ages of the depression, the theater revived in Dallas, along with the revival of "the Road." A new generation of stars—Otis Skinner, Minnie Maddern Fiske, Jessie Bartlett Davis and Barnaby's Bostonians, and others—came to fill the ranks thinned of the older personages of the stage. Cycle Park near the Fair Grounds was converted into the home of a resident stock company in 1898, although it retained its name from the days when it had served the bicycle fans.

The year before, on February 3, 1897, Edison's latest invention of the Vitascope had been displayed to "a well pleased audience at the Opera House" as a feature of the bill presented by a vaudeville troupe. Perhaps these first motion picture films ever shown in Dallas are worth noting—"a watermelon contest, a Mexican duel, scenes from Hoyt's 'A Milk White Flag,' Broadway and Fourteenth Streets, a hanging scene, scene in a blacksmithy shop, haymakers' umbrella dance, lynching scene, fire rescue and 'Niagara Falls.' " Already the basic elements of a great industry had been born.

The fine arts came in for a larger share of attention in THE NEWS. In March of 1900, Paderewski gave his first concert in Dallas. The Sunday editions began to be filled with more extensive chroniclings of the art, musical and theatrical worlds. Frank Reaugh, a young artist who had recently discovered the possibilities of subject matter for the painter in Texas, was added to the staff as weekly art commentator and reporter. "So far as concerns scenery and material for an artist to work up," he said, "I have not found anything equal to Texas. In Chicago and the East they do not have the coloring, nor the beautiful skies that we are blessed with, to say nothing at all of the sunsets."

THE NEWS stimulated the public's interest in books. Its weekly review of current literature, usually published on Monday mornings, was marked by discrimination and judgment. THE NEWS reviewer, for example, discussed Ellen Glasgow's "The Voice of the People" in July, 1900. "In the present state of Southern fiction," he wrote, "we are disposed to base much on this as yet young authoress. . . . The book begins and ends in Virginia, which is another way of saying that the author does not substitute what she thinks she knows for what she really does know." Nor were the literary sights trained only on Southern or American figures. Discussing a new novel shortly afterward by a "red bearded, fearless Irishman living in London," the reviewer pointed out that Bernard Shaw's better known plays were "no milk and water diet for women's clubs" and one of his works, "Candida," was "one of the first-rank plays that this generation has seen."

No reflection was intended, however, on either the intelligence or importance of women's clubs. THE NEWS, on the contrary, considered such groups of great value in promoting civic welfare. The paper's own woman's page enjoyed distinction and wide influence through the work of its editor, Mrs. W. A. Callaway. Writing usually under her pen name of Pauline Periwinkle, Mrs. Callaway helped shape for many years the outlook and interest of thousands of her sex in the Southwest toward public affairs. Through her,

THE NEWS was a primary moving force in the establishment and development of the woman's club movement in the Southwest. As early as 1897, she could write in THE NEWS that "the rabid, unreasoning prejudice against the 'woman movement' has almost entirely disappeared. . . . We have become familiar with the literary, scientific, reformatory, religious and political phases of the woman's movement. It is a sign of the times that a National Council of Mothers, to be organized in February of this year in Washington, D. C., will draw indiscriminately from the constituencies of all these other bodies. It affords indisputable evidence that the cultured and directed mind of womankind is the one most keenly alive to the responsibilities of the sex and their highest fulfillment."

A more local evidence of the ability of organized groups of women to promote civic causes was furnished shortly afterwards. The clubwomen of Dallas, marshaled by Mrs. Henry Exall, Mrs. George K. Meyer and Mrs. J. C. McNealus, turned their energies toward the goal of a public library. The earlier, volunteer library assembled during the 'Eighties had largely been dissipated through neglect. Mrs. Exall started the movement for a publicly supported library in 1899. Encouraged by THE NEWS, which headed the list with a personal subscription of $1,000 from Colonel Belo, a campaign netted $11,000 in donations from the public to buy the library site on the southwest corner of Commerce and Harwood. With the acquisition of the land, the clubwomen next turned to Andrew Carnegie, who made a gift of $50,000 for a library building in Dallas. His gift was contingent, however, upon an agreement by the city to appropriate at least $4,000 a year toward the maintenance of the library. A special library tax was voted on April 7, 1900, along with other special taxes endorsed by the Cleaner Dallas League and the Commercial Club—those to provide a better water supply, larger school facilities, more street paving and collection and incineration of garbage by the city itself.

"At any rate," THE NEWS was able to say on May 14, 1899, "all hands must admit that diversification of crops and the promotion of sanitary improvements in the cities and towns beat the same old politics, the same old quarrel over a few public offices."

CHAPTER XV

THE GALVESTON STORM

1900–1901

As THE YEAR 1900 opened, the great question agitating Christendom was whether or not the Twentieth Century had been born. There were strict constructionists of the calendar, such as the Vatican, who held that the Nineteenth Century would survive until January 1, 1901. THE NEWS, weighing the evidence, finally sided with the Papacy. But the year was to prove more epochal in the history of Texas, for toward its close, the State would be visited by the most destructive tropical cyclone in its history, the storm which centered over the city of Galveston and almost destroyed it.

THE NEWS at Dallas entered the new year in a mood of expansion. Still held in the closest association with its parent at Galveston, the duplicate at the Three Forks of the Trinity, nevertheless, far exceeded its original in circulation, size and advertising revenue. Yet the leased wire stretching the 315 miles between the two offices—irreverently referred to as the "umbilical cord"—continued to symbolize the close union of the publications. Colonel R. G. Lowe, vice president at Galveston, and Thomas W. Dealey, the secretary and treasurer, had exercised close supervision over the expansion required to take care of the great growth of the business at Dallas. A new Scott multiple press had been added in 1899 to raise the total printing capacity to 60,000 completed 8-page papers an hour. The new press alone was able to print 34,000 copies an hour. THE NEWS recited that "these facilities are not equalled by any paper south of St. Louis and not excelled by any newspaper in the South or West." In the summer of 1900, THE NEWS finished construction of a new three-story home in Dallas on the northwest corner of Commerce and Lamar, a fireproof building of steel, brick and stone, that was one of the most nearly complete newspaper plants in the country at the time. This adjoined the original NEWS building at Dallas, a "jerry built" structure in the middle of the block on Commerce Street and just west of the City Hall and Central Fire Station of 1885, on which latter site the new building had been erected. By 1938 the gradual expansion of THE NEWS plant would call for nine different contracts for the construction of physical plant. Improved mechanical facilities enabled the paper to present its first half-tone photographic reproduction, which happened to be that of General A. P. Cronje, a prisoner taken by the British in the Boer War.

While control of the purse strings had remained in Galveston since 1885, direction of news, editorial and other policies had been largely centered in and from Dallas since that time. Colonel Belo's official residence was in the North Texas city, and the editor-in-chief of all publications also lived in Dallas. An important change occurred in January, 1900, when Donaldson C. Jenkins, editor-in-chief for the last twenty-six years, resigned, and Luther W. Clark was named as his successor. Jenkins was the only surviving partner of Colonel Belo from the reorganization that followed the death of Willard Richardson in 1875. Now in poor health himself, Jenkins had been relinquishing his hold on editorial views for several years prior to his resignation. But it was his wife's ill health that immediately impelled him to resign, sell his interest in the company to Colonel Belo and remove to Southern California. The exchange of letters between Jenkins and Colonel Belo revealed the secret of their long and harmonious association, the genuine mutual regret over its dissolution.

"Well do I remember the first day when we met in New Orleans in 1873," Colonel Belo recalled, "and how refreshing it was to me to find a journalist of your experience so thoroughly in accord with the views I entertained. . . . We have so fully understood each

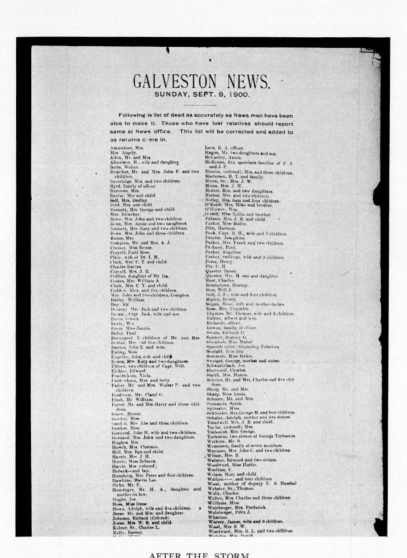

AFTER THE STORM

With its main presses waterlogged, THE GALVESTON DAILY NEWS could issue no more than the above handbill from a hand press on the morning of Sept. 9, 1900.

Main Street, Dallas, west of Akard, in 1885, the year in which THE NEWS was
established in the North Texas town

Photograph by Rogers

Main Street, Dallas, west of Akard, in 1938

other and been so thoroughly in accord in our purpose to publish a purely independent, fearless newspaper."

But it was the storm at Galveston rather than any changes at Dallas which would make the year memorable in the history of the institution. For the storm, one of the most horrible of peacetime disasters, was also the greatest news story in which the paper itself figured as a principal. THE NEWS at Dallas was so intimately and so vitally connected with its parent at the time that it shared directly in the calamity.

Recorded history is full of accounts of severe coastal storms breaking over the Island of Galveston. As early as 1521, the first white man to tread Texas soil, Cabeza de Vaca, landed there unintentionally because of a shipwreck in such a gale. In more modern times Galveston had suffered, although not seriously, by being on the edge of the storm which wiped out Indianola on Matagorda Bay in 1872. But, in spite of the island's vulnerability—nowhere did it rise as much as twelve feet above high tide and most of the area was even flatter—Galvestonians had little fear of the wind and waters from the Gulf of Mexico. There had been several proposals for a sea wall during the 'Nineties, but none had been entertained seriously. Citizens were totally unprepared, therefore, both physically and psychologically, for the great catastrophe of 1900.

September opened auspiciously for Galveston. THE NEWS issued its annual September 1 commercial edition to reveal that business and industrial prospects there were the brightest on record. Figures disclosed that the city was now the chief cotton exporting seaport in the world, and rising grain elevators pointed toward the possibility of equal world supremacy in flour and wheat. The Southern Pacific Railway system had recently decided to make extensive investments in terminal railway and steamship-loading facilities. The Census Bureau at Washington had just announced that there were 37,789 men, women and children in the island, a gain of almost thirty per cent in population since 1890.

The worst calamity imaginable to the proprietors of THE NEWS lay in the remote chance that William Jennings Bryan might, on his second try for the Presidency, unseat William McKinley.

As early as Tuesday, September 4, the Galveston weather bureau received its first message regarding a West Indian hurricane, then moving northward over Cuba. Each day thereafter bulletins were posted. By Thursday the slow moving tropical cyclone (as such disturbances are known to meteorologists) was over southern Florida, from which it changed its course by heading westward in the Gulf. It was centered off the Louisiana coast on the morning of Friday the seventh. The Federal weather reporting station on that day ordered up northwest storm warnings for Galveston. But the great majority of Galvestonians paid little attention to these signs and reports. The first public recognition of the disturbance was in THE NEWS on Friday morning. Two short, single-paragraph stories on Page 3 reported, under small headlines, that a cyclone had destroyed crops and left natives destitute in the Cuban province of Santa Clara and that the storm, "which has been raging on the South Florida coast for twenty-four hours, is now said to be north of Key West." Even the Saturday morning issue of THE NEWS contained only a small story on Page 2, also relative to the damage already done by the storm on the Florida coast.

When Galvestonians awoke on the fateful day of Saturday, September 8, the storm was even then upon the city. A high wind was blowing, and the waves on the Gulf side began pounding and wrecking the wooden beach resorts. A heavy tropical rain began to fall. Still, the early morning life of the city moved in its accustomed orbit, although many curious citizens went to the beach to see the grand fury of waves and wind. But weather bureau men on the fifth floor of the Levy Building watched the ominous sinking of the barometer, checked the constant increase on the wind gauge and then noted at 10:10 a.m. that the wind veered suddenly from north to northwest. There was no doubt now that the hurricane (as the dreaded tropical cyclone is known popularly) with its opposed quadrants of wind, had borne straight in on the city and enveloped it. It was apparent, in fact, to these trained observers that the whole island was now endangered. Telephone calls poured into the weather bureau office. To the hundreds of anxious inquiries, there was a single answer: "If you live in a low part of the city, move at once to high ground. Prepare for the worst, which is yet to come."

The normal life of Galveston had been paralyzed by early afternoon, with citizens attempting to reach their homes on foot, in carriages, wagons, boats—any way to get through the mounting tide. Half of the city was covered by tidewater at three o'clock; an hour later and the entire community lay buried one to five feet. The wind was howling at more than fifty miles an hour, while the rain continued to fall in blinding sheets. Telegraph connections to the mainland snapped shortly afterward as railroad and wagon causeways swayed and then slumped under the flood; for the first time since the "Old Lady by the Sea" had established her offspring in North Texas fifteen years earlier, wire communication between the two offices was broken. In Dallas, worried department heads hovered around the dead telegraph instrument and sought vainly for news of the beleaguered city by way of Beaumont, Houston and even Vera Cruz, Mexico. But the cable between Galveston and the latter city had also lapsed into silence. At the moment communication was severed City Editor William O'Leary was in the office of Manager G. B. Dealey, proving by Maury's Geography that the destruction of Galveston by tropical storm could not happen.

And thus while the world waited and wondered, Galveston passed into its greatest ordeal. By mid-afternoon heads of families who had delayed leaving for home plunged into the storm, wading through water almost to their necks, dodging flying slate from roofs and other missiles whipped through the air by the storm. Several years before Galveston had suffered a disastrous fire; subsequently a city ordinance had been passed requiring slate shingles to be substituted for wooden. A great many people were killed by pieces of slate flying through the air and cutting like so many knives. Still the wind increased in velocity—from sixty to seventy, to eighty, to ninety miles an hour—until at 5:15 p.m. the anemometer on top of the Levy Building registered 96 miles an hour, at which time it was torn from its perch. The wind appeared to begin shifting constantly, calming for a second or two, then resuming with terrific jerks so powerful that it seemed no building could withstand it.

Yet the climax of the storm came only after nightfall. By 8 o'clock, the wind reached a velocity of from 110 to 120 miles an hour, it was estimated by the weather bureau man who stuck to his post in the Levy Building. At the same time the general direction of the wind shifted once more, now from east to southeast and, simultaneously, a tidal wave four to six feet in height swept over the already inundated city. As THE NEWS reported later in its graphic, first-hand account, this was the moment of greatest destruction. "With a raging sea rolling around them, with a wind so terrific that none could hope to escape its fury, with roofs being torn away and buildings crumbling all around, men, women and children were huddled like rats in the structures. As buildings crumpled and crashed, hundreds were buried under the debris, while thousands were thrown into the waters, some to meet instant death, others to struggle for a time in vain, and yet other thousands to escape death in miraculous and marvelous ways."

☆

Throughout the remainder of Saturday night, there was gradual abatement of the storm. Terror-stricken survivors in homes and buildings that had withstood the elements noted that waters in the first floors began to lower inch by inch. The flood fell back into the bay and into the Gulf more rapidly than it had risen. Sunday morning dawned clear, with bright sunshine flooding the scene of the holocaust. Survivors at first could not comprehend the magnitude of destruction. As yet there was no realization of the frightful toll of life, although soon it was seen that more than a fourth of the area of the city, that nearest the Gulf, had been scraped clean of homes, stores, schools, churches and orphanages. A huge embankment of compressed wreckage marked the line of the storm's greatest advance toward total annihilation of the city.

The work of rescue and removal of bodies began. Moment by moment the proportions of the tragedy bore in on the dazed minds of the living. By tens, by scores, by hundreds and then by thousands the death toll mounted. Hospitals were jammed with the injured and dying; public buildings and warehouses were thrown open to provide first aid stations and temporary morgues. With the hot September sun beating down, quick burial of the dead became a necessity. The needs of the living were an even greater problem. With no bridges or wire connections left, word could not be flashed to the outside world of what had happened, yet it was obvious that relief must come, and come quickly, if starvation and pestilence were not to compound the horror.

W. L. Moody's yacht *Pherabe* had miraculously weathered the storm. At 10 o'clock Sunday morning it left the battered docks at Galveston, its improvised crew and passengers hoping to reach Houston fifty miles away by way of the Buffalo Bayou. Richard Spillane and William Delaney were aboard this first vessel, but the ship was unable to go farther than Texas City across Galveston Bay, from whence the two men began walking over five miles of flooded coastal prairie along the railroad track in the direction of Houston. They arrived in time to give details of the destruction to a mass meeting of Houstonians late Sunday afternoon. Shortly before daybreak on Monday a special train left Houston for the stricken city, carrying foodstuffs and clothing and 225 militiamen. Meanwhile, THE NEWS at Dallas sent two of its most able staff men, Colonel Sterett and George M. Bailey, on the night train for Houston and Galveston.

From late Saturday afternoon the world at large sought an authentic picture of the disaster. By Tuesday a telegraph line had been strung across from the mainland, and one of the first messages was from Charles S. Diehl, general manager of the Associated Press in New York, asking for a statement from Colonel R. G. Lowe. The operating head of THE NEWS answered with the first authentic estimate of the loss of life and property.

"A summary of conditions prevailing at Galveston is more than human intellect can master," telegraphed the old Scotsman. "The loss of life cannot be computed. No lists could be kept and all is simple guesswork. Those thrown out to sea and buried on the ground wherever found will reach the horrible total of at least three thousand souls. My estimate of the loss of the Island of Galveston and surrounding district is between 4,000 and 5,000 deaths. I do not make this statement in fright or excitement. The whole story will never be told, because it can not be told. The damage to property is anywhere between fifteen and twenty million.

"The necessities of those living are total. Not a single individual escaped property loss. The property on the island is wrecked, fully one half totally swept out of existence. Whatever our needs are can be computed by the world at large from this statement much better than I could possibly summarize them. The help must be immediate."

The response to this cry of distress by State and nation, as well as distant parts of the globe, was memorable and commensurate with the proportions of the disaster. The New York *Herald* took the lead among newspapers of the eastern part of the nation in raising relief funds by popular subscription. To expedite the wise and quick expenditure of relief funds, the New York paper called on THE DALLAS NEWS through its manager, G. B. Dealey, to make purchases and dispatch them to Galveston. Dealey called in the mayor of Dallas, Ben Cabell, and the County Judge of Dallas, Kenneth Foree, to administer these funds with him. Large sums were raised over Texas, and Dallas citizens responded generously to the call for help. Before the task was completed many thousands of dollars were spent in providing emergency relief. The first $500 received were spent for ten car loads of lime, which moved by special train to Texas City and were thence ferried across to Galveston. Dallas drugstores and warehouses were emptied of medicines and disinfectants. For the aftermath of the storm was ghastly, due to the disruption of civic facilities and to the fact that thousands of bodies carried out to sea for burial were washed ashore again by the tide. But martial law was proclaimed by Governor Sayers, threats to public order and public health were soon checked by armed authorities, and within a week the worst of the crisis was over. By September 18, Clara Barton of the American Red Cross had arrived to coordinate disaster relief on the island itself.

☆

The presses of THE NEWS at Galveston had been stalled, of
course, on the afternoon and night of the storm, since the flood
waters surrounded the building and climbed well toward the ceil-
ing of the first floor. The customary Saturday night scene of newspaper making had been transformed into one of defenseless watching and waiting, not only by members of THE NEWS' organization
but also by hundreds of other refugees. THE NEWS' building was
perhaps the strongest of its size in Texas and so well built that it
went through the storm with damage of only $50—and that was
to the iron shutters to doors and windows on the outside. No Sunday paper could be issued, but a small handpress began grinding
out handbills later that day. These attempted to list such of the
dead as could be identified. It was not until Wednesday morning
that THE NEWS could publish even a semblance of its ordinary
edition, yet herein is to be found the first complete story of the
catastrophe. What is more, this first edition crystallized the spirit
of Galveston, which refused to accept defeat in the face of the appalling experience. Thus its hastily written editorial did as much
to restore shattered morale and to plot the future of the seaport as
all other agencies combined :

What THE NEWS desires most to say to the surviving victims of
last Saturday's catastrophe is that, in the knowledge of a world-wide
sympathy which is encompassing us, we must not give way to despair.
If we have lost all else, we still have life and the future, and it is toward
the future that we must devote the energies of our lives.

THE NEWS also answered the panic of the moment, which counseled removal of the entire city to the mainland :

Tears and grief must not make us forget our present duties. The
blight and ruin which have desolated Galveston are not beyond re-
pair. We must not for a moment think Galveston is to be abandoned
because of one disaster, however horrible that disaster has been. . . .
It is time for courage of the highest order.

As days and weeks went by, Galveston rapidly righted herself
and prepared to make the most of the future. Out of her physical
helplessness arose the plan for a great seawall and the raising of the
level of the city by hydraulic fill, a protective scheme which proved

its success in 1915 when a storm of even greater intensity failed to produce more than a fraction of the havoc of the 1900 hurricane. And, out of the disrupted civic economy, was to evolve the Galveston Plan of city government—a more efficient system of municipal administration which proved a notable advance on the older aldermanic form and was widely adopted in this and other countries. In these and other rehabilitation moves, THE NEWS again asserted its old leadership on Galveston Island. No better answer could have been given to the report that THE NEWS would abandon Galveston and "go to live with her daughter at the Three Forks of the Trinity River." But, to scotch the rumor finally and unequivocally, THE NEWS at Galveston declared in an editorial:

The Old Lady by the Sea has lived a long time, and she is able not only to hold her own but she has had a life work which she has no idea of abandoning because of the late catastrophe to her people. She will stand with them in the future as she has stood with them in the past; that is until death doth them part.

THE NEWS at Dallas was drawn closer than ever before to its counterpart at Galveston by the tragedy of the storm. The two papers joined a few weeks later in observing a double anniversary in their own history. October 1, 1900, was significant, first for the fact that on that date thirty-five years ago Colonel Belo had begun his long connection with the institution. It was also the fifteenth anniversary of the birth of THE DALLAS MORNING NEWS. The paper called attention to the occasion in a lead editorial which, in phraseology as well as in thought, recalled the continuity of the institution through floods, wars and pestilences, as well as the more tranquil eras of the past. Even the wording of the editorial was made up largely of words and phrases taken from earlier editorial pronouncements. The result formed both a summary and a prophecy:

The master mind and the guiding hand of THE NEWS in those early days was found in the person of Willard Richardson, who devoted his maturer years to the upbuilding of Texas through the col-

umns of THE NEWS. The value of his assistance and the strength of
his name to THE NEWS were always appreciated, and after he was
gone was felt the want of counsel from "his good gray head which all
men knew."

All those connected with THE NEWS at its outset have left the scene
of their labors. Their successors have never swerved from the path
blazed out, ever preferring public duty to personal favor. . . .

Today THE NEWS enters upon a new cycle under the present chief
proprietor. Few are left who were with him thirty-five years ago. . . .
Yet there are men faithful at the helm. Many of them have served
the property zealously for years and have learned to love the institution which in their humble way they have helped to foster and build
up.

In all probability before the close of another twenty-five years, the
present guiding hand will have sought retirement so justly won.
Others will follow in his footsteps, building along the lines blazed
out by the pioneers gone before. As they stop at various stages of
growth for a brief retrospective view, they will realize that success in
those days of glorious superstructure is resultant in no small degree
from the sturdy foundation builded by the founders, verily the works
of whose hands shall survive them.

This prophecy of retirement justly won for Willard Richardson's successor was much closer than anyone could possibly have
known. Yet, as 1901 turned up on the calendar, there was a re-
minder of human frailty and mortality. In January, THE NEWS
chronicled the death of Queen Victoria, whose reign had been almost concurrent with the life thus far of THE NEWS. The Legislature of Texas adjourned for a day out of respect for her memory,
and THE NEWS gave its opinion that her reign "had covered the
most progressive period in the history of mankind. . . . The truth
is that Victoria was not merely a gracious queen. She was a good
woman."

☆

Texas was prosperous in the early part of 1901—"even the most
pessimistic had to agree." The new electric railway between Dallas
and Fort Worth was under construction. "The city has a promising decade ahead," said THE NEWS, "and the thing to do is for
everybody to work with determination to bring Dallas round to

the 100,000 mark by the time the next census is taken." The discovery of oil in gusher proportions at Spindletop near Beaumont in January had set the pace. Soon the whole State seemed to be embarked on a frenzy of oil speculation. "Texas is as crazy as a loon on the subject of oil," said THE NEWS in a story describing the excitement in Dallas. Soon it was retailing how young fortunes had been made by bootblacks as well as merchants, farmers and others. As the oil advertisements poured into its columns, THE NEWS expanded in average size from ten to sixteen pages.

As summer approached, Colonel Belo and his family left Dallas for their summer home in Asheville, N. C. In more fragile health than ever, he was not considered, however, to be in an alarming condition when he departed. Yet he had scarcely reached the end of his journey when he died in Asheville on April 19. A few days later the funeral was held in his birthplace, nearby Winston-Salem. It was attended by representatives from widely separated parts of the country, as well as by a host of friends and relatives. Melville E. Stone, general manager of the Associated Press, and the editor of *Harper's Weekly* represented the press of the nation. Vice President Lowe and Secretary Thomas W. Dealey hurried from Galveston to represent THE NEWS family. The remnants of Colonel Belo's old Forsythe Rifles were drawn up beside the grave for the final military tribute. From his retirement at Princeton, former President Grover Cleveland voiced the sentiment of thousands by saying "this is a personal loss, as he was a friend to whom I was warmly attached. He was a chivalrous, high-minded man, an exceptionally able, fearless and conscientious journalist. His death is a loss to the entire country."

The officers and employees of THE NEWS at Dallas assembled on April 20 to honor the memory of their dead chieftain. Tearing aside for a moment the curtain of anonymity which was traditional with the paper, THE NEWS the next morning revealed the grief and keen sense of personal loss felt by the organization. Instinctively, the office of spokesman for the group fell to G. B. Dealey. Not only was he the ranking officer in the Dallas group; he was also the closest personal associate of the deceased. Luther Clark, the editor-in-chief; Arthur Geen, chief bookkeeper, and Thomas

M. Rinehart, press foreman, were named a committee to draft a formal expression. But, in the off-hand, brief and deeply personal remarks of G. B. Dealey, were summed up the sentiments of the entire staff.

CHAPTER XVI

PROBLEMS OF A NEW CENTURY

1901–1906

ALFRED H. BELO, JR., trained from birth as his father's successor, became president of THE NEWS in 1901. The five short years in which this young man fulfilled his destiny were marked by unusual tranquillity within both the institution and the larger community of Texas. Galveston recovered rapidly from the near death blow of the storm, and both State and nation enjoyed increasing prosperity. Under the governorship of Joseph D. Sayers, then that of Samuel W. T. Lanham, Texas passed into a period almost devoid of rancor and turmoil over public office. And, as politics receded further from the concern of THE NEWS, the paper was able to give almost all of its attention to the more cherished task of promoting internal development.

Late in the summer of 1901, William McKinley made his only visit to Texas. It was part of his swing around the country that was to terminate tragically at Buffalo. Texans cordially greeted the presidential party as it passed westward from Louisiana to the New Mexico borders. The only intimation of regret was voiced in THE NEWS by Larry Chittenden, the Cowboy Poet, who wrote: "We're monst'rous glad ter meet you, but whar's your running mate?" When, therefore, Teddy Roosevelt fell heir to the presidency a few weeks later, Texans were among the first to evince their good will. Roosevelt gathered additional favor in 1903 by his quick recognition of the Republic of Panama, by which the construction of an isthmian canal was assured. "That Texas of all States in the Union will be the quickest and most benefited by this waterway" was the belief of THE NEWS.

President Roosevelt gained first-hand proof of his popularity in the Lone Star State in the spring of 1905, when he journeyed to San Antonio for the reunion of his famous Rough Riders. The News reported one of the greatest popular demonstrations ever given an individual in Texas. Entering the State at Denison, the president received a continuous ovation along the 400-mile journey to San Antonio. The trip was broken at nightfall at Dallas, where 25,000 Texans crowded the streets to welcome him. Former Governor James Stephen Hogg came from retirement at Houston to bestow his approval upon the Rough Rider at a banquet that night at the Oriental Hotel. Conspicuously absent was United States Senator Joseph Weldon Bailey, whose forces had gradually routed the Hogg dynasty from power in Texas. The year before Bailey had stumped the nation in opposition to Roosevelt's re-election, making an issue of the Panama adventure. There were instant repercussions, therefore, in the Texas political scene when Hogg, at the banquet, congratulated Roosevelt on the achievement at Panama, lauding him as "the great President who had the manhood, without resorting to diplomacy or the complications of red-tapeism, to strike back the dough-faced pirates who have fettered commerce for a hundred years." Colonel Sterett noted in The News at once that this foreshadowed a mighty contest, a final trial by arms between the Bailey and anti-Bailey men.

More significant was the act of the Legislature in 1905 in legalizing, at last, a system of State banks. More than half a century had passed since The News first advocated this reform. The paper also took pride in the passage of the Terrell Election Law that same year, one that provided a direct vote in the party primary elections. There was satisfaction, furthermore, in the decision of the same Legislature to permit Dallas County at least to issue and sell bonds for the improvement of its highways. From the turn of the century, the automobile had been slowly forcing itself upon the attention of Dallas and Texas people. There had been six or seven of these horseless contraptions in Dallas as early as June, 1901, when the first auto races in the State were held at Fair Park. By the middle of 1903, The News reported the automobile "fad"

had reached such proportions that there were "over forty automobiles owned in Dallas at this time, more than in any city of its size in the South." The retail price of gasoline rose from 65 to 85, and then to 95 cents per gallon. The increasing band of motorists were the wheel horses in the local good roads movement. By 1905, THE NEWS began to see tangible results in its long campaign for better highways.

"In time," the paper that year remarked, "we may all have autos, and when it comes to racing and fun, we may then outstrip even the French. In the meantime the use of public highways must be wisely and fairly regulated so that the casualty list may be kept at least in decent bounds."

Even more challenging to the imagination of NEWS readers were efforts made at this time to realize man's age old dream of human flight. The plans of Professor Langley to launch a heavier-than-air machine near Washington made front page news in 1903. But the skepticism of the nation was rewarded on December 8, when Langley's folly wrecked itself on its second unsuccessful attempt and sank in the Potomac River. When, therefore, two unknown mechanics of Dayton, Ohio, were reported ten days later to have soared successfully into the air in a gasoline-powered aeroplane near Kitty Hawk, N. C., the telegraph editor of THE NEWS relegated the freak yarn to an obscure column on Page 3. This Associated Press dispatch of December 18, 1903, from Norfolk, Va., told of the fantastic flight of Wilbur and Orville Wright. It is doubtful if THE NEWS would have printed the story at all, had not a zealous news editor made independent inquiries of Dayton, which drew an assuring response that the Wrights were "intelligent mechanics, sons of Bishop Wright of the United Brethren Church, and members of a well known family." The airplane had been born, but it would be lost sight of for the next five years. Not until 1908 would the Wrights, before United States Army authorities near Washington, D. C., thoroughly and publicly demonstrate their ability to fly.

The prosperity that rolled over Texas during the first seven fat years of the Twentieth Century was based, in part, on the revival in agriculture but stimulated immensely by the discovery of oil at Spindletop near Beaumont. THE NEWS itself enjoyed remarkable prosperity from the oil boom, due to the great amount of oil stock advertisements which flowed into its columns at this time. Revenues from this source were large for several years after 1901— throughout the incumbency of Alfred H. Belo, Jr., as president, in fact—but dividends of the company fell off markedly after the oil excitement died down. The paper learned much from the experience; when the next oil boom hit Texas some ten years later, the policy of THE NEWS was much stricter in the matter of acceptance of such advertisements.

Cotton in the first years of the century sold at high prices in spite of, or perhaps because of, the inroads which the boll weevil was making into the total volume. THE NEWS harped on the theme of crop diversification, adding endorsement of the "improved seed" movement for cotton producers which arose in 1903. In the same year, THE NEWS offered cash prizes for the written experience of growers on how they made farming profitable in spite of the boll weevil. But even greater prosperity was noticeable in the towns and cities of Texas.

Dallas during these years boomed again. In 1903 the trans-river, suburban city of Oak Cliff surrendered its autonomy and merged with Dallas. By 1905, many of the more enthusiastic boosters were convinced that the next Federal Census might show 150,000 residents, if something were only done about it; thus they banded together in the "150,000 Club" to work toward that objective through a community advertising program in national publications. At a meeting of the club in the Harvey Restaurant in the old Santa Fe passenger station, G. B. Dealey cautioned the boosters to remember that a clean and wholesome city was fully as important as a large one. He cited the example of the housewife who first puts her house in order before receiving guests. He argued that

the campaign to rid Dallas of drab, dirty streets, poor housing conditions and unsightly and insanitary conditions in general should
be speeded up and that such action naturally would bring additional population.

His talk represented the school of civic thought in Dallas which
insisted that social and human values were more important than
mere size of population. Through G. B. Dealey, THE NEWS was
now more than ever committed to this sounder concept of civic development. The reunion of Confederate veterans in Dallas in
May of 1902, which THE NEWS helped celebrate by issuing a 72-
page souvenir edition, had emphasized the need for a better street
system, a cleaner and more attractive city. The large crowds
brought from all parts of the South—more than 100,000 people
gathered in Fair Park for several events—indicated that Dallas,
perhaps, was not ready for a permanent population of 150,000.

Under the leadership of THE NEWS, a second important step
was taken to better living conditions, the organization on Decem-
ber 10, 1902, of a local branch of the American League for Civic
Improvement. The sponsors were such civic leaders as L. M. Dab-
ney, Epps G. Knight, R. E. L. Saner, E. J. Gannon, A. Harris, W.
O. Connor, Alex Sanger, M. M. Crane, M. H. Thomas, J. B.
Adoue, Sydney Smith, A. V. Lane, G. H. Schoellkopf, E. O. Teni-
son, Henry D. Lindsley, G. A. Trumbull, G. B. Dealey, G. R.
Scruggs, A. A. Green, Sr., B. M. Burgher, Alfred H. Belo, Charles
L. Dexter, W. H. Atwell, Barnett Gibbs, Edward Gray, Charles F.
Bolanz and others. In congratulating the new organization, THE
NEWS laid down a five-point program of objectives that should be
sought: an adequate water supply and distribution system, a modern fire department, a sanitary sewer and disposal system, well
paved streets with ample provision for keeping them scrupulously
clean and, finally, a system of parks. This last objective, THE NEWS
believed, should be tackled at once. "Dallas needs a great many
things badly but nothing more than parks and plazas," the paper
said. In 1903 it felt the taxpayers were ready to accept a small
mill tax to acquire and maintain a park system, but the proposal
was rejected at the polls in August. The next year, though, the
State Fair of Texas faced a financial crisis, and its continued exist-

Cartoon by John F. Knott, containing his well-known character
'Old Man Texas.'

REMEMBER THE TWO DONKEYS?

Cartoon by Jack Patton, staff cartoonist of THE DALLAS (Evening) JOURNAL

ence was threatened. THE NEWS now took the lead in rescuing the State Fair from chaos, devoting an enormous amount of space in news and editorial columns to the campaign which the paper fostered and saw through to a successful conclusion. A refinancing plan named for the chairman of the committee, E. M. Reardon, was agreed upon, and the citizens voted to buy the fair grounds as a public park, accepting at the same time a small tax for maintenance. From this the city park system of today was born and the first park board created. In addition to Mayor Bryan T. Barry, its personnel included M. N. Baker, W. O. Connor, Emil Fretz and J. J. Eckford.

But THE NEWS came to realize that the objectives of the League for Civic Improvement, like those of the earlier Cleaner Dallas League, hinged on improvement in the city government itself. The weaknesses in the old aldermanic form were more obvious than ever. Beginning in August, 1903, the paper ran the first of a series of educational articles on the success of the Galveston commission form of government, then three years old. These were written by Tom Finty, Jr., formerly of the Galveston staff, later legislative correspondent for both papers at Austin, and attached to the Dallas office as an editorial writer at the time.

Evolved out of the necessities left by the storm of 1900, the Galveston city commission, Finty wrote, had become "a model municipal administration. By the application of honorable business methods it has redeemed the city from financial bankruptcy." THE NEWS continued its fight for adoption of the plan at Dallas, "repeating that the first thing is to secure legislative permission to establish a government in Dallas modelled after the Galveston elective commission." At last the Legislature authorized the voters of Dallas in 1906 to say whether they wanted the innovation or not. On the eve of Dallas' acceptance of the new form, THE NEWS made the obvious but important observation that any form of government depends in the final analysis "upon the attention given to it by citizens and taxpayers and upon the exercise of the powers of government possessed."

THE NEWS recorded marked evidences of the commercial growth of Dallas during the first years of the century. By 1904 the

wholesale business had exceeded $67,000,000 a year, "eclipsing all
former records," and definitely establishing Dallas as the jobbing
mart of the Southwest. Three years before, in May of 1901, the
first annual trade trip of the Commercial Club had been made by
special train, the itinerary taking the trade evangels into the Indian
and the Oklahoma Territories. The Dallas Fall Market had been
established by 1904, under the auspices of the Trade League, and
visiting buyers were sufficient in numbers to fill the Cycle Park
theater one evening as guests of the League at a special performance of "La Mascotte," the master work of the Lyric Opera Company. Postal receipts by 1905 justified the construction of the
second, or Main Street, annex to the post office at Ervay, Commerce and Main. The American and Exchange national banks
had been consolidated to form the largest financial institution in
the State. That same year citizens were raising with a fair degree
of ease some $100,000 for a new Young Men's Christian Associa-
tion building, which was built on the south side of Commerce
Street between St. Paul and Harwood. Then, on March 24, 1905,
City Building Inspector L. L. Bristol announced that the fraternal
order of Praetorians had been issued a permit to erect a skyscraper,
a fourteen story office building outtopping anything in the city.
The first residential suburb in Dallas, with restrictions in the deeds
to control the nature and cost of homes, was also opened that
year as Munger Place.

Amusements continued to fill a large place in the life of the city,
as the pages of THE NEWS indicated. Increasingly the paper gave
more space to sports, to theatricals, to social events. In this period
converts to the ancient but imported game of golf were made by
the score. In 1903 H. L. Edwards, founder of the Dallas Golf and
Country Club and Texas State golf champion, played in the
Southern Association's tournament in Asheville, N. C. In 1904,
the Dallas group had erected their first clubhouse in Oak Lawn on
grounds lying between Turtle Creek Drive, Lemmon Avenue,
Reagan, Throckmorton, Gilbert and Blackburn Streets.

As before, the stage continued to hold an important place in the
affections of Dallas people. On May 22, 1901, THE NEWS reported the loss by fire of the old, admirably constructed Opera

House on the southwest corner of Commerce and Austin Streets. But a new playhouse was soon completed on the northeast corner of Main and St. Paul Streets, and attractions such as "Ben Hur," Anna Held in "The Little Duchess," or Fred Hemlin in "The Wizard of Oz" were on the boards. In 1903, C. E. Bray, resident manager of the New Orleans Orpheum Theater, announced that Dallas would soon have its own vaudeville house. He took pains to explain to Texas patrons that "a vaudeville show is different from a variety show." Then, on October 30, 1905, the Majestic Vaudeville Theater was opened on the northeast corner of Commerce and St. Paul Streets with Karl Hoblitzelle as manager. This introduced a man who later was to have a great part in the subsequent development of amusement enterprises in the Southwest. The opening bill of ten acts included a showing of the "kinetograph," forerunner of the motion picture feature.

Music, also, came into a golden age of its own in Dallas during the first half of the decade. The greatest artists of the day were attracted to "the Road." Among those heard in Dallas were Paderewski, the composer- pianist Edward MacDowell, Ernestine Schumann-Heink, Carl Rosenbecker and the Chicago Symphony Orchestra; Walter Damrosch and the New York Symphony Orchestra; Nordica, Melba, Heinrich Conried and the Metropolitan Opera Company. But the height of interest was reached in the Golden Jubilee of the Texas State Saengerfest, held in Dallas in 1904. For this, Marcella Sembrich was engaged as guest artist at the then record fee of $7,000 for her part in the two-day festival. The success of this great event was due chiefly to the work of Charles A. Mangold and Will A. Watkin.

Under the guidance of young Belo, THE NEWS as an institution continued to prosper. Nearing thirty years of age when the chief responsibility fell upon him, he proved a capable and modest executive who justified the long training that had been given him.

After graduation from Yale in 1896, he had entered the Dallas office, familiarizing himself with the work of various departments.

He was not headstrong by nature and he drew heavily upon the experience and counsel of those who had been longest associated with his father. In Colonel R. G. Lowe and Thomas W. Dealey at Galveston, and in G. B. Dealey at Dallas, he had a general staff that assured continuation of the traditions and ideals of the institution.

Circulation and other factors testified to the growth of THE NEWS at Dallas during these same years. From a daily average of 25,000 copies in 1901, the paper reached an average of 38,000 five years later. Departmentalization was carried further in March of 1904 when an eight-page Sunday magazine section was added. Harry Lee Marriner, first editor of this section, also began publication of his daily weather column verse on Page One—a feature which was to prove one of the most popular ever published by THE NEWS. Even Colonel Lowe's long stand against colored comics crumbled at this time before the pleas of the circulation department; two of the eight pages of the Sunday magazine were given over to the antics of Foxy Grandpa and to a mule named Maud. The prosperity within and without THE NEWS also led to the revival of THE TEXAS ALMANAC AND STATE INDUSTRIAL GUIDE in 1904. Once more this yearbook did its part in recording and promoting the growth and development of the State.

With Luther Clark as editor-in-chief and Colonel Sterett and Tom Finty, Jr., as editorial writers, the policy of the paper fitted in admirably with the spirit of the times. The news department saw several changes. On the resignation of Hugh Nugent Fitzgerald in 1902, D. Prescott Toomey began his long and memorable tenure as managing editor. The first directing head of the news department to have been trained exclusively within the organization at Dallas, Toomey had risen from the mailing room by way of the art department to this ranking position. George M. Bailey, later widely known as a brilliant editorial writer and paragrapher on the Houston *Post,* had served as Washington correspondent of THE NEWS since 1899. He resigned in 1904 and once more Colonel Sterett, for a brief time, returned to the national capital. At the insistence of Colonel Sterett and R. G. Lowe, vice president and general manager, J. J. Taylor, editor and part owner of the

Clarksville *Times,* was now persuaded to join THE NEWS as an editorial writer, then Sunday magazine editor, later to begin his long reign over the State Press column and, in turn, to be named to his present place as editor-in-chief. In 1905 Alonzo Wasson began his long and faithful career with THE NEWS as Washington correspondent.

☆

The two ranking executives at Galveston, Vice President Lowe and Thomas W. Dealey, secretary and treasurer, occupied peculiarly important positions during the regime of Alfred Belo. To them fell the increasingly difficult task of co-ordinating the Galveston and Dallas branches of the business. Although Colonel Lowe insisted upon Alfred Belo's taking more and more responsibility, he nonetheless exercised his own authority when he considered it necessary.

Typical of Colonel Lowe's attitude toward journalism was his decision toward the State's last major yellow fever scare in 1904. Numerous communities were threatened with quarantine, coincident with the outbreak in New Orleans. While no cases developed in Dallas, the State Fair was postponed more than a month that fall at the insistence of State health officials. The publisher of a paper in Houston urged Colonel Lowe and other executives to censor or omit all references to the threatened epidemic, even to the point of refusing to print official articles by health authorities. Colonel Lowe refused to approve such a boycott, answering:

Of course the newspapers of the State by general agreement could minimize the action of so-called yellow-fever experts, but to minimize the experts themselves is the serious matter. State and Federal authorities are now engaged in the work of preventing the spread of yellow fever, and these authorities will work in common after their fashion towards the desired end. The newspapers of the State cannot well afford to ignore the action of these experts, no matter what we may consider the effects thereof when inserted by the press.

The Scotsman was chiefly concerned with the management of the editorial and news departments, and he never hesitated to call the editorial department to taw when he felt it was veering from the true policy of THE NEWS. Thus, in correction of an editorial paragraph, he wrote on the margin of the proof in July, 1905:

You will observe the statement that THE NEWS "merely alluded remotely to an accusation which got abroad during the session of the legislature." This is not the right kind of matter to make editorial charges upon. Referring remotely to accusations don't go. . . . Never permit the editorial department to enter the field of innuendo or personal motive unless it is prepared to make specific charge. Then when it does, fight it to the tail end of the whole business as hard and as strong as it can.

The diversity of the commercial interests of Dallas and Galveston sometimes made for slight but annoying estrangement between the two branches. Particularly, Colonel Lowe sometimes felt that the chief editorial writers, who were attached to the Dallas end, were not always alert to protect the commercial interest of Galveston. At his insistence, THE NEWS began more vigorously to demand that the Texas Railroad Commission abolish the rate differential between Galveston and Houston, then in favor of the latter city. Stronger in circulation, advertising volume and revenue, THE DALLAS MORNING NEWS at times, or so it appeared to Colonel Lowe, had a tendency to forget the needs of its parent paper. For the Twentieth Anniversary issue of THE DALLAS MORNING NEWS on October 1, 1905, Colonel Lowe wrote:

The Old Lady by the Sea congratulates THE DALLAS MORNING NEWS on its twentieth anniversary. You were never a real baby. You came into existence quite capable of taking care of yourself, with muscle and brain well developed, and with an ancestry that is no discredit to you. You displayed good sound sense in the selection of your parentage; likewise as to the place of your birth. Dallas and its people have done well by you, and you have done your duty by Dallas and its people. Your "auld mither" is proud of you and pleased beyond measure to know that her offspring gives promise of days without number and usefulness without limit.

More privately and not for publication, Colonel Lowe about this time complained against what he considered neglect of the Galveston end. In a letter to Alfred Belo he wrote:

My kick of yesterday is still registered. Please see to it that your people at Dallas give this end attention when they have anything good on hand. I know you are very busy and likely to overlook our requirements. Still, we took good care of you when you were beginning to toddle along and you ought not to forget the Old Lady when she needs a lift. . . .

The personal relationship between Colonel Lowe and the young titular head of the business was such that the older man could speak in the sternest of terms if need be. But most of his counsel was given in a kind and often bantering spirit. He insisted that Alfred Belo should "run down to Austin for some little time and get acquainted with the young men of the State now taking part in her politics." The set "that I knew," added Colonel Lowe, "is passing away and the new generation is on the boards." The two men met in Austin in January of 1905 during a session of the Legislature, and Colonel Lowe showed his pupil the ropes. When they had returned to their respective homes, the 69-year-old vice president was satisfied. "I think you will turn out a pretty good mixer, if you keep it up," he wrote Belo.

To no one was the blow more personal than to Alfred Belo when Colonel Lowe died suddenly of a heart attack in Galveston on January 15, 1906; young Belo broke down when word of his death was flashed to the Dallas office. Two weeks later, rising from an attack of influenza and still far from well, Alfred Belo went to Galveston to attend the annual meeting of stockholders and directors of A. H. Belo & Company. The death of Colonel Lowe, he said, had caused "a large vacancy in our organization." THE NEWS, though, "as an institution, having closed up the ranks as best it can, must go marching on. THE NEWS is fortunate in having a large corps of loyal workers, who, having been trained in the policies of those who have gone before, will take up the work and carry it on to the best of their ability."

At the same meeting Alfred Belo announced that Thomas W. Dealey, continuously with THE NEWS for the past thirty-six years, insisted upon resigning as secretary and treasurer. Declining health required his removal from Galveston to the health resort of Mineral Wells, where he was even then undergoing treatment. The president announced, however, that he had persuaded Thomas W. Dealey to remain as a director of the company, "so that we may still have the advantage of his advice and counsel."

The concluding matter of business was the selection of successors to Colonel Lowe and Thomas W. Dealey in the roster of officers. G. B. Dealey, a director since 1901, was now named vice president and general manager. John F. Lubben, identified with the Galveston end since 1881, was elected secretary and treasurer. A quarter of a century had passed since these two offices in the corporation had been created, and these were the first changes in them.

One month to the day that Colonel Lowe was stricken, Thomas W. Dealey died in his new home at Mineral Wells. Alfred Belo, in the meantime, had suffered a relapse from his earlier illness, and physicians had diagnosed it as cerebro-spinal meningitis. Thus the president of the company lay desperately ill in his Dallas home and could not even be told of the death and funeral of this second official of the company.

For twelve days longer the thirty-three-year-old head of THE NEWS made an heroic fight against the disease. Everything that medical science, care and attention could offer was done to aid him. A special train was chartered to bring specialists from a distance to aid those on the ground. Doctors, nurses, friends and family marveled at the spirit and stamina of the young man in his fight for life. But, on February 27, the fight was lost, and this "most rare and promising example of untainted youth" was dead.

The death of the three highest ranking officers within the short span of six weeks was the severest blow ever sustained by THE NEWS in its corporate history. From this time forward the main weight of executive direction of the properties fell upon the vice president and general manager, G. B. Dealey, who was also the ranking member in length of service in THE NEWS' official family.

It became necessary to effect a reorganization. The Belo family invited Dealey to become the president. This he declined, suggesting instead that Colonel Belo's widow, Mrs. Nettie Ennis Belo, be named titular head. This step was taken. In his will, or otherwise, Colonel Belo had advised his family, in the event of a serious calamity, to seek the advice of their relative, C. Lombardi. So the latter was sent for and asked to connect himself with the institution. After several conferences, he agreed to this and, on the strong recommendation of G. B. Dealey, consented to take an official position in the active management. The by-laws of the corporation were changed to meet the new conditions, and officers were elected as follows: Mrs. A. H. Belo, Sr., president; C. Lombardi, vice president; G. B. Dealey, vice president and general manager. Lombardi established his office on the editorial floor and was given supervision over that department, while G. B. Dealey took general supervision over all other departments.

A native of Switzerland, Cesar Lombardi—or C. Lombardi as he invariably referred to himself—had emigrated to Texas as a youth and had married a younger sister of Mrs. A. H. Belo, Sr. Identified for many years with W. D. Cleveland & Company of Houston, he had rounded out a successful mercantile career in Texas when he moved in 1900 to the Pacific Coast. On being called back to Texas to assume the vice presidency of THE NEWS, he began an experiment fraught with disturbing possibilities for more than one party. That C. Lombardi promptly and tactfully made himself one of the most valuable members of the organization in its history is a testimonial to unusual qualities of mind, heart and character. Throughout the next thirteen years he would contribute a graciousness of spirit, an urbanity and a liberalizing influence that would leave an indelible impress upon THE NEWS.

CHAPTER XVII

"THE SCARLET WOMAN"

1906–1912

THE ERA of good feeling in Texas politics came to an abrupt end late in 1906. THE NEWS had its part in that conclusion. But the long truce scarcely seemed threatened as the year opened. That spring and summer, Tom Campbell of Palestine and three other candidates, the strongest of whom was Railroad Commissioner O. B. Colquitt, sought the Democratic nomination for Governor. In addition, Joseph Weldon Bailey, completing his first term as United States Senator, announced that he would submit his candidacy to the direct primary, then being given its first trial in Texas. No one offered to contest his re-election, so that his name stood alone in the place on the ballot assigned to the senatorial office.

THE NEWS expressed gratification on July 17, just a few days before the primary, over the way in which the political campaign was being waged:

There are two ways to look at a campaign like the present. Shall it be the ordinary, hot, unfair and desperate contention of bitter partisans over men, or shall it be a decent contest in which all the men are fairly heard and in which intelligence and good conscience will be given a show? . . . THE NEWS is not displeased with the failure of those who would bring the people down to a condition of untimely and intense excitement over immaterial differences.

The primary election in July disclosed that neither Campbell nor Colquitt, the two high men, had won a majority. At that time no provision was made for a run-off primary, and thus the final settlement of the nomination was again cast back on the State convention. It was noted that the votes cast for Senator Bailey in the primary were more than those cast for all four candidates for Governor.

The State convention met in Dallas on August 14, and, after some listless jockeying, Campbell received the nomination. The convention itself was a tame affair, except for the incident in which Senator Bailey threw his support to Campbell during a speech to the delegates. His recitation of the siege of Lucknow, with its stirring climax of "The Campbell's Are Coming," furnished the single exception to what Colonel Sterett described as being otherwise a "peaceful, placid, perfunctory meeting."

Beneath the surface, however, there were forces at work to revive partisanship. Largely under the impetus of Roosevelt's trust-busting activities in the nation at large, there was a resurgence of feeling in Texas against corporate wealth, particularly that in the form of oil companies and railroad corporations. More especially was the Waters-Pierce Oil Company under fire. The suit brought by the State of Missouri some months before to dissolve the company was soon reflected in Texas. A suit was filed by Attorney General R. V. Davidson, who sought forfeiture of charter and heavy penalties for violation of Texas laws. A native of Asheville, N. C., Davidson many years before had been a solicitor in THE NEWS' office at Galveston, his first job in Texas. Throughout, this legal fight was predicated on the charge that the Waters-Pierce Oil Company had gained readmission to Texas six years before on the false affidavit that it was not a part of the Standard Oil combine. Bailey's endorsement of the reformed Waters-Pierce Oil Company in 1900 had been used quietly against him by his opponents.

Public sentiment in Texas had been worked up to a fitful pitch by September when Henry Clay Pierce, on the witness stand in St. Louis, announced that Senator Bailey had been his attorney in the handling of several large business transactions, although none of them in connection with the Waters-Pierce Oil Company. This furnished the spark to set the large, smouldering opposition to Bailey aflame. Soon mass meetings were being held throughout the State, petitioning the approaching Legislature to disregard the primary vote on the senatorship and to defeat Bailey. THE NEWS on September 29 took cognizance of this anti-Bailey movement. Without approving all that Bailey had done since the first fight on him in the Legislature of 1901, the paper insisted, nevertheless, that the instructions of the people themselves in the primary should not be overridden by mass meetings.

The opposition to Bailey increased, and soon M. M. Crane, Attorney General in the first prosecution of the oil company, took the stump in favor of his defeat. In October, a joint debate between Bailey and Crane was held in Houston, one of the more memorable political encounters in the State's history. The next morning readers of THE NEWS in all parts of the State were furnished with a live, running story of the debate, a thirty-thousand-word verbatim report, which made history in the journalism of the Southwest. The debate itself did not end until midnight. The Houston municipal auditorium was two miles from the telegraph office. No advance copies of speeches had been made. Yet so perfected was the task of direction of the stenographic reporting, of relaying to the wires and thence in telegraphing to the Dallas and Galveston offices that the last "take" of the twenty-four-column report had been handed to telegraphers sixty-seven minutes after the debate ended, and the whole story had cleared the wire thirty-seven minutes later, reaching both publication offices in time to catch the first State editions. The system of stenographic reporting by court stenographers working in relays was evolved by Tom Finty, Jr., whose work in this instance was typical of his reportorial genius. He was in general charge of THE NEWS' staff at Houston with E. B. Doran, city editor of THE DALLAS NEWS, second in command. Alonzo Wasson, Washington correspondent, wrote the general lead. K. K. Hooper, city editor of THE GALVESTON NEWS, J. A. Lord, C. I. Evans, Jr., J. A. Feagin, J. W. Neeld and A. J. Rosenthal were other members of this special staff.

In the meantime Attorney General Davidson presented his charges against the Waters-Pierce Oil Company of Texas in a district court at Austin. He now called on Bailey, in a public letter, to explain his part in the re-entry of this company into the State six years before. The issue, in the final analysis, narrowed down to a question of Bailey's veracity; whether he had been the paid attorney of the oil company in 1900, or, as he asserted, whether he had aided the company without accepting employment. So began the exchange of public letters between Davidson and Bailey, the latter indignantly denying the allegations of the former, which raised the Bailey issue to the plane of a first-class political dog fight.

THE NEWS on December 7 contributed its own part to this eleventh-hour sensation. Less than a month remained before the Legislature would meet to re-elect or defeat Bailey. After Bailey had responded to a series of questions asked by Davidson covering the Senator's connection with Pierce, THE NEWS reversed its editorial position of September and called for Bailey's defeat in the Legislature. Referring to the latest exchange of letters, THE NEWS added:

At this point THE NEWS felt inclined to say that there should be a legislative investigation; that the time for *ex parte* statements had passed. Nevertheless it has waited to hear Senator Bailey's rejoinder. This statement from Senator Bailey appears elsewhere. It speaks for itself.

In so far as Senator Bailey's eligibility is concerned, THE NEWS does not now deem an investigation necessary. . . . He may be judged by his own statement. It is this statement which convinces THE NEWS that no investigation is necessary, because it furnishes the reason why the Legislature should not re-elect Senator Bailey.

THE NEWS is extremely reluctant to reach such a conclusion in the case of a man of Senator Bailey's brilliant attainments, and it is not unmindful of the displeasure it will incur in certain quarters by making this declaration. Nevertheless it does not shrink its duty as a public journal.

It does not consider Senator Bailey's explanation satisfactory and is convinced that his influence and usefulness have been so sadly impaired by the charges against him and by his own responses and explanations that the Democracy of Texas should unite upon some other man for the high place he now holds.

Now the "hot, unfair, desperate contention" erupted in earnest. Throughout the remainder of December, Bailey answered his critics from the stump, while the opposition to him waxed in fervor. Editorially THE NEWS supported its declaration of war, daily ap-

pealing to Texans to persuade the Legislature to turn Bailey out
of office. The junior Senator replied by attacking the honor and
reputation of THE NEWS, digging back into the 1890's to revive
the charge of its sale of influence to the railroads. He also charged
that THE NEWS had supported "the craven hearted Davis against
the lion hearted Coke" during Texas' fight to emerge from the
horrors of Reconstruction. And, from a hundred platforms, he
denounced "this journalistic Hessian," this "hyena," usually
concluding with the thought that:

"Texas Democrats will not take their lessons from the polluted
columns of THE NEWS—the scarlet woman of Texas journalism."

THE NEWS, for its part, kept its temper better than did Bailey.
But, as the time approached for the convening of the Legislature
and it was evident that the fight would be continued in that body,
THE NEWS replied:

His is the desperation that comes of guilt, of exposure, of confession, or popular condemnation. While pretending to serve two mas-
ters he has served the wrong one by betraying the true one. As if by
providential design he has been brought face to face with retributive
justice.

The legislative investigation of Senator Bailey in January and
February of 1907 failed to halt his re-election. This, as THE
NEWS viewed it, however, was merely "the culmination of a costly
farce." Even to Bailey's friends the outcome in the Legislature
seemed a draw. Not until the spring of 1908 was the Bailey issue
submitted directly to the people to pass on, in view of all the charges
and counter-charges made since the primary of 1906. Bryan once
more was seeking the Democratic nomination for the presidency.
Texans generally, including, strangely enough, both Bailey and
THE NEWS, were now agreed that Bryan should be nominated.
The junior United States Senator announced that he would be a
candidate for delegate-at-large to the Democratic National Convention. His opponents were asked to set up an opposition slate of
delegates-at-large, thus providing a referendum by the people on
the Bailey issue. For he promised, if defeated for delegate-at-
large, to resign from the Senate.

The contest that ensued set a new high water mark of political bitterness in Texas, exceeding that of even the Hogg-Clark campaign of 1892. THE NEWS again marshaled the forces opposed to Bailey and editorially warned Texans that to approve "the things Senator Bailey has done, which he declares were not wrong, would disarm Mr. Bryan, defeat and possibly destroy the Democratic party itself." Thus, by the intensity of its aversion for Bailey, was THE NEWS hurled completely into the camp of William Jennings Bryan and into the circle of the more rabid trust busters and trust baiters in Texas. But the State-wide vote on the delegates to the Denver national convention proved to be a thorough victory for Bailey; the Senator and his friends construed it as a complete vindication.

The panic of 1907 had, in part, raised the hope of Democrats for victory in the national campaign of 1908. This currency shortage had inconvenienced Texans, but it had not been felt as severely in the agricultural Southwest as in most other parts of the nation. The nation-wide recovery also was fairly rapid. Although all urban banks in Texas were thrown on an emergency basis, with restricted withdrawals of currency deposits, failures were relatively few.

THE NEWS believed that the only way to prevent the recurrence of money panics lay in the adoption of some form of guarantee of individual deposits. C. Lombardi, the new vice president of the company, was responsible for the intensive campaign which the paper inaugurated. From his long experience in the mercantile world he felt that a mutualization of risks and losses constituted one of the bulwarks of economic life. He contended that the Federal government already required insurance of its own deposits with commercial banks, and he considered it only a logical extension of a soundly proven principle to give the same protection to the individual's deposit. "Whatever may be proposed or done in the way of banking and currency reform," the paper declared as early as November 14, 1907, "the result will never amount to more than a palliative unless it is coupled with some method of insurance whereby the depositor feels as secure against loss as the householder does when he is insured in a reliable fire insurance company."

The paper continued to argue along this line during the next eighteen months through more than fifty editorials and special articles. Both the Democratic and Republican platforms of 1908 paid lip service to the idea of national bank insurance. But the only tangible result was the adoption of the plan for State bank deposits by some five commonwealths, among which was the State of Texas. The Texas system lasted from 1909 until 1927, when it finally lapsed, due to its defect of being applied only to State banks. It was not until 1933, after the worst financial crisis in the history of the country, that deposit insurance was revived and made applicable on a nation-wide scale. The work of C. Lombardi and THE NEWS in pioneering the agitation for this reform was acknowledged in the discussions which led to the present banking law.

THE NEWS accepted Bryan's defeat in 1908, as it had that of Alton B. Parker four years before, with a fair degree of resignation. It even proposed in November that the President-elect, William Howard Taft, "whom we all recognize as a man of charming personality and exceptional experience and ability," be invited to visit Texas. It was not until a year later, however, that Taft, en route from his meeting with President Diaz at the international bridge between El Paso and Juarez, was able to accept the hospitality of Dallas and other Texas centers.

Preparation for the reception of the President went ahead in Dallas, with the greatest responsibility resting on the committee in charge of the banquet. This committee was headed by G. B. Dealey, assisted by J. L. Brown, Albert Linz, C. H. Platter, and R. H. Stewart. For they were instructed in advance that the food must be plain; the President, it was explained, was "trying to keep his weight down and hence prefers such plain food as ham and eggs, corn beef and cabbage." Although the committee did not follow instructions literally, it set a local precedent for an official banquet, in that no alcoholic beverages were served. It was a lavish affair, tickets costing $25 each; the elaborate souvenir menu

Removal of railroad tracks on Pacific Avenue, bringing about the present boulevard, followed John Knott's depiction of the proposal to elevate the same tracks.

Underpass of Commerce, Main and Elm Streets, before and after construction, showing new traffic outlet between the business district and the reclaimed area of the Trinity River valley.

was typical, handsomely engraved and containing six miniature silk flags, one for each of the sovereignties in the history of Texas. These souvenirs cost $5 each. Taft's reception in Dallas rivaled that given Roosevelt four years earlier and was greatly pleasing to the visitor himself. To an audience at the State Fair he admitted that one of the chief duties of a President was to visit such expositions and thus help swell attendance. More seriously, he declared the Texas exposition to be the finest of its kind yet visited by him. The banquet wound up in a pleasant and jovial mood. Next to the temperament of the guest, this success was due in large part to the ease, the grace and the humor of the chief spokesman for Texas, the venerable Bishop A. C. Garrett of Dallas. President Taft was so pleased with the banquet and reception that he summoned Otto Praeger, Washington correspondent of THE NEWS, who was accompanying the President on his trip, and that night before leaving Dallas gave him a special interview expressing his appreciation of the courtesies shown him. Major Archie Butt, presidential aide, and others confirmed the fact that "the Chief" was greatly pleased.

Politics failed to furnish all the major news stories that crowded across the pages of THE NEWS toward the end of the first decade of the century. In 1908 aviation once more caught the imagination of the country as the Wright Brothers carried out their successful demonstration before United States Army officials at Fort Meyer. But even more earth-shaking—or so it seemed at the time—was the discovery of the North Pole, first reported in the fall of 1909. Dr. Frederick Cook, backed by a Brooklyn capitalist, was first to claim this victory over geography. He was being feted in the Danish capital when, on September 6, a wireless message came out of the fog of Labrador stating that Commodore Robert Peary of the United States Navy had nailed the Stars and Stripes to the North Pole.

Then began the noted conflict of claims as to which of these dis-

coverers was to be credited with the achievement; the battle of
words raged for weeks across the front pages of American newspapers. Each contestant told his own, exclusive, copyrighted story
—Peary, through the syndicate headed by the New York *Times*
and the London *Times;* Cook, through the New York *Herald* syndicate. THE NEWS, with generous impartiality, bought both sides
of the argument and ran them with equal prominence on the first
page. For a time, in this period of the birth of newspaper ballyhoo
and exploitation of exploration, the contest seemed to be between
rival journals and syndicates. Not until a number of years later
would the argument be settled.

The dreaded word revolution was heard in Texas as 1910 prepared to give way before 1911. In a strictly political and domestic
sense the revolution was not alarming. Taft's first two years in office
had been far from happy ones, due principally to the resentment of
the nation over the excesses of the Payne-Aldrich tariff bill. On
March 30 THE NEWS printed a first-page story with photograph
about the president of Princeton University, in which Dr. Woodrow Wilson assured the Democracy of the nation that "the day
when the Democratic party must take charge of this country's affairs is almost at hand." From that moment this university official
roused the deepest allegiance of THE NEWS, an allegiance which
two years later would touch the course of history itself in the part
Texans played in the nomination of Wilson for President.

Just before the general elections of 1910, in which the lower
house of Congress would be captured by the Democrats and Democratic governors would be elected in five pivotal States of the East
and Middle West, THE NEWS said in October:

> The election of Dr. Woodrow Wilson to be Governor of New Jersey
> would be, to our way of thinking, about the most inspiring event that
> it is possible for the ballot boxes to give forth next Tuesday. It would,
> for one thing, be enlarging the list of available men, increase the like-
> lihood that the Democratic party will have as its nominee for the
> presidency two years hence a man who can appeal to the best senti-
> ment and intelligence of the country. . . .
> Of all the men in public life, Dr. Wilson is perhaps the profoundest,
> ripest scholar, and one who unlike Senator Lodge, is not burdened by
> a puerile love of pedantries. . . . Dr. Wilson is a thinker; his mind is

no mere sepulchre. He is not one who makes a procrustean bed of precedent to which all the problems of today must be fitted.

Revolution in a more fundamental sense, though, was brewing even closer to Texas. In 1910 the centennial of Mexican independence was celebrated in the ancient Aztec capital, although some misguided patriots probably thought it was the celebration of one hundred years of rule by President Diaz. For thirty-three years, however, the Iron Man had been the master of Mexico, with an iron peace and surface indications of prosperity prevailing for that time. But Porfirio Diaz was now an old man whom the years had enfeebled, and, in the progressive, modern State of Nuevo Leon, Francisco I. Madero, scion of a wealthy family of Northern Mexico, was seeking the presidency. Arrested and jailed by Diaz forces for his effrontery, Madero in October escaped into Texas. He established headquarters in San Antonio and organized the revolution which finally unseated Diaz.

THE NEWS, in November, 1910, began publication of a series of articles on Mexico by Colonel Sterett; these were based on an extended tour of the Republic. Colonel Sterett raised the question in his introduction as to what would happen in Mexico, once the firm hand of Diaz was stilled or withdrawn. At that very moment the Diaz regime was hard put to down outbreaks in Puebla and other central Mexican points; Troop L of the Third United States Cavalry was rushed from San Antonio to the border, and THE NEWS was constrained to admit that "all one can feel sure of is that there is rather a large volume of discontent in Mexico."

Not until May 10, 1911, however, with the capture of Juarez by Madero revolutionists, did prospects of insurgent success become apparent. John Sneed, staff correspondent of THE NEWS at El Paso, began sending his colorful, personal impressions and interviews with the revolutionary chieftains. News on the Mexican situation poured in by wire from every direction. On March 8, Washington announced that 20,000 United States troops were being moved to the Mexican border. The clamor for American intervention became louder but not in the columns of THE NEWS; the paper, therefore, was happy to report late in April that Congressman John N. Garner of Uvalde, a die-hard opponent of intervention, had been added to the House Foreign Affairs Committee. Then, late in May, Diaz capitulated, fled to Europe and on June 8 Francisco I. Madero entered Mexico City in triumph.

"The question of most concern now," said THE NEWS, "must be that of Madero's ability to control the forces he has awakened. . . . It remains to be seen whether he is cast to be the hero or the victim of his triumph. . . ."

☆

All the while the progressive revolt in American politics forged ahead. Early in 1911 THE NEWS' antagonist, Senator Bailey, resigned from the Senate in protest against the political and economic heresies which he felt to be gaining the ascendancy in American life. At the same time, he assured Texans that Governor Woodrow Wilson of New Jersey was much too revolutionary to be the standard bearer of the party in 1912. To which THE NEWS replied with a eulogy of Wilson and added that "the Democratic party is not so super-abundantly supplied with presidential material that it can afford to have a man of Dr. Wilson's type damned with a dictum. . . ."

By August of 1911 THE NEWS was "gratified to learn" that the first of the Wilson-for-President clubs had been organized in Texas. By every legitimate means the paper furthered the political fortunes of this man, whose "general political attitude [THE NEWS believed] is more in accord with the inclination of Texas Democrats than any other possible nominee."

The height of Wilson enthusiasm was reached in Texas in the fall when the candidate made a pilgrimage to the State Fair at Dallas; he was acclaimed by thousands on Woodrow Wilson day, October 16. This event, THE NEWS reported, "inspired one of the most extraordinary gatherings of political leaders ever seen in Texas." In addition to insuring the solid support of Texans at the national convention, Wilson's pilgrimage had the further benefit, in the eyes of THE NEWS, of solidifying the anti-Bailey elements in Texas. Although the junior Senator was voluntarily resigning from public life, THE NEWS desired to see him permanently eliminated from influence in Texas.

As the presidential year swung into line, Governor Judson Harmon of Ohio and Speaker Champ Clark invaded the State in an effort to garner convention support. Courteous to these visitors, THE NEWS insisted, however, that Wilson would make the best candidate, and, on the eve of the Texas presidential primary in May, the paper urged Texas Democrats to declare for Wilson. In that event, the journal was convinced, "the nomination of that gentleman could be regarded as a very likely probability. Certainly the result of tomorrow's contest in Texas will be fateful on the candidacy of Woodrow Wilson." By May 9, the landslide for Wilson at the ballot boxes of Texas had been determined, and John Knott's cartoon, "After the Storm," was gracing the first page of THE NEWS.

The story of the Baltimore convention of the Democratic party in 1912, and the part played by Texas' "Immortal Forty" delegates in that protracted struggle, may be found in the day by day accounts in THE NEWS. With D. Prescott Toomey, managing editor, and Otto Praeger, Washington correspondent, on the scene, Texas readers were furnished a running inside story to supplement the general wire reports. Among syndicate features used were special articles by William Jennings Bryan. From the opening of the convention on June 25 until the nomination of Wilson seven days later on the forty-sixth ballot—an epochal event which THE NEWS announced with an extra at 3:00 p.m. on July 2—the excitement in Texas was great. The next morning, for the first time in more than a quarter of a century, THE NEWS appeared with a front-page "encyclical":

In the opinion of THE NEWS the worst criticism to be made of the Baltimore convention is that it did not do on Thursday, June 27, what it did on Tuesday, July 2. . . .

Of all the gentlemen who sought the party's nomination, he was the only one who had silhouetted his personality on the imagination of the millions of people who feel that the great need is to restore the conditions of equal opportunity. . . . A Democrat not in the merely conventional meaning of that word, but in its literal and spiritual meaning. . . .

THE NEWS thinks it would be no exaggeration to say that his nomination is an epochal event. Not since Thomas Jefferson died has the Democratic party been able to boast a follower of such virile intellect. . . . The Democratic party has redeemed itself at the very moment when thoughtful men had reason to fear that it was about to pass out of existence. . . .

Five months later, THE NEWS was able to jubilate in the election of President Wilson—"the hour and the man have met." Not since the days of Reconstruction had THE NEWS been in closer rapport with the overwhelming majority of the Texas Democracy. In voicing the following opinion on the 4th of March, 1913, THE NEWS spoke the faith of Texas and Texans:

"Few Presidents have gone into the White House so heavy burdened of responsibility. It is time of flux. A revision of formulas that have served their occasion has been decreed. The hopes and aspirations born of a decade of agitation and strife are to be made articulate in acts. We stand on the threshold of an age of social amelioration, and to many of us Woodrow Wilson typifies that age in all its intensity. . . . He enters the White House today armed with the faith of a nation, and thus armed, we believe he will be invincible."

CHAPTER XVIII

TOWARD A CITY PLAN

1907–1912

AFTER 1906, THE NEWS redoubled its energies toward the goal of a model city. In doing so, its influence for civic betterment spread gradually from the two publishing centers of Dallas and Galveston to affect many parts of Texas and adjacent territory. This work was practically all done at Dallas. There, under the unremitting drive of G. B. Dealey, the more marked results were achieved.

The voters, it has been seen, acted on the advice of THE NEWS in the spring of 1906 by deciding to adopt the Galveston Commission Plan of city government. But the decision to change was only half the victory. A greater task lay ahead, the drafting of a charter in the spirit of the new plan and the selection of city officials who would carry it out conscientiously. THE NEWS continued its educational campaign throughout that year and into the next. A representative banker, J. A. Pondrom, headed the committee to draft the charter. He was aided by other such non-political figures as T. L. Camp, Gilbert H. Irish and George Clifton Edwards.

Economic conditions in Dallas were favorable during most of 1907. Already the contract for the construction of the second interurban line, that between Dallas, Sherman and Denison, had been let. In addition to the Praetorian Office Building, an eight-story steel-and-brick fireproof hotel, the Southland, was soon under construction. On March 21 the cornerstone of another landmark, the Scottish Rite Cathedral, was leveled in ceremonies conducted by Sam P. Cochran, president; Louis Blaylock, vice president; M. H. Thomas, Eli Sanger, John M. Spellman, A. V. Lane, G. B. Dealey, members of the board of directors, and J. L. Stephens, secretary, of the Scottish Rite Cathedral Association.

☆

On March 31, 1907, the Flippen-Prather Realty Company announced the opening of the first 100 acres of Highland Park, a restricted residential suburban development which was to have wide influence not only in the history of Dallas but in the city planning movement throughout the Southwest as well. It was the outgrowth, largely, of the foresight and enterprise of John S. Armstrong, a pioneer industrialist and banker of Dallas.

Much of the land later embraced in the Town of Highland Park was granted to settlers by the Republic of Texas, either for homestead purposes or in recognition of military services in the Battle of San Jacinto. In 1888 Colonel Henry Exall, one of the more farsighted civic leaders of a generation ago, became attracted to the Highland Park area as a residential development. In the year following, while in Philadelphia, he persuaded a group of capitalists, including certain members of the Biddle family, to form a syndicate with him under the name of the Philadelphia Place Land Association. From the Cole, Caruth and other estates, they acquired 1,326 acres five miles north of the courthouse. Colonel Exall laid some gravel streets and built on Turtle Creek what was then, and for many years afterward, known as Exall's Lake—a favorite picnic ground of an earlier generation, now part of the emergency water supply of the Town of Highland Park. But the Panic of 1893 halted this development.

In 1906, John S. Armstrong, who had disposed of his interest in the Armstrong Packing Company and retired from other business and banking connections, became interested in developing this suburban area. At his suggestion Colonel Exall went to Philadelphia and effected a sale of the land by the original syndicate to Armstrong. Back in the 1880's and 1890's Armstrong had been a business associate of T. L. Marsalis, the "Father of Oak Cliff" and the first civic leader of that era. That earlier example of trans-river development undoubtedly influenced Armstrong to dream of a planned city north of Dallas. Accompanied by one of his sons-in-law, Hugh E. Prather, he went to Los Angeles and saw the laying out of what is now Beverley Hills. He next engaged Wilbur

David Cook, designer of the California suburb, who was soon at work on the Dallas project. The first section of Highland Park, a 100-acre tract lying just west of the Katy railroad between Armstrong Avenue, St. John's Drive and Gillon, was opened in the spring of 1907. Another son-in-law of Armstrong, Edgar L. Flippen, was associated in the realty development company. Sites in this area were advertised in THE NEWS as just beyond the city's smoke and dust, where summer temperatures were "ten degrees cooler." Rapid progress was made in putting in paving and utilities and this first installment was sold out quickly. At the time of Armstrong's death in 1908, a substantial start toward the fulfillment of his dream for a model, suburban city had been made.

Successively other sections of Highland Park have been opened through the years, until it now covers an area many times the size of the original; it is distinguished for its natural and created beauty in both landscaping and homes. Since 1913 it has been an incorporated city. Incorporation was effected December 22 of that year with W. A. Fraser as the first mayor. Other officers were Frank McNeny, marshal; W. O. Connor, L. M. Lennington, Frank O. Witchell, P. G. Claiborne and Frank M. Gray, aldermen.

The cornerstone of the Highland Park Town Hall was laid on Thanksgiving Day, 1923. This structure of Spanish colonial design is built of brick, interlocking tile and stucco. It was designed by Lang & Witchell and constructed at a cost of $65,000. It was formally opened on the evening of October 30, 1924, in public ceremonies presided over by G. B. Dealey. Mayor Pro Tem A. T. Powell, officiating in the absence of Mayor Frank M. Smith, welcomed citizens to the new community house. Edgar L. Flippen spoke on the history of the suburb. Other brief talks were made by F. O. Witchell, P. G. Claiborne, Frank M. Gray, W. I. Ford, W. T. Harris and John W. Kizer, former aldermen.

In order to "awaken our people to a fuller appreciation of art, music and all things cultural that make for a finer citizenship," Mayor Frank M. Smith, prior to the opening had appointed a committee to plan programs and otherwise insure the greatest possible community benefit from the new building. G. B. Dealey accepted the chairmanship of this committee, on which were also

Mrs. A. H. Bailey, Mrs. Warren Jones, E. B. Doran, R. H. Morton, D. L. Whittle, F. E. McLarty and Don L. Sterling. As a result of arrangements by this committee, a series of popular lectures was presented in the winter of 1924–25 and twilight musical concerts were held on two Sunday evenings a month. Early in 1925, the Highland Park Society of Fine Arts offered a course of morning art lectures at the Town Hall. The use of a part of the town hall as an art museum was begun at that time.

The Highland Park Independent School district, which includes both Highland Park and adjacent University Park, was formed in 1914. It has more than $1,000,000 invested in buildings, grounds and equipment.

The opening of Highland Park was only one of the notable events of 1907. In Dallas proper THE NEWS and other civic leaders pushed forward to insure a proper inauguration of the commission form of city government adopted by the voters in 1906. Soon the new city charter was ready for adoption. It was necessary to set up machinery which would make certain that a non-political group of city commissioners would be chosen. The Citizens Association came into being on March 4, 1907. With Henry D. Lindsley as its president, the association of about 100 members numbered among its backers such men as Royal A. Ferris, J. B. Wilson, Alex Sanger, E. M. Kahn, C. Weichsel, Arthur A. Everts, George S. Leachman, George W. Loudermilk and Sam Dysterbach. It was nothing short, THE NEWS believed, of the birth of the Greater Dallas movement:

The interest and enthusiasm manifested by those who attended the first meeting of the Citizens Association should be highly gratifying to all those who approve the purpose of making Dallas a model city.

Nobody who appreciated the material growth of Dallas and considers the present provisions for water, for an adequate sanitary sewer system, for clean streets and the safety of the city, can have left in his mind any doubt whatever that there must be an abrupt and absolute departure from the old policy of temporizing, if the Greater Dallas movement is really to mean more than a costly joke.

We are going to have a new charter, a better system to begin with, and the wonderful growth of the city adds the necessary element of power that has never before been enjoyed. Progressive citizens of Dallas are determined to concentrate the means and forces . . . to unite the people at this most opportune time upon all the hopeful mottoes and movements of the past and upon the flattering opportunities of the present.

Under the managership of Will T. Henry, the Citizens Association offered a slate of candidates which included S. J. Hay for mayor. The four candidates for commissioners were D. F. Sullivan, Charles B. Gillespie, William Doran and Harry L. Seay. The older political group made some resistance. The incumbent mayor, Curtis P. Smith, sought re-election under the new form, but, at the election on May 21, the Citizens Association came into control by a large majority. Two days later THE NEWS said:

Dallas has joined heartily in the movement looking toward better municipal government. The success of the Citizens Association ticket indicates very clearly a popular determination to let the office seek the man a while. . . . The controlling purpose of the people is to intrust the public service to business men upon their pledges to conduct it according to business principles.

On October 1, 1907, THE NEWS at Dallas was twenty-two years old. Symbolic of the fact that it had reached its "majority" in completing its first twenty-one years, all advertisements from that date were excluded from the first page of THE NEWS. This was done at the order of the new vice president and general manager, G. B. Dealey. Whether within THE NEWS itself, or in the life of community and State, reform was uppermost in this executive's mind. Closest to his heart, though, was the proposed reformation of living conditions in Dallas. The change in the form of the city government became the signal for a general frontal attack by THE NEWS on civic sloth and indifference.

☆

It was given to a public calamity, however, to furnish the immediate spur toward civic reform. On April 18, 1908, the mild, slug-

35,000 DAYS IN TEXAS

gish Trinity River, lying as a perpetual threat between Dallas and
Oak Cliff, rose from its bank to a flood crest of 35.6 feet at the
Commerce Street Bridge, flooding the lowlands and destroying
cattle and houses to the west. This was inconvenient and costly,
although not alarming. But, slightly more than a month later,
Oklahoma and northern Texas were swept by torrential rain
storms, and, on Monday, May 25, the river at Dallas went on a
record-breaking rampage. The new flood spread death and destruction over an enormous area, drowning five persons and causing
4,000 others to flee from their homes. The flood damage totalled
$2,500,000 in the city proper, chiefly in the overflow of the lower
end of the business district. With the central power plant in North
Dallas submerged, electric lights and street-car service were paralyzed. Except by boats, communication was cut between Oak Cliff
and the main part of Dallas. Telephone and telegraph lines broke
down, all roads and bridges were covered with water. The Texas
& Pacific Railway's causeway crumbled and floated away in the
flood.

Within five days, civic leaders in Oak Cliff were calling a mass
meeting to plan the construction of an all-weather, flood-proof
viaduct to link the two halves of the city. Thus was initiated the
movement that would lead to the completion four years later of
the Houston Street Viaduct, built at a cost of $750,000 by county-
wide bond issue, and for many years the longest concrete structure
of its kind in the world. At the same time the newly formed West
Dallas Improvement League petitioned Governor T. M. Campbell for State aid in flood control through levee construction. Dallas, Fort Worth and other communities suffering from the disastrous floods were now convinced that the Legislature should at
least authorize the creation of levee and drainage districts. The
Thirty-first Legislature in 1909 passed the Levee and Drainage
Act. Fort Worth set about at once to authorize and sell $250,000
of levee district bonds for the harnessing of the Trinity River
through that city.

Meanwhile, Dallas business interests perfected other machinery
for co-operative effort. In 1909 there was formed a modern
Chamber of Commerce. This resulted from the merger of the

old Commercial Club, the Trade League, the 150,000 Club and the Dallas Freight Bureau. L. O. Daniel, long a leader in the wholesale market, was named the first president of this united organization. J. R. Babcock became its first secretary.

Now that the city government and civic interests were more efficiently organized, THE NEWS insisted that all civic improvements should be made in accordance with a long-range, carefully designed plan. As early as 1908 the paper urged Dallas to emulate the example of other cities, notably Los Angeles, which had engaged Charles M. Robinson to draw up a plan for that city. In February of 1909, G. B. Dealey read a paper before the Critic Club, an organization numbering some of the leaders of Dallas, in which he advocated a city plan as an immediate objective. In May of that same year the new Coliseum at Fair Park was opened for use. This was the first major improvement on the fair grounds since the reorganization of 1904. THE NEWS displayed prominently the report by Francis H. McLean, special agent for the Russell Sage Foundation, who had come to Dallas to suggest steps for bettering civic and social conditions. An article by Charles M. Robinson on "Planning a City's Growth with Some Thought for Appearance" attracted much attention from NEWS readers.

The development of Fair Park had ever been close to the heart of THE NEWS. The paper contributed directly to it in 1909 by presenting a replica of the Alamo. Built exactly to scale but only half as large as the original at San Antonio, this replica was to be visited during the next quarter of a century by millions who might otherwise never have visualized the shrine of Texas liberty.

The city plan for Dallas became a reality in 1910. Perhaps the best summary of this achievement has been given by the man most responsible for it. In a paper read before the American Civic Association in Washington in 1910, G. B. Dealey reported:

"Civic improvement, and all which that term implies, had for years been one of my hobbies. In May, 1899, I was instrumental with the help of THE DALLAS NEWS in organizing the Cleaner

Dallas League. Later on it occurred to me that another organization on broader lines could accomplish more, and again through the instrumentality of publicity in THE NEWS, it was my privilege to assist in organizing on December 2, 1902, the Civic Improvement League of Dallas. . . .

"Further sporadic efforts were made from time to time for civic betterment. As far back as February 28, 1908, I corresponded with the American Civic Association and procured through J. Horace McFarland, president of that association, twenty-five copies of 'The Awakening of Harrisburg,' which I distributed among some of the most progressive citizens of the city, urging them carefully to read it. . . .

"In its issue of May 16, 1909, THE NEWS commended the city plan idea and suggested that the larger cities of Texas ought to have such a plan idea and use it as a chart for development. Then beginning in its issue of January 1, 1910, THE NEWS asked quite a number of leading citizens to express themselves through its columns on what civic improvement works Dallas should take up. . . . This campaign brought splendid results. Civic improvement became the talk of the day.

"At this juncture a council of the editorial staff was called and the suggestion that the psychological moment had arrived to strike for a city plan was unanimously approved. The president and the secretary of the Chamber of Commerce were then called into consultation, and it was proposed that the Chamber of Commerce should take up the project and work it to a finish. These gentlemen readily and enthusiastically acquiesced.

"On January 28, 1910, at a meeting of the directors of the Chamber of Commerce, the movement was presented and met with unqualified support. A committee consisting of Rhodes S. Baker, Alex Sanger, J. B. Wilson, Henry D. Lindsley and G. B. Dealey was appointed to consider ways and means of carrying out the project. On February 3 this committee further suggested that the Chamber of Commerce appoint a City Plan and Improvement Committee as comprehensive in it personnel as the plan for the city of Dallas will be in its scope.

"Arrangements were now made to bring down President Mc-

Farland of the American Civic Association. That gentleman arrived on February 25 and the same night lectured at the First Baptist Church. Prior to the lecture Mr. McFarland was entertained with a luncheon at which there were present some fifty leading citizens, including the Mayor, City Commissioners and the Park Board. After the lecture the mass meeting endorsed the action of the Chamber of Commerce in appointing a city-wide organization to be known as the Dallas City Plan and Improvement League. President of the Dallas Chamber of Commerce at the time was L. O. Daniel, with J. R. Babcock as secretary. Mr. McFarland was presented by Rhodes S. Baker.

"Soon afterward this league, of which Henry D. Lindsley was chairman, invited George E. Kessler to visit Dallas. It was also decided that the league should appear before the City Commission and the Park Board to urge adoption of a city plan for Dallas, urging the employment of competent city designers and municipal engineers to prepare for a proper plan.

"In the meantime city officials were being told of the advantages of the movement. At one time the mayor and city commissioners were entertained at the home of G. B. Dealey where C. Lombardi, Tom Finty, Jr., and the host discussed throughout an entire evening just what the forward step would mean to the city. Then on March 9 the matter was presented officially to them. The City Commission expressed sympathy with the movement and decided to accept the recommendation.

"During this period frequent meetings were held and many articles and illustrations on city planning were reproduced in THE NEWS. Tom Finty, Jr., wrote a series of articles on 'The Replanning of a City.' Special magazine articles from the city plan number of the *Survey* and from the *American City* were reproduced.

"For months in every day's issue of THE NEWS a picture two to five columns wide was run under the head of 'Examples of Civic Attractiveness.' Altogether some 400 of these illustrations were printed that year and in four months' time some 900 columns of civic improvement matter were printed in THE NEWS.

"Then began the publicity regarding Mr. Kessler, telling of the wonderful work he had accomplished in various cities. He reached

Dallas May 23, 1910, and made a tour of the city. Afterward he met at the city hall with the municipal commission and the Park Board. The latter consisted of the mayor as ex-official chairman; Murrell L. Buckner, E. L. Pike, M. N. Baker and Emil Fretz. After an hour's joint conference it was unanimously decided to engage Mr. Kessler to prepare a city plan, the cost to be divided between the City Commission and the Park Board."

☆

After months of study, Kessler in October of 1910 offered the basic lines of his plan for the city of Dallas. The major improvements provided for in this Kessler Plan were: flood control and land reclamation of the Trinity River valley between Dallas and Oak Cliff; a union passenger terminal, removal of Texas & Pacific Railway tracks from Pacific Avenue between Lamar and Central, elimination of other dangerous railroad grade crossings and construction of a belt line surrounding the city; a civic center; numerous street openings and widenings; parks, parkways and boulevards and the establishment of additional playgrounds.

Significantly enough, first place in the Kessler Plan was given to the flood control project in the Trinity River valley. Although Kessler throughout his lifetime always considered this the key to a Greater Dallas, the improvement was to be delayed almost twenty years and accomplished finally in the face of greater misunderstandings and antagonisms than any of his other proposals. THE NEWS from 1910 threw its full weight and influence behind the levee reclamation. But with the exception of the union passenger terminal and a few street widening projects, the Kessler Plan remained largely unrealized until after 1920. The delay was due chiefly to the outbreak of the World War and to America's part in that conflict.

There was no slackening of interest on the part of THE NEWS in rural welfare. In 1910 De Witt McMurray, editor of THE SEMI-WEEKLY FARM NEWS, began another campaign for crop diversification. The paper continued its advocacy of cooperative marketing of fruits and vegetables. G. B. Dealey made talks over

Headline display and front page make-up of THE NEWS since 1889

Members of The News organization with more than twenty-one years of continuous service on Oct. 1, 1935, fiftieth anniversary of the establishment of The Dallas Morning News.

Front Row (*left to right*)—Robert Cherry, C. M. Seay, Mark L. Goodwin, W. E. Graul, W. M. Davis, Chas. Blake, Pope Armstrong, Jennie Hogg, K. A. Ward, W. L. Maynard, Sr., W. M. Thornton, H. W. Leggett, A. C. Weaver, Edwin B. Doran.

Second Row—Shivers Boykin, H. C. Scott, Sam Rollins, W. W. Dathe, J. Homer Reilly, F. B. Richmond, Ralph R. Gillham, Cecil O. Hill, Harvey Stephenson, W. W. Truax, E. W. Hatton, Ben Whitehead, H. R. Greer, G. B. Dealey.

Third Row—Geo. H. Rheinlander, W. A. Page, H. C. Withers, R. J. Murray, J. F. Lubben, Ray McMurray, Frank Brown, J. E. Taggart, Ed Hall, Sam Moxley.

Fourth Row—Will T. Richardson, Harold Ward, W. J. McClellan, W. H. Benners, LeRoy Thomasson, Herman Butters, L. E. Hamilton, Sterling M. Hart, Arthur M. Allen, John F. Knott, Sherman Reed.

Fifth Row—DeWitt McMurray, Alonzo Wasson, J. J. Taylor, Miles Norcom, A. P. Vaughan, H. D. Guy, J. E. King, Walter K. Thomas, Tom Porter, Leven T. Deputy, C. H. Taggart.

the State on problems of rural sociology and of the value of attractiveness on both towns and country. George Waverley Briggs, formerly of the San Antonio *Express* and the Austin *Statesman,* joined THE NEWS in 1911 as staff correspondent; his first assignment was to write a series of articles on housing in Texas which was printed in both THE GALVESTON NEWS and THE DALLAS NEWS. Briggs capped a brilliant career in journalism by serving as editor of THE GALVESTON NEWS between 1913 and 1918, at which time he became assistant manager for the Southwestern division of the American Red Cross. He served as State Commissioner of Insurance and Banking in 1919–20 and has since been a vice president and trust officer of the First National Bank in Dallas.

Reform in the State government was urged in a series of special articles published in THE NEWS in 1911 and written by Dr. James Quayle Dealey, then head of the political and social science department of Brown University, later to become editor-in-chief of THE NEWS. Tom Finty, Jr., then as later one of the most valuable and influential members of the staff, analyzed the revised State government of Wisconsin in another series printed about the same time.

In Dallas THE NEWS gave wholehearted support to the formation and work of the Dallas Playground Association which Elmer Scott, then head of one of the larger mercantile houses in the Southwest was persuaded to head. In announcing publication in 1911 of a series of articles on how to improve the smaller city, G. B. Dealey in a letter to Texas newspaper editors summarized the activity of THE NEWS :

This is a continuation of a work started by THE NEWS on January 1, 1910, in behalf of civic improvement in Texas, and since that time this paper has run over 1,200 columns in behalf of this interest. No newspaper in the United States, or in the world for that matter, has devoted as much space continually to that subject as has THE NEWS. We are going to keep it up because we know that the results will come and that they will be worth while.

CHAPTER XIX

THE WORLD WAR

1913–1918

TEXAS AND THE NEWS were to find the second decade of the century far different from the first. The outbreak of the World War profoundly affected local plans, State policies, national concerns. But as the Wilson Administration took office in 1913 there were few reasons to anticipate a world upheaval. Domestic reforms instead, ranging from tariff reduction to the creation of a Federal reserve banking system, were uppermost in the mind of the average citizen.

The year was marked within THE NEWS by the death of Mrs. A. H. Belo, Sr., president of the company since 1906. She died on February 3, 1913, at the home of her daughter, Mrs. Jeannette Belo Peabody in Cambridge, Mass. Never active in the management itself, she had won, however, the admiration and respect of the organization on the score of her personal qualities. An editorial in THE NEWS expressed the warmth of this feeling:

The best part of the life record of a noble woman is by many considered too nearly sacred for publication, and this view is at least in harmony with the character, desire and quiet service to humanity of the good woman who has gone to her reward. . . .

It is enough to say that the news of her death has brought sadness to the heart of every person connected with THE NEWS, to many others who knew well of her sympathy and kindness, and to a host of life-long friends in Texas and other States.

☆

The passing of Colonel Belo's widow failed to alter the management in any material aspect. G. B. Dealey continued as vice president and general manager. C. Lombardi, the brother-in-law of Colonel Belo, was asked to take the presidency and Mrs. Peabody, a daughter of Colonel Belo, a member of the directorate, became a vice president as well. There had been few changes since 1906 in the office personnel of THE NEWS. Since that year Luther Clark, the editor-in-chief, and Arthur Geen, chief accountant, had served on the board of directors. The latter died of a heart ailment while at his desk in 1910. W. H. Benners, a member of the Dallas organization since 1893, had been named business manager. In 1912 Walter A. Dealey, elder son of G. B. Dealey, began his career with the organization.

THE NEWS was perfecting plans for expansion of plant and facilities at the time of Mrs. Belo's death. Two years before it had been necessary to add a sextuple press with color attachment, capable of printing 72,000 copies an hour of a twelve-page paper. This high-speed, three-deck press, installed in the fall of 1911, was the largest ever brought to Texas before that time. The adjoining property on the northeast corner of Commerce and Austin Streets was next purchased, and in 1913 the four-story and basement, fireproof annex was completed on that site. Here the mechanical departments, from the linotypes and stereotypes on the fourth floor to the presses and power plant below were housed. With the first unit completed some twelve years before, THE NEWS at Dallas now possessed one of the finest and most nearly complete newspaper plants in the country.

Then on April 1, 1914, the first issue of THE DALLAS (Evening) JOURNAL came from the presses of THE NEWS. With Tom Finty, Jr., as editor, E. B. Doran as managing editor and Harry Withers as city editor, this latest offspring rapidly achieved success in its particular field. The corporation was commended widely for this step. The afternoon paper was started for a number of reasons. The main cause, however, was the practice introduced by other daily newspapers in Texas of issuing "bulldog editions" of their papers; that is, pre-dated copies which were printed the day before and mailed out over the State for next-day delivery. These editions carried the closing market quotations of the previous day, particularly of the cotton exchanges. THE NEWS preferred not to issue similar editions of its own and hence decided to use an after-

noon edition under the name of THE DALLAS JOURNAL to meet
this competition. Likewise, it was felt, the growth of Dallas called
for a live, aggressive and essentially local paper that would serve
the city and immediate environs in the afternoon field.

The birth of THE JOURNAL came in the midst of an area of rapid
physical growth in Dallas. The city had reached a population of
100,000. A series of national conventions from the Elks in 1908
to the Associated Advertising Clubs of America in 1912 and the
Shriners in 1913 had served to focus attention on the North Texas
city. The Busch interests of St. Louis announced in 1912 that they
would build a skyscraper hotel in Dallas. This was contingent
upon the citizens raising a $300,000 bonus, which was forthcom-
ing. This assured the first unit of the Hotel Adolphus.

☆

In the same year the railroads entering Dallas began work on a
$6,000,000 union passenger terminal on South Houston Street
in accordance with Kessler's plan. The decision and final completion of the building two years later culminated a long-drawn-out
community effort in which THE NEWS took the leadership from
the start.

As early as 1895 citizens had hoped that a union station might
result from the Dallas Terminal Railway & Union Depot Company, but it did not materialize. In May, 1903, Benjamin F.
Yoakum, then president of the Frisco system and influential in
other Southwestern lines, fanned the flames of local hope by announcing that such a facility should be constructed in Dallas.
Again in 1909 prospects brightened with the passage of a law by
the Texas Legislature empowering the Texas Railroad Commission to order joint passenger terminal facilities when found desirable. But the issue dragged out in talk as the carriers found
additional reasons for postponing a decision at Dallas. Meanwhile Kessler urged that a union station be located at the foot of
Main, Elm and Commerce Streets and in December, 1910, the
City Plan and Development League approved the idea. It was
not, however, until officials of THE NEWS, particularly G. B.

Dealey, became vitally interested in getting relief from terminal deficiencies then existing, that the movement advanced into its final phase.

Late in 1910 Albert P. Foute, official of one of the larger wholesale distributing houses, visited Dealey in the latter's office and pointed out that local freight service was as distressing as that available to passengers. This conversation led to a conference between THE NEWS and a large group of shippers, at which a vigorous crusade was agreed upon. THE NEWS assigned a staff writer, K. K. Hooper, to investigate the local situation and to write a series of articles pointing a way to its solution. These were published each day for about a month beginning on Christmas Day, 1910. Among the woes of passengers stressed in this series was the fact that railroads used five separate stations, only two of which had sheds to protect travelers from the rain. Also, but two of the stations were served directly by street-car lines, and bus operators charged twenty-five cents for each passenger and the same amount for each piece of baggage in making transfers. The Missouri, Kansas, & Texas lines then used their own station at Pacific and Market; the Texas & Pacific depot was on Pacific Avenue, between Lamar and Griffin; the Southern Pacific lines, jointly with the Texas & Pacific, used the original Central Depot in East Dallas at Pacific and Central Avenues; the Gulf, Colorado and Santa Fe, the Frisco and the Rock Island lines used the Santa Fe depot on Commerce Street where the present Santa Fe office building and terminal warehouse now stand; the Cotton Belt lines used the right-of-way of South Lamar Street to Commerce, where its depot stood on the southwest corner of Commerce and Lamar (now occupied by the Union Bus Terminal). The grief of those whose freight was handled in and out of Dallas was also pictured by THE NEWS. To show what other progressive cities had already accomplished, THE NEWS published numerous pictures of new union stations in various parts of the country.

This educational effort led to the convening of the largest number of important railroad executives which had ever met in Dallas up to that time. These officials were persuaded by important shippers in Dallas to attend the conference, which was held February

8, 1911, in the Southland Hotel. After a general discussion with Dallas business leaders, which was harmoniously conducted with George E. Kessler as a "surprise" speaker, the railway and local groups held separate meetings to choose representatives for further negotiations.

Presiding over the Dallas business men was J. C. Duke. On nomination of G. B. Dealey, a committee of four citizens was named to represent Dallas. These were Alex Sanger, A. P. Foute, Louis Lipsitz and Royal A. Ferris. Each of these men was fairly small in stature and this fact, combined with their results, led to the characterization of them as "the biggest little committee" in the history of Dallas. Sanger was named chairman with Ferris as secretary. F. G. Pettibone, vice president and general manager of the Gulf, Colorado and Santa Fe, was advanced as spokesman for the carriers. Before that same day was over, Pettibone announced that the railroads had decided to build a station in Dallas, although they did not set any specific date to start construction.

As might have been expected, a vast amount of work remained to be done, particularly by the Dallas citizens' committee of four. The committee during the next twenty-four months held 263 meetings, conferring not only with railroad officials but also with city and county officials, property owners, real estate men and engineers. A staggering number of details of a physical property nature had to be arranged in advance, including the option purchasing of the land, before work could start. The committee's hardest problem was to provide a traffic outlet westward on Commerce Street from Houston, due to the great concentration of tracks. After half a dozen meetings with the County Commissioners' Court, they succeeded in getting an order for a bond election to provide for an overpass. The election campaign was successfully managed by Ben E. Cabell. The overpass served until 1935 when it was razed in connection with the three-way underpass at Elm, Main and Commerce.

Construction started on the union terminal in January, 1914, and the structure was formally opened on October 14, 1916. Approximately 120 visiting railway officials participated in this ceremony, which was also coincident with the opening of the 1916

State Fair of Texas. It was held out of doors with G. B. Dealey as master of ceremonies. W. M. Holland, former mayor and chairman of the committee to arrange for the ceremony, wrote that Dealey was unanimously selected for this honor "on account of the splendid work done by him personally and through THE NEWS in behalf of the new station." Governor James E. Ferguson, accompanied by his staff in uniform, attended. Later the same day the Governor and the staff were present in Fair Park when a monument to Sydney Smith, first secretary of the State Fair, was unveiled in ceremonies presided over by G. B. Dealey.

During this same period THE NEWS saw another of its long cherished objectives realized. This was the opening of Southern Methodist University in 1915. As early as 1874 Dallas had sought to interest one of the major religious bodies of Texas in locating a university in its midst. At that time inducements were offered to the Presbyterians to locate Austin College when it was moved from Huntsville. But Sherman on the north won out over its rival. In 1900 the University of Dallas was established, at least on paper, and its departments of medicine and pharmacy were actually started. Three years later these were taken over by Baylor University of Waco and have developed into the Dallas units of Baylor, the colleges of medicine, dentistry and nursing associated with Baylor Hospital. Also in 1903 the Methodist institution of Southwestern University at Georgetown opened Southwestern Medical College in Dallas, with Dr. J. O. McReynolds as dean. It was housed in the structure on Hall Street, between Bryan and San Jacinto, now occupied by the Baylor University School of Dentistry.

For a number of years the Rev. W. H. Clagett, a Presbyterian minister, had been working to establish an educational institution in Dallas. In 1907 his dream appeared near realization, for John S. Armstrong, in connection with the development of Highland Park, donated a tract of 100 acres of land in what is now Highland Park West to the proposed Presbyterian University. But various factors defeated the plan. Armstrong, however, had been imbued with the idea of a local university, and on his death in 1908 it was found that his will provided for a bequest of 100 acres to any religious denomination that would act on the plan. This second tract lay just northeast of Highland Park in what is now University Park.

By 1910 the Methodists of Texas were actively considering the establishment of a new university at some place in North Texas. At this point THE NEWS and Dallas interests generally, especially the Chamber of Commerce, began working for the selection of Dallas. H. H. Adams headed the Chamber of Commerce committee and Dr. John O. McReynolds and John R. Babcock, the secretary, worked closely with him. Mayor Stephen J. Hay and THE NEWS participated actively in the campaign. And in June the Dallas committee offered $325,000 in subscriptions and 125 acres in land, or $400,000 in subscriptions and only fifty acres. This was in fact an offer to relocate Southwestern University in Dallas, which was rejected by a vote of twenty-one to thirteen in the board of trustees.

But the minority of thirteen appealed this decision to the five Texas conferences of the Methodist Episcopal Church, South. Among these dissenters were Judge M. M. Brooks of Dallas, chairman of the board, and Dr. Robert S. Hyer, then president of Southwestern University. Out of this appeal came an authorization by the Methodists of Texas that, while Southwestern University would remain at Georgetown, a second university should be established. The commission in charge was headed by Bishop James Atkins. It held its first meeting in Austin on January 18, 1911, and its second meeting in Dallas on February 1. Dallas now offered $300,000 in subscriptions and 662½ acres of land, all within six miles of the post office. The principal tracts were donated by Mrs. John S. Armstrong and William W. Caruth. Dr. Hyer was elected president of the new institution with H. A. Boaz, now Bishop, as vice president; A. V. Lane of Dallas, treasurer, and Frank Reedy, bursar. In this organizational phase Colonel C. C. Walsh, then a banker of San Angelo, later chairman of the board of the Dallas Federal Reserve Bank, was instrumental in securing funds from the General Education Board to be matched by funds raised in Texas.

The opening date of Southern Methodist University was set tentatively for September, 1912, but various factors delayed the event and it was not until September 23, 1915, that opening exercises were held in Dallas Hall. An unexpectedly large registration delayed the convening of classes until September 28 when the University had 456 students. On October 12 Reedy reported to The News that this number had increased to 551, and total registration for the first year mounted later to 706. The original faculty, engaged on June 15, 1915, included President Hyer as professor of physics and three teachers whom he brought from Southwestern University: John H. McGinnis, professor of English; John Reedy, professor of chemistry, and Frank Seay, professor of theology. Some twenty other members of the faculty were engaged before the opening of the university.

The essential part played by The News, particularly in securing the location of the new institution in Dallas and in promoting the campaign to raise the large amount of subscriptions, is testified to in a typical letter of the period from Frank Reedy, bursar, who wrote to G. B. Dealey:

"I know I am expressing the sentiment of every official and friend of Southern Methodist University over the entire Southwest," he wrote, "when I undertake to say that largely to you, personally, and to your fellow officials is due the credit for the success and program of Southern Methodist University.

"President Hyer has repeatedly commented upon the future of our institution as being largely in your hands. I beg to earnestly co-operate with you in this movement, in which you are in a sense the leader, and which has for its object to the completion of the university as second to none."

☆

A second, equally notable, victory was celebrated by The News in the selection of Dallas as headquarters of the Eleventh Federal Reserve Bank. The law providing for not less than eight nor more than twelve regional banks was passed by Congress in 1913. In the spring of the next year Secretary of the Treasury William Gibbs McAdoo, Secretary of Commerce David F. Houston and Comptroller of the Currency James Skelton Williams held regional hearings in various parts of the country to aid in making final selections. Financial and business interests of Dallas appeared at the hearing in Austin to present the case, first, for the location of one bank in Texas, and second, in Dallas if possible. Houston and Fort Worth groups joined in the first half of this representation, differing, naturally, on the matter of where in Texas the bank should be placed. The brunt of the fight for Dallas fell upon J. Howard Ardrey, an officer of the City National Bank. While in Austin he conferred with the late Colonel E. M. House, the Texan who had already become one of President Wilson's closest advisers. Ardrey also worked closely with Washington and Texas officials of THE NEWS. For use over the private wires of the newspaper between Texas and Washington, a confidential code was devised to keep G. B. Dealey and Ardrey informed of backstage developments. The President was referred to as Allah, Colonel House as Tacitus, Secretary McAdoo as Croesus and Postmaster General Albert S. Burleson as Mercury. Otto Praeger, former Washington correspondent of THE NEWS, who had been named postmaster of the capital city by Burleson and Mark L. Goodwin, his successor for THE NEWS, worked day and night.

Feeling that the locating committee and Colonel House were favorably impressed with the arguments and briefs in behalf of Dallas, Ardrey and Dealey next turned to Postmaster General Burleson in an effort to secure his deciding vote in the selection. The administration's chief liaison officer with the Democratic majority in Congress, Burleson was one of the most influential officials in Washington. When the Dallas proponents learned therefore by code message that he was en route to Texas, G. B. Dealey suggested that Ardrey and Tom Finty, Jr., meet him at St. Louis and discuss the matter during the remainder of the journey. In a private conference in the drawing room of a Texas-bound Pullman car, Ardrey and Finty were able to lay all facts and arguments before him. "I think that conference on the train completed the job," Ardrey related a number of years later.

When the selection was finally made, the Postmaster General on April 2, 1914, telegraphed G. B. Dealey as follows: "I am gratified that Texas has obtained a regional bank and congratulate Dallas upon the selection as the center of this reserve region. It is only fair to say that the Dallas and Galveston NEWS contributed more through the assistance rendered than any other agency or person toward this great service to Texas. Please extend my congratulations to all concerned."

In reviewing the matter in the retrospect of more than two decades, J. Howard Ardrey later said, "As a matter of fact, throughout the preparation for the hearings and the time we were working on this objective, the organization of THE NEWS was the most effective instrument we had. In view of the interest Mr. Dealey took in it, the great work done by the Washington representatives of the paper, that by Mr. Finty and, above all, the prestige of the paper, I think that THE NEWS was the principal factor in securing the location of the Federal Reserve Bank in Dallas."

THE DALLAS JOURNAL was only a few months old when the European War flashed across the pages of the newspapers of America in unprecedentedly large headlines. But, at the time, the emergence of James E. Ferguson, banker and farmer of Bell County, as a new star in the firmament of Texas politics seemed almost as important. As early as April, three months before his virtual election in the contest that named the Democratic nominee for Governor, THE NEWS examined his candidacy; it found that the worst that might be said of Ferguson was that he betrayed himself a Socialist by advocating a law to limit what landlords might charge their tenants. "But those of us who recall the several things which the State does to limit the charges of individuals and institutions," continued THE NEWS, "must think that this is not so highly criminating as it is made out to be." The editorial concluded:

All we feel certain of is that the Hon. James E. Ferguson has proved himself to be a most interesting and potent political phenomenon. Unasked and unaided, he has given his ambition to be governor a plausibility and a formidableness which made it an unsurmountable obstacle to the purposes of a political faction which boasts that it constitutes a majority of the people of the State. . . .

Soon, however, the war in Europe was producing acute distress in Texas. THE NEWS on July 29, commenting on Austria-Hungary's declaration of war on Serbia, promptly decided where guilt lay "for letting loose these furies: upon Austria and her Triple Alliance." Almost immediately unemployment mounted sharply in Dallas as the war halted building operations. THE NEWS urged a local public works program to provide relief. What was worse, the bottom dropped out of the cotton market and distress spread into every corner of the Cotton Belt. It was then that the "buy-a-bale" movement was launched. THE NEWS endorsed this effort to tide the farmer over the emergency.

The editorial course of THE NEWS in regard to events leading up to America's entry into the World War closely paralleled that of President Wilson. When the President severed diplomatic relations with Germany in February of 1917 over the issue of unrestricted submarine warfare, THE NEWS declared that he had the unanimous support of the country "out of intellectual conviction, out of faith in his patriotism and wisdom." When the German plot to dismember Texas and return the State to Mexico was revealed in March, THE NEWS felt that "even the pacifists must see the folly of half measures and even the agents and sympathizers of Germany in this country must now be convinced that their efforts to restrain and fetter the President have all the consequences, if not the purposes, of disloyalty." When war was formally declared and President Wilson called for the first contingent of volunteers, THE NEWS said:

The man whose patience and forbearance have won the plaudits of pacifists and the execrations of chauvinists has bidden the people of the United States to enter the most devouring war the world has known. This alone proves the abundance of our provocation and establishes our justification in a way that will withstand the utmost scrutiny of history.

☆

In the midst of the war excitement a more local concern troubled Texas. When President Wilson was re-elected in 1916, James E. Ferguson at the same time was given a second term as Governor. But he had raised a host of opponents who took advantage of every possible mistake in office to rouse sentiment against him. Most notably had Ferguson offended the powerful group of former students of the University of Texas by his attacks on that institution. By April 9, 1917, THE NEWS had risen to the defense of the university. When the Governor in June sought to close the doors of the institution by vetoing its appropriations, THE NEWS termed this act a challenge "to the self respect, the pride and the patriotism of the people of Texas." The Legislature met in special session on August 1 when impeachment charges were filed against the Governor. Then for more than a month the fight continued at Austin, judgment finally being voted by the Senate of Texas on September 25 that James E. Ferguson might nevermore hold any office of honor, trust or profit under the State of Texas. THE NEWS felt that the ends of political justice had been served:

While Mr. Ferguson was the defendant, it was the fame of the people of Texas which was on trial. The Senate could not have acquitted Mr. Ferguson without impeaching the moral responsibilities of Texas before the bar of intelligent public opinion. . . .

His conduct toward the University has been that of an autocrat. The success of his usurpation would have been ruinous to the University and that fact alone would have been sufficient reason for impeachment and conviction, in THE NEWS' opinion. . . .

THE NEWS believes that an overwhelming majority of the people of this State will approve the verdict. The Senate and the House are to be congratulated for the courageous manner in which they have discharged a duty which must have been painful to every member. They have done something which will have a salutary effect on the politics of Texas.

The full resources of THE NEWS were enthusiastically pledged to the winning of the war. In all, some sixty-three members of the organization at Dallas joined the armed forces of the government and saw service at home or abroad. An equal proportion of the working staff at Galveston enlisted. THE NEWS early saw the advantages of the selective service or universal draft act passed by Congress. While the measure was pending before Congress the paper conducted a campaign urging its readers to "let your representative in Congress know" that Texas favored this democratic method of filling in the ranks of the army and the navy. Other measures in behalf of victory won equal support from the newspaper. The war was covered as ably as the regular and special press services made possible. Interest in the day-by-day developments on various war fronts mounted, so that the circulation of THE SUNDAY NEWS went over the 100,000 mark for the first time, in March of 1918. The war cartoons of John Knott were in themselves notable contributions to the maintenance and upbuilding of the morale of those on the home front.

The first sign of the end of the war came on October 5, 1918, when the Austro-Hungarian minister at Stockholm asked the Swedish government to transmit a proposal for an armistice to President Wilson. "While these signals of despair are not the acknowledgment of defeat," remarked THE NEWS, "they are recognition of the fact that defeat is inevitable and at an early date." Just after midnight on November 10 the German Emperor fled across the Dutch frontier and the next day at 11 o'clock in the morning firing ceased on the western front. Oddly enough, the actual signing of the Armistice occurred at the eleventh hour of the eleventh day of the eleventh month, a fact impressively received by many a person of a religious turn of mind because the three numbers added up to the age of Christ at the time of his crucifixion. The official Armistice Celebration was held in Dallas on November 13, with a parade through the business district which surpassed in size and enthusiasm anything similar in local history.

A welter of international, national and State problems followed in the wake of victory. There were great obligations resting on the victors in making peace, THE NEWS believed, among which was the duty to exercise "moderation and forbearance" on the vanquished. There was the problem of Russia, now that "a cabal" of Bolsheviks had seized the power. There was the resurgence of Prohibition sentiment during the war itself when the Texas Legislature on March 4, 1918, had ratified the Eighteenth Amendment to the Federal Constitution. THE NEWS, still opposed to the principle of Prohibition, ironically remarked on the circumstance that "this despotism of the majority should attain its culmination at a moment when we are fighting to make the world safe for democracy and to establish the supremacy of right over might." Women were making a bid for the suffrage and THE NEWS supported the Nineteenth Amendment in the belief that "fundamental justice demands for women the same opportunities in self-government that custom and laws afford men."

But the greatest concern of THE NEWS as the war ended and reconstruction began was what the country would do to prevent the collapse of economic activities which ordinarily followed a war. The paper believed that the war itself had pointed the way to stabilization of economic life through the functions of the State. "Never before," said THE NEWS on November 14, 1918, "has the State attempted and succeeded in eliminating economic waste in the larger things involving the welfare of society. That the successes which have come of it are greater than the people had reason to expect is proof of the capacities of the democratic State." The editorial continued:

So the end of the war finds the people of all countries that have been aligned for civilization speculating upon the extent to which things learned and demonstrated under stress of war may be made available for progress during peace. . . .

The war brought need for new and bold methods on the part of the State. The methods have worked out as expected. Have the principles behind these methods taken such root during the war as to survive in the new era that is to follow? Are regulations of business methods, profits and prices likely to be forgotten on tomorrow as instruments in statecraft? These questions import the thought of co-operation and of labor's share in the management and profits of industry. And they bring forth the companion thought of industrial stabilization. . . . That is the problem of so-called reconstruction.

CHAPTER XX

BOOM YEARS

1919–1929

THE END of the World War unleashed new energies, new tendencies and new problems in the life of Texas and THE NEWS. America's immediate, post-war boom reached its climax in 1919, followed by swift deflation in 1920. But the nation righted itself rapidly, due chiefly to the stabilizing influence of the Federal Reserve Banking System. Then began the near decade of steadily mounting prosperity which is associated chiefly with the name of Calvin Coolidge.

The war had furnished new ties between Texas and the rest of the nation. As early as 1916, when threatening difficulties with Mexico brought national guardsmen from all parts of the country to the Southwestern border, the influx had started. Training camps and flying fields established in various parts of Texas during the war gave other thousands a first-hand knowledge of the State. Many an ex-soldier returned to make his home in Texas. The discovery of several large pools of oil and gas at Ranger, Burkburnett and other West Texas fields during and just after the war also gave Texas another large-scale industry to match its cotton, cattle and lumber. Oil explorations continued, leading to development of richly productive areas in every section of the State during the 1920's.

Although THE NEWS had felt the great stimulus of intensified reader interest and business revenue which war times produce in modern journalism, the organization adjusted itself rapidly to post-war conditions. It also had a more personal adjustment to make. On June 23, 1919, the regency of Cesar Lombardi as president of THE NEWS ended with his death in California.

The passing of Cesar Lombardi was greatly mourned within THE NEWS because of the close affection with which he was held by all of his associates. A measure of this feeling is reflected in the following excerpts from the editorial which appeared the day after his death:

. . . Mr. Lombardi was the directing editor of THE NEWS and its allied publications as well as chief executive of the publishing company. In the latter capacity he was notably wise, as he was firmly grounded in long business experience; but it was in his capacity of editor that he took the greater pleasure and to which he gave the best of his unusual endowment. His were earnest convictions, and he wished for nothing so much as to be instrumental in forwarding those interests which he regarded as fundamental in the development of human character and equitable government.

He was by nature and preference a democrat, and he had a veritable passion for freedom and fair play for every element of the population.

His business brought him to Texas and his tenacity, faithfulness and inherent ability advanced him steadily until he won a liberal material prosperity. But he seemed never covetous of money for money's sake. . . .

By nature a gentleman, he was considerate and accessible to every attache of THE NEWS at any hour of the working day, and unaffectedly sincere in his friendships.

Although never unmindful of a newspaper's duty to itself, Mr. Lombardi sought above all ends to make the papers over which he presided something more than dividend-earners, or vehicles of current news. He conceived it to be the duty of a medium of public information to afford constructive inspiration and to reflect social, political and cultural progress. He believed wholeheartedly in public education, and considered a newspaper which catered to ignorance or demagogy as guilty of a gross violation of its implied obligation to the public that supported it. Such was Cesar Lombardi as editor and business man. . . .

G. B. Dealey, vice president and general manager since 1906, now became president as well as general manager. Policies and principles of management for which he had in fact been chiefly responsible since 1906 were continued, although modified and given new directions, as will be seen, under the demands of new times and conditions.

To meet changing economic conditions in Texas and particularly to serve more effectively the growing needs of its own immediate territory at Dallas, THE NEWS in 1923 sold THE GALVESTON DAILY NEWS to W. L. Moody, Jr., of Galveston. Corporate headquarters were transferred to Dallas, along with all office records and files of THE NEWS. THE SEMI-WEEKLY FARM NEWS of Galveston, the direct continuation of the original NEWS dating from 1842, was likewise transferred and combined with the edition of the same name at Dallas. Two long-valued members of THE NEWS' family, Louis C. Elbert and Silas B. Ragsdale, remained with THE GALVESTON DAILY NEWS under its new management. As general manager and managing editor, respectively, they have piloted the "Old Lady by the Sea" on its notable, present-day success. But John F. Lubben, manager of THE GALVESTON NEWS, secretary and treasurer of the publishing company since 1906, moved to Dallas to continue in his official capacity in the corporation. For him as for THE NEWS, severing of immediate ties with Galveston and the "Old Lady by the Sea" was saddening. The decision had been made, however, only after long and careful consideration, as the following editorial in THE DALLAS NEWS of March 23, 1923, reveals:

For many years it has been evident to us that it would be desirable from a business standpoint to dispose of THE GALVESTON DAILY NEWS. The factors leading to such belief are the continuous and rapid expansion of our interests centered in Dallas, the distance covering Dallas and Galveston, and the seeming necessity of making THE GALVESTON DAILY NEWS partially a duplicate of THE DALLAS MORNING NEWS so long as common ownership existed, notwithstanding the disparity in the potentialities of the respective communities.

Nevertheless, we have never offered THE GALVESTON DAILY NEWS for sale, but on the contrary have discouraged overtures for purchase until the present. We were reluctant to think of parting with ownership of our original newspaper, which is interwoven with the history of Texas and with which tender memories are associated, and we were firmly resolved that we would never permit it to pass to interests that could not be relied upon to maintain it in accordance with its honorable traditions, or that would imperil the interests of the people of Galveston.

We have listened to and accepted Mr. Moody's offer to purchase because we believed that the conditions that we had imposed upon ourselves were met in him. He is a native of Texas—born in Fairfield, Freestone County—and from infancy Galveston has been his home. His large and varied interests center in that city. Moreover, at the outset we received satisfactory assurances from him that he would not lower the standard that we had maintained, his own phrasing, as published in Thursday's NEWS, being:

> "It is our purpose to continue THE GALVESTON NEWS on the high standard of conservatism, accuracy and impartiality so ably maintained by A. H. Belo & Company. We are to present a newspaper that will represent impartially all creeds, races and individuals."

The sale of THE GALVESTON DAILY NEWS does not lessen our affection for, nor our interest in Galveston and South Texas. THE DALLAS MORNING NEWS, THE DALLAS JOURNAL and THE SEMI-WEEKLY FARM NEWS will continue to be all-Texas newspapers serving, as they always have, all parts of the State and the people of Texas in general.

But even as the long dual operation of THE GALVESTON NEWS and THE DALLAS NEWS drew to a close, the institution was laying the foundation for a notable expansion of its facilities at Dallas. After 1920 the radio was brought out of the laboratory and radio telephonic broadcasting placed at the disposal of the public. A rare toy at first, not many newspaper executives could envision this new agency as of lasting merit either in the field of public education or public entertainment. Walter A. Dealey, elder son of G. B. Dealey, who had been named an executive of THE NEWS in 1920, was one of the first newspaper officials to realize the potentialities of the radio. He early interested THE NEWS in establishing a broadcasting station, and his name and memory will always be identified with STATION WFAA, the first newspaper-owned radio station in the Southwest.

STATION WFAA began broadcasting from improvised studios in THE NEWS building on June 26, 1922. Its power was only 100 watts and the transmitting aerial was strung from the smokestack on the Katy building to the Mercantile building half a block away. Popular interest had already led THE NEWS to inaugurate first a weekly radio page each Sunday and then a daily feature which listed available programs for the listener. Then on October 30, 1922, the new 500-watt transmitter built by the Western Electric Company was installed; THE NEWS' station received a Class B rating from the Department of Commerce. The Rev. William M. Anderson, pastor of the First Presbyterian Church of Dallas, dedicated the station to the public. He was followed by G. B. Dealey, who, in a brief talk through the microphone, explained the purposes of the publishing company in expanding into this new and untried field.

I am glad to say a few words on the general subject of the relation of the radio to a newspaper [said the president of THE NEWS]. There are a great many misapprehensions in the public mind. We have invested a good many thousands of dollars in the radio plant. But while the cost is large, operation is the main item of expense. We have at present a radio staff of six persons—a supervisor, an operator, a man in charge of programs, a radio reporter, a radio editor and a stenographer.

Why, then, should we get into the radio game? What do we get out of it? The answer is simple. The chief asset of any institution is the good will of the public. From the beginning we recognized that radio was not only a remarkable scientific discovery, but it also presented an opportunity for public service that would be recognized and appreciated by everyone. If we obtain the good will of our listeners we are content. We are more than content; we are immensely pleased. This station belongs to the great American public of the Southwest.

Eight years later, after the Federal Radio Commission had been created, STATION WFAA was increased in broadcasting power to 50,000 watts, thus becoming the first newspaper-owned super-power station in the United States and the first station of this size in the South. A modern transmitting plant was built at that time in the northwest part of Dallas County, near Grapevine. Modern, scientifically designed broadcasting studios were also installed in the Baker Hotel and the station continued to expand into its present range, popularity and influence as one of the nation's key stations. The rise of radio broadcasting as a medium of advertising has also given the station its place in the revenue-producing units of THE NEWS.

☆

About the time that the radio first began to make inroads on the popular fancy, an organization formed in the Old South began to spread over Texas. This was the Ku Klux Klan, ostensibly a revival of the Klan of Reconstruction days but in reality more of a spiritual descendant of the Know Nothing political movement of the 1850's which THE NEWS had opposed strenuously. As in 1857, so in 1921, THE NEWS denounced the movement as un-American. But by May of that year the white-hooded organization had won converts by the thousands in Dallas and had staged its first torchlight parade. THE NEWS commented:

The spectacle of 800 masked and white-gowned men parading the streets of Dallas under banners proclaiming them Knights of the Ku Klux Klan and self-appointed guardians of the community's political, social and moral welfare has its ridiculous aspects. . . . But it also has a serious significance which will not be lost on the minds of men who cherish the community's good name and have the intelligence to understand how well designed that exhibition was to bring it under reproach.

It was a slander on Dallas because the only conditions which could be given to excuse the organization do not exist. . . . White supremacy is not imperiled. Vice is not rampant. The constituted agencies of government are still regnant. And if freedom is endangered, it is by the redivivus of the mob spirit in the disguising garb of the Ku Klux Klan.

Thus began the three-year fight between THE NEWS and the Klan, a fight which ended in final triumph of the principles championed by the newspaper. The Klan quickly rose to almost complete power in city and county governments; only the city public school system withstood the shock of its assault. Its influence in Texas politics reached a high-water mark in the race for United States Senator in 1922. Senator Charles A. Culberson, continuously in the office since 1898, was in poor health and thus unable to make a personal campaign. He announced for re-election, however, and was ably championed in the field by Barry Miller of Dallas and others. Culberson early ranged himself in opposition to the Klan. Clarence Ousley, Cullen F. Thomas, Sterling P.

Strong and R. L. Henry—the last two openly friendly toward
the Klan—announced for Culberson's seat.

But it remained for two other political figures to make the
strongest bid for the Democratic nomination. Former Governor
James E. Ferguson, following his removal from office by the Texas
Senate in 1917, had renounced the Democratic party in 1920 by
offering himself for the presidency on his own American Party.
He returned, however, to the fold in 1922 as a senatorial candidate. A younger man, Earle B. Mayfield of Tyler, nephew of the
beloved chairman of the Texas Railroad Commission, Allison B.
Mayfield, and himself a member of the regulatory body, became
this second chief contender. THE NEWS attempted to smoke out
all candidates on the Klan issue by means of a questionnaire.

☆

The July primary narrowed the field to Mayfield and Ferguson.
The former had made no effort to rebuff Klan support, while
Ferguson continued to attack Ku Kluxism. But THE NEWS and
many other conservatives failed to warm up to either candidate.
Early in August, Tom Finty, Jr., explained in THE NEWS how in-
dependents might nominate someone to oppose the winner in the
November general election. Sentiment of this kind grew as the
August run-off primary gave the nomination to Mayfield.

Sensing this split within the ranks of Democracy over the Klan
issue, Republican leaders such as R. B. Creager of Brownsville
moved cautiously. A young attorney of Houston, George E. B.
Peddy, announced in September that he would oppose Mayfield as
an independent. Anti-Klan forces rallied to his support, and, in
October, following the discreet retirement of Dr. E. P. Wilmot of
Austin, the official Republican candidate, the State Executive
Committee of that party announced unqualified support of Peddy.

This contest between the regular nominee and an independent
Democrat moved toward its conclusion. But the final stages of the
battle were fought more in court rooms than on the husting, for
there now unfolded an amazing series of court duels involving the
principals. Represented by Luther Nickels of Dallas, a group of

citizens went before Judge Hawkins Scarborough of the Thirteenth District Court at Corsicana on October 3 and secured a temporary injunction which restrained State officials from placing Mayfield's name on the ballot. Action was sought under a State law of 1919 designed to limit the expenditures of senatorial candidates to $10,000. It was alleged that Candidate Mayfield had exceeded that limit.

Concurrently, Peddy forces, on learning that State officials would not permit his name to be printed on the November 7 ballot, entered Federal Court seeking a mandamus to the same State officials. The Peddy case worked rapidly toward a decision, and, to the accompaniment of screaming headlines in THE NEWS and other Texas papers, it was disposed of by a three-judge Federal Circuit Court at New Orleans on October 23. The Court held that it was powerless to instruct State officials on the matter. It was now seen that if Peddy were to win, his adherents must conduct a write-in campaign of staggering proportions.

Mayfield forces—represented by the redoubtable W. P. Mc-Lean, Jr., of Fort Worth—appealed to the State Circuit Court of Appeals at Dallas for a stay of the Corsicana injunction. This intermediate court refused, whereupon the appeal was rushed to the State Supreme Court at Austin. Back in Corsicana the case went to jury trial in the hearing on the petition for a permanent injunction. E. M. (Ted) Dealey, who had been almost constantly in the field that summer and fall with various candidates, was detailed to the trial.

For more than a week the testimony and argument provided one of the more exciting of Texas political shows. Candidate Mayfield took the stand and by admission of former membership in the Ku Klux Klan, narrowed the issue unmistakably between himself and Peddy. On October 26 the jury at Corsicana decided twelve out of twenty-one special issues submitted by the court in favor of the plaintiffs, and Mayfield's name, it now appeared, must also be written in if it were to show up on any ballots. Two days later, however, the Supreme Court at Austin ruled that proceedings at Corsicana were null and void, on the ground that the plaintiffs were not qualified parties to bring the action.

Undaunted, Peddy forces the next day entered a second district court, that presided over by Judge A. M. Blackmon at Groesbeck, and secured a second temporary injunction. By Saturday, November 4, an appeal was acted on by the Dallas circuit court which, this time, gave a temporary victory to the Mayfield forces by dissolving the Groesbeck injunction. The appellate court convened again on Sunday—two days before the election—and overruled a motion for rehearing. This cleared the right-of-way for a final appeal before the Supreme Court. Both sides raced to Austin where, at 3:30 o'clock on the eve of the election, the Supreme Court chopped away any and all legal obstructions to the certification of Mayfield's name on the ballot. And, in the ensuing election, despite an unprecedented write-in of Peddy's name, Mayfield won the senatorship by a majority of two to one. The victory of the Klan was unquestioned.

By 1924 the Klan was ready to take over the State government. THE NEWS refused, however, to ask any quarter, despite the victories already chalked up by its opponent. The newspaper published the syndicated, serial exposé of the Klan which had been originated by the New York *World*. Every known instance of lawlessness attributed to the Klan was given daily publicity in the columns of the paper. The newspaper lashed away editorially even though thousands believed, as it confessed, "that THE NEWS is headed straight for bankruptcy if it persists in its opposition to the lawlessness and impossible hatreds that have sprung up everywhere the Klan has cast its fatal shadow." Many of these prophets of doom did their part in an unsuccessful attempt to make the prophecy come true.

The Governor's race of 1924 proved the turning point in the fortunes of the Klan in Texas. District Judge Felix D. Robertson of Dallas asked for the Democratic nomination. He was backed, it was commonly believed, by the hooded organization. Although barred from holding any State office by the impeachment verdict of 1917, James E. Ferguson was once more a power in Texas poli-

tics. He took the field against the Klan. Or, rather, he was represented by his wife, the actual candidate, who won over Robertson
in the Democratic primaries. At this point the Republican party,
always a negligible factor in Texas since Reconstruction days,
thought it saw its opportunity. It decided to contest the matter by
offering a candidate of its own in the November general election
against Miriam A. Ferguson. The Republicans picked therefore
a well-regarded private citizen, Dr. George C. Butte of the law
faculty of the University of Texas. No Klansman himself, Dr.
Butte was expected, however, to furnish the Klansmen their chance
for revenge by defeating the anti-Klan Democratic nominee. THE
NEWS did not hesitate in its choice. It felt that Butte's election
would give a new lease of life to the secret organization in Texas
politics; thus it threw its unqualified support to the Fergusons.
The influence of THE NEWS, particularly in the heavily populated
north-central counties, proved decisive. Mrs. Ferguson in November became the Governor of Texas, and with her election the power
of the Klan began to recede. Years later G. B. Dealey, in an address
dealing with an experience of fifty years of newspaper publishing,
declared:

Perhaps the most courageous thing THE NEWS ever did was to fight
the Ku Klux Klan. The paper realized the danger and counted the
cost. A large part of the population, and even many of the paper's
own employees, had been swept off their feet by the tidal wave of
Klan favor and were eager to join in its spectacular pageants, to
revel in its alliterative titles and to glory in its assumption of authority
over the morals of the community. But THE NEWS saw the menace
to representative government and constituted authority, and the
threat to personal and religious freedom. It therefore fought against
a tyranny that threatened the destruction of democratic principles.
This course of action was financially and in other ways much more
serious to THE NEWS, whose constituency was largely pro-Klan, than
it was to the New York World, another anti-Klan newspaper, whose
constituency contained a large foreign born element.

Having aided the Fergusons to return to office, THE NEWS soon
felt called upon to oppose their administration. The young red-
headed Attorney General elected with them, Dan Moody, soon
broke with the Fergusons. He attacked the conduct of the high-

way department by the Ferguson administration and in 1926, with
the support of THE NEWS, defeated Mrs. Ferguson for Governor
by an impressive majority.

☆

National politics impinged on Texas in a direct way in 1928.
Largely through the enterprise of Jesse H. Jones, the city of Houston, by spirited financial bidding, secured the Democratic National Convention. Its meeting there in June was the first national
conclave of any major party on the soil of the State. The party
was in need of funds for other than convention purposes, but
through the work of Jouett Shouse, aided by John J. Raskob and
other men of wealth, it was well on the road toward rehabilitation.
Nation-wide resentment against the Eighteenth Amendment continued to grow and the new "Liberal"—that is, the repealist, or
modificationist—element within the party had gained the ascendancy. Governor Al Smith of New York, a lifelong opponent of
prohibition, early became the favored candidate. He did not attend the convention, but his cause was advanced brilliantly there
by Franklin D. Roosevelt, whose "happy warrior" speech nominating his old friend Smith gave political wiseacres in Texas something to talk about. T. Whit Davidson, and others, at once spotted
this New York delegate as a rising figure in national politics.

The nomination of Al Smith to oppose the Republican standard
bearer, Herbert Hoover, resulted almost as a matter of course. The
prohibition issue was neatly saddled. On what should have been
a matter of graver concern—the virtual abandonment of the historic opposition of the party to the high tariff system—the convention acted hastily. The outcome of the contest between Smith and
Hoover was never seriously in doubt; the Republicans were riding
high on the bull stock market, and when Candidate Hoover predicted a perpetual New Economic Era by references to two
chickens in every pot and two cars in each garage, the mass of
voters was willing to accept the heir of Harding and Coolidge.
But in Texas—and throughout the Solid South, in fact—the campaign developed subterranean fires and possible explosions. Nom-

inally aroused over the selection of Smith because of his well-known anti-prohibition views, there were large sectors of Southern voters who also objected to him because of his membership in the Catholic Church.

Republicans once more scented a possible break within the ranks of Texas Democracy. As in the Hogg-Clark, the Mayfield-Peddy and the Ferguson-Butte campaigns, they made an open bid for Democratic votes. This time, however, they asked Democrats to vote Republican only in the national contest for the presidency. Governor Moody was seeking a second term and his partisans made no strenuous campaign to carry the State for Smith. THE NEWS put no premium, then or before, on party regularity, but it is doubtful if it would have remained fully as neutral as it did, if the result in Texas could have been predicted. For, when the ballots were counted in November, it was seen that Texas, along with Virginia and two other Southern States, had swung into the Republican presidential column. This was accomplished in the face of the fact that Governor Moody and other Democratic candidates for State offices were elected by the usual majority. In view of Smith's defeat, well might undergraduates at the University of Virginia drape the statue of Mr. Jefferson in deep black; never since before the Civil War had the Solid South been so "rocked and riven."

In its purely local, home sphere, THE NEWS was able, during the prosperous 'Twenties, to realize its greatest success in the field of civic improvement. After 1927, Kessler's city plan for Dallas began to take tangible form. Simultaneously, THE NEWS directed an assault against inefficiency in city government, with the result that in 1931 the city manager form replaced the outmoded city commission.

The union passenger terminal, as has been seen, became the first item in Kessler's plan to be completed—as early as 1916. The next objective was the removal of the tracks of the Texas & Pacific Railway from that portion of Pacific Avenue which bisected the business district from Lamar to Central Avenue. It is difficult today, with a broad bouvelard rapidly becoming one of the main thoroughfares of the city, to realize what an unsightly and dangerous traffic hazard Pacific Avenue presented only so short a time ago. With freight and passenger trains thundering down this east and west artery, it was a constant threat to the life of pedestrians and to vehicular traffic. Kessler in his 1911 report had advanced the track removal plan with some trepidation; there was opposition in the city council to this radical idea, but, as one councilman explained, it was so "advanced" that it seemed impossible of realization. Therefore, largely to humor the city plan enthusiasts, it was left in the city plan and thereby adopted. But the mounting toll of grade crossing fatalities in the heart of the city made some sort of action imperative, while the potential increase of value to abutting property by such removal made it financially possible. For these reasons THE NEWS urged the improvement as a basic, first step in bringing about the proper development of the downtown district. There were powerful forces in opposition. It is not necessary here to recall the many vested interests which threatened to throttle this proposal. Typical, however, was one large national concern whose branch warehouse had been located on Pacific Avenue and served for years by the switching facilities of the Texas & Pacific Railway and, by trackage rights, of the Santa Fe Railway as well. There was a time during the Federal control of railways, in 1919, when a group of Dallas citizens, including G. B. Dealey, went to Chicago to confer with the regional director. In conversation with rail officials, Dealey said that the project was so vital to Dallas that it would finally prevail "despite the opposition of this powerful national concern." The conference was a success, and finally all opposition from shippers and railroads subsided. At one point a compromise plan was suggested, the elevation of the tracks on Pacific Avenue. But a graphic picture of this clumsy arrangement, presented in THE NEWS in a cartoon by John F. Knott, coupled with strong editorial opposition, overwhelmingly demonstrated the drawbacks to this plan.

Meanwhile a representative committee of citizens worked tirelessly on the project. This was headed by Harry L. Seay and included J. Early Lee, Rhodes S. Baker, Hugo Schoellkopf, Hugh

Prather and M. H. Mahana. The Texas & Pacific Railway finally agreed to removal upon certain conditions. The head of the railroad, J. L. Lancaster, became one of the most enthusiastic proponents of the plan. The chief condition was the provision of a wholesale industrial district in lower North Dallas to replace the area which the railroad would lose by the track removal. This meant the raising of a fund of approximately $700,000 from property owners. Two youthful and enterprising real estate dealers, Frank and Fletcher McNeny, were retained to effect the program of this wholesale district committee. THE NEWS counseled acceptance of this costly plan because "the removal of perilous grade crossings in the heart of Dallas will mark an episode in the civic accomplishment of the Southwest."

Eleven years after it was first broached and after "186 final conferences" had been held by interested committeemen, the Pacific Avenue track removal project at last became a reality on June 30, 1921. With befitting ceremony the first spike was pulled from the roadbed by Chairman Seay. The physical job was completed two years later on October 11 when another celebration of the completion of paving was held on Pacific Avenue and the new boulevard thrown open to the public. A miniature, rubber-tired railroad train headed the parade. On this "last train" were five early day residents of Dallas who had aided in securing the original right-of-way for the railroad in 1873—Alex Sanger, W. H. Gaston, William G. Sterett, B. S. Wathen and W. H. Adams. In these same years the City of Dallas widened North Lamar between Pacific Avenue and Elm Street and projected similar work on South Lamar. THE NEWS evidenced its good faith in these expensive widening projects by cheerfully as well as promptly bearing its part of assessments levied against adjoining property owners.

The death of George E. Kessler at his home in Indianapolis on March 19, 1923, served to remind the citizens of Dallas further that his great plan for the city as a whole was still largely on blueprints. In the following year the Kessler Plan Association was formed to popularize it and to carry on the enormous amount of education necessary to bring about its financing by the city. Then as before THE NEWS took the lead in this educational work. Efforts at last began to bear fruit. The example of St. Louis, which had recently voted an $87,000,000 bond program for similar improvements, proved a stimulating one. The City Plan Commission of Dallas was headed at this time by a tireless advocate of the plan, John J. Simmons. The planning body took the initiative on June 4, 1925, by recommending that the City Commission appoint a committee of citizens "to devise ways and means of carrying out the Dallas city plan along lines adopted at St. Louis." A series of conferences followed between Mayor Louis Blaylock, Chairman Simmons of the Plan Commission, T. M. Cullum, president of the Dallas Chamber of Commerce, and Charles Sanger, president of the Kessler Plan Association. As a result Mayor Blaylock in July named Charles E. Ulrickson, Harry A. Olmsted, Leslie A. Stemmons, Frank L. McNeny and Alex Weisberg as this special planning committee.

The Ulrickson Committee, as it was subsequently called, was assisted by the best engineering talent available, including City Plan Engineer E. A. Wood, who had worked directly with Kessler in years past. Studies by the committee continued for more than eighteen months. The committee at last made its report. Based primarily on Kessler's plan, it called for $23,900,000 in bonds to be issued and sold over a period of nine years. THE NEWS and other Dallas papers fully explained the details of this long-range bond program, printing the report in full to provide the widest possible understanding. Copies of this simply worded but comprehensive report were also mailed separately to every qualified voter in the city by the city government in advance of the bond election, which was held December 1, 1927. The radical revision of the street system of Dallas in the form of street openings, widenings and grade separations; the major improvements to the city water system; the public building program to provide more schools, public libraries, central fire station, public art gallery and downtown auditorium—these and other items were explained in full. The response of the voters was overwhelmingly in favor of the program.

☆

Now it should be kept in mind that the heart of Kessler's plan for Dallas had been the harnessing of the Trinity River by levees for flood control and the consequent reclamation of the noxious and disease-breeding swamps between Oak Cliff and the remainder of Dallas. This was obvious in view of the central, north-and-south position of the river in the layout of the city. Then as always, short of a geological cataclysm, the river would serve as the main interceptor of the city's storm sewer system. Without the flood control and land reclamation, the street system of Dallas would forever remain chopped almost in half. Other public services could be vastly improved, chiefly in the laying of water main connections, if the levee project were carried out:

As Kessler stated in his original city plan report of 1911 :

It is proposed to move the present channel of the Trinity River toward the Oak Cliff side and to confine it there by means of levees approximately twenty-five feet deep and 1,200 feet apart. The earth between these levees should be dredged out so as to give ample and uniform depth and should, in turn, be utilized for the building of the levees and for filling in the adjacent low ground in the river bottoms. On the levees there should of course be provided ample space for tracks and for all the operations attendant in the handling of freight from barges when the Trinity Canal is in operation. . . .

The Trinity River bottoms, with its wide flood area, together with the railroads on its left bank, strongly illustrate the barriers surrounding the business district of Dallas. On the west side of the river within ten minutes walking distance of the highest valued lands in the city, is a great area having practically no more than farm values, upon which a great city will spring up immediately upon the construction of one or two more highways safely above the floods and railroads.

The river, instead of remaining upon the western border of the city and a constant menace to it, would, in such a case, become nearly the center of a great city, with Oak Cliff and West Dallas integral parts instead of segregated units. If Dallas were to remain a city of 100,000 people, such development would be useless. As it will, however, continue to grow, it is essential to its expansion that the west shall have equal consideration with every other direction.

Kessler in 1910 did not outline the method of financing this great city plan project. He believed, however, that even the Fed-

eral Government should participate in the enterprise because of
its connection with the proposed Trinity Canal. He stated then
that "this particular improvement, which is an absolute essential
to the city, county and State and Federal governments, and in
addition thereto, to all the railroads entering the city, can be
accomplished only by united and harmonious action on the part
of all."

☆

The World War intervened, however, and when Kessler returned in 1919 he found nothing had been accomplished toward
elimination of the swamp lands and the menace of floods between
Dallas and Oak Cliff. In the meantime the urban development
of areas west of the Trinity River had gone forward at an unprecedented rate. After one ride over the city, Kessler promptly reiterated that "the Trinity River project is the biggest problem you
have today in Dallas." He now believed the improvement to be so
vital to a proper unified growth of the city and county as a whole
that the taxpayers of Dallas should bear the entire cost of the job.

But by the time that the Ulrickson Plan was evolved in 1927,
owners of land within the area to be reclaimed agreed to shoulder
the full cost of straightening and leveeing the river and filling in
the adjacent lowlands. They accepted this task at a direct cost of
$6,500,000 and agreed to spend $3,000,000 for other improvements within the area. This was conditioned, however, upon a
three-way agreement among the city, the county and the property
owners in the proposed industrial district. In accordance with the
voted Ulrickson Plan, the city agreed to spend some $3,200,000
to realize its portions of benefits. Practically all of this amount was
for improvements to the city's storm and sanitary sewer and street
systems. Included in the latter were five major underpasses of the
passenger terminal railroad tracks on the west end of the business
district to provide new street connections with the area west of the
river. The County of Dallas for its part agreed in 1928 by a vote
of the people to issue $3,339,000 in bonds to build four additional
viaducts over the new river channel together with three low water

W. L. MOODY, JR.
[Publisher]

LOUIS C. ELBERT
[General Manager]

SILAS B. RAGSDALE
[Managing Editor]

Executives of THE GALVESTON DAILY NEWS since its purchase in 1923 by W. L. Moody, Jr.

Starting the presses for the Fiftieth Anniversary edition of THE DALLAS NEWS—Oct. 1, 1935. (*Left to right*—G. B. Dealey; the late John F. Lubben, secretary and treasurer of the company; E. M. (Ted) Dealey, vice president; J. M. Moroney, now secretary and treasurer; Leven T. Deputy, superintendent of the mechanical department; John E. King, managing editor; the late James Q. Dealey, editor-in-chief; the late E. B. Doran, business manager.

crossings, and to construct an arterial highway, all of which would tie in with the improvement program of city and levee district. The Houston Street viaduct had long since become inadequate to handle traffic created largely by the growth of Oak Cliff into a suburban area of 100,000 people. Because the levee project would shorten the floodway from 6,000 to 2,000 feet, the county was able to build these additional viaducts at approximately the cost of one duplicate of the old Houston Street viaduct. Railroads and utilities likewise joined in the co-ordinated program, spending some $5,405,000 for the new railroad, street car and interurban viaducts and bridges, as well as in conforming their underground and overhead facilities to meet the plan of reclamation.

Although the engineering work on the levees was completed in 1931, final completion of the comprehensive flood-control and reclamation project hung fire, chiefly due to delays on the part of the city of Dallas in carrying out its part of the original agreement. In 1935 the State Highway Department, using State and Federal funds to match city expenditure, advanced the underpass program by construction of the $1,000,000 triple underpass which provides access to the west for traffic on Commerce, Main and Elm Streets. The city park board has also converted space on the east approach to create Dealey Plaza, latest of small park areas in the business district and named for G. B. Dealey.

While the leadership of THE NEWS admittedly has been the driving force in this great civic improvement, a large number of other civic leaders had a part in the development. The landowners within the City and County of Dallas Levee Improvement District itself assumed the greatest financial burden and therefore are entitled to the most credit. They have also planned a modern industrial district in the reclaimed area which will be second to none in the country and will bring greater benefits ultimately to the community of Dallas than can be measured today in dollars and cents. It would be unfair, however, not to single out a few of those who have fought longest and hardest for the final realization of this dream. Chief among these are Leslie A. Stemmons, John J. Simmons, W. J. Wyatt, John E. Owens, E. J. (Ward) Gannon, A. P. Rollins, W. J. Powell and Tom Tipton.

Between 1920 and 1930 Dallas experienced much of the physical expansion that its most ardent boosters had long striven for. Population within the city proper increased from 158,000 to 260,-000, while the metropolitan area registered a commensurate increase. The Ulrickson program was initiated in the midst of this urban boom, at a time when the downtown sky line was being transformed by new office structures, hotels, business houses and new factories. THE NEWS came to realize, however, that the future progress of the community was threatened by the near breakdown of efficient, non-partisan city government. As early as 1911 the paper had predicted that Dallas would some day adopt the city manager form. It said editorially at that time:

Twelve years from now, or twenty at the utmost, the commission form of government will be as much an obsolescence as it is now an innovation. It will be succeeded by some form which still more nearly recognizes the fact that management of a municipality's affairs is purely a matter of business. To predict such an evolution within twelve years is not rash. Already there are two towns in this country whose chief executive is called a manager rather than a mayor. There will be a board of directors who will hire a city manager and the whole scheme of corporate management will be applied to the affairs of the city.

Tom Finty, Jr., "Elder Statesman" of the editorial department of THE NEWS, directed the energies of the paper in 1926 toward the adoption of the council-manager form in Dallas. A member of the staff, Louis P. Head, was assigned to the large task of educating the electorate to this change. In 1927 a series of fifteen articles by him on "Measuring the Efficiency of a City's Government" appeared in THE NEWS. This series graphically and unanswerably revealed the weaknesses in the commission form in the face of modern needs.

The first step was taken in January of 1928 when Mayor R. E. Burt appointed a commission of fifteen citizens to draft a proposed new city charter. Hugh Grady was named chairman.

Although invited to a place on this charter commission, Finty declined, and Head was appointed in his stead. The sub-committee concerned with drawing up the charter comprised Louis P. Head, chairman; Hugh Grady and C. F. O'Donnell. Technically an amendment to the existing charter, their report in fact called for a sweeping alteration. The administration of Mayor J. Waddy Tate, elected in 1930, refused to submit the proposal to the voters, whereupon the charter commission by a referendum petition containing more than 10,000 names of qualified voters forced an election in December of that year. The council-manager plan was adopted by a majority of more than three to one.

A non-partisan Citizens Charter Association was formed to assure a favorable start of the new system. Its ticket of nine councilmen was elected in April of 1931 and John N. Edy was installed as the first city manager on May 1. The new government set to work in earnest. Its main achievements were the reorganization of fiscal affairs through the introduction of strict budgetary control and the institution of civil service among all employees of the city.

At the time the bull stock market of the 'Twenties and the hectic prosperity of urban, industrial areas created the fiction of a new economic millennium, the American farmer, notably the cotton grower, failed to enjoy any part in the boom. And, as before in its long history, THE NEWS sought to offer a remedy for the plight of the farmer.

Early in 1924, Victor H. Schoffelmayer became agricultural editor of THE NEWS. As did Colonel Sterett more than a quarter of a century before, he began studying the forgotten man with the hoe in the cotton field. The resulting series of articles on farm tenancy revealed the near-ruin which dependence on cotton had brought nearly half the rural population of Texas. Obviously, the way out for the cotton farmer in 1924, as forty years before when THE NEWS termed it a hackneyed but none the less effective plan, was crop diversification. Genuine diversification, Schoffelmayer contended, could only come from the determination of the farmer to live at home, giving less acreage to cotton and thereby securing a larger and more dependable cash income from the staple. Interestingly enough, this was the same purpose behind the plan of farm relief adopted by the Federal government during the great depression of the 1930's. The end result of these studies and deliberations was the "More Cotton On Fewer Acres" contests sponsored by THE NEWS in co-operation with agricultural and business leaders.

"The idea behind the contest," Schoffelmayer explained later, "was to reward honest, intelligent effort toward producing the highest yield per acre, the grower in the contest being encouraged to keep complete records of operations, together with their cost. These records were to become the property of THE NEWS, but they were to be analyzed at the end of each year's contest, as they were, by economists of the agricultural college. They were subsequently printed in annual bulletins and widely distributed, not only throughout the entire cotton belt but also abroad in Egypt, India, Brazil, Mexico and to many foreign authorities on the crop."

THE NEWS in the spring of 1924 announced that a grand cash prize of $1,000 was offered for the highest yield of lint cotton grown that year on any five acres of non-irrigated land in the State. Before the time for entry closed, 3,018 farmers in 170 cotton-raising counties had entered. The contest had been endorsed by Henry C. Wallace, Secretary of Agriculture, by officials of the Federal Reserve Bank, Texas Bankers Association, American Cotton Growers Exchange, Texas A. and M. College and its extension service, Texas Farm Bureau Cotton Association and most of the Chambers of Commerce in Texas. Local, county-wide contests were also launched by business men in some fifty counties, so that $60,000 in all were posted as prizes that year.

☆

The first award in THE NEWS' "More Cotton On Fewer Acres" contest was made at a banquet in Dallas at the Baker Hotel in December of 1924. John W. McFarlane of Palestine, Anderson

County, who harvested 5,081 pounds of lint from a five-acre plot, was acclaimed first place winner. Second and third places were won by F. H. Littleton of Vernon, Wilbarger County, and by Philip Noto of Bryan, Brazos County.

McFarlane's yield of ten bales from five acres gave him a net profit of $193.27 per acre. His family exemplified the live-at-home philosophy, making sales of other farm and dairy produce averaging $100 or more a week. The cost of raising his prize-winning cotton had been five cents a pound compared with an average for the State of twelve cents a pound. Cotton sold that year for twenty-three cents a pound. It was noted that five of the six high men in the contest that year had used commercial fertilizer in making their records.

☆

The results of this initial contest stirred great interest throughout the cotton belt.

The winner of the second "More Cotton on Fewer Acres" contest in 1925 was G. Mont Adams of Tyler, Smith County, who produced sixteen bales on his five-acre plot. This not only broke all previous records for production but also upset the generally accepted belief that standard length varieties of cotton would not yield as well as shorter varieties, for his sixteen bales were all of standard 1-1/16 inch staple. His cost of production was five cents a pound.

An important new factor was added to the cotton contest for 1926—that of quality. Whereas East Texans had been winners of the first two contests, a West Texan, F. B. Littleton of Willbarger County, won the grand prize of 1926. But the gross income prize went to Mrs. F. O. Masten of Collingsworth County, also in West Texas, who had raised 5,719 pounds of 1-5/32 inches staple cotton. Smith County, in behalf of East Texas, won the $1,000 community prize on the basis of turning in forty-seven completed crop records. In all 7,416 Texas farmers participated in the contest.

The final contest in 1927 contained another rule which emphasized the main purpose of the series. This stated that no entrant would be eligible for any prize "whose completed crop record does not show that he has raised his living at home, either through the direct use on his farm of home grown feed and food crops or from their sale." The contest committee thus was bound "by the fair requirements of an average farm family as to feed and food for one year." John W. McFarlane, winner of the first contest, was again first prize winner in 1927. M. F. Sulser of Tyler, Smith County, won the $1,000 State-wide prize for upland staple cotton. The gross income prize of $1,000 was won by Will Johnson, a Negro of Smith County. The awards were again made at a dinner given by The News in Dallas. As in former years, attendant ceremonies were broadcast over Station WFAA.

CHAPTER XXI

FACING THE FUTURE

1930–1938

THE STOCK MARKET panic of 1929, sounding the death knell of The New Economic Era less than eight months after Herbert Hoover became President, was to affect profoundly the course of nation and State in the next decade. It was likewise to subject THE NEWS to a host of problems both within the organization and among its "constituency."

There was a certain good fortune, therefore, in the turn in purely corporate affairs which occurred three years earlier—in the same prosperous year of 1926 which was to be used as the measure of longed-for prosperity under the recovery efforts of the administration of Franklin D. Roosevelt. This was the reorganization of the publishing institution, by which the enterprise was better able to weather emergencies that were to arise in the desperate years ahead.

The heirs of Colonel Belo, after the death of C. Lombardi in 1919, were no longer represented directly in the management of the business, although Mrs. Jeannette Belo Peabody remained as a vice president and Ennis Cargill of Houston, a relative by marriage, was added to the directorate. The latter had long been prominent in the printing trades and banking industries of South Texas. All parties came to realize, therefore, that the best interests of the historic corporation would be served by a reorganization, whereby control would vest in those directly engaged in managing the enterprise. Thus on March 10, 1926, it was announced that G. B. Dealey and associates had purchased stock control of THE NEWS.

Salient points in the reorganization were stated as follows:

"A. H. Belo & Company is the oldest publishing house in Texas, dating from 1842, and its newspapers are institutions in the State of Texas and in the Southwest. The management has spent a lifetime in upholding the high ideals of those publications, and the primary purpose of the reorganization is to secure the continued and permanent maintenance of those ideals.

"For this purpose and also to stabilize their investment, a substantial majority of the present stockholders has agreed with the management upon a plan which, in brief, contemplates that the interest of the present stockholders not connected with the management shall be represented hereafter primarily by bonds and preferred stock and that the control of the institution shall vest in G. B. Dealey and associates active in the management, as the holders of all voting stock, a majority of which will be owned by Mr. Dealey. Such an arrangement as this was deemed wise in order to protect the personnel of the business from any fear of a change of management and policy. . . .

"The value of the property in the reorganization has been fixed at $2,725,000. Aiding in the determination of this value were Don C. Seitz, formerly of the New York *World* and now with the *Outlook;* Sam P. Weston, a newspaper engineer of New York, and James W. Brown, publisher of *Editor & Publisher.* Among those active in constructing and forwarding this plan of reorganization . . . are Mr. Ennis Cargill of Houston, related by marriage to and representative of the Belo family; Messrs. Baker, Botts, Parker & Garwood of Houston, his attorneys acting for the Belo family; Mr. Owen D. Young, chairman of the board of the General Electric Company, formerly a resident of Boston and a personal friend and business adviser of the Belo family; George Waverley Briggs, vice president and trust officer of the City National Bank of Dallas, formerly identified with the management of A. H. Belo & Company; R. H. Stewart, chairman of the board, and J. A. Pondrom, president of the City National Bank of Dallas, and Louis Lipsitz, all business advisers of the management, and Locke & Locke of Dallas, who throughout all the negotiations have acted as attorneys of the management."

These same attorneys have continued as counselors to the management in its corporate affairs.

☆

As in previous economic depressions Texas was slower than the more industrialized areas to feel the full effect. At the beginning of the third decade of the century—it was revealed in the Federal Census—the State was fifth in population among American commonwealths, with more than 5,821,000 people. This was an increase of 25 per cent over 1920. Manufacturing, particularly in the extractive industries of lumber from East Texas, sulphur from South Texas and oil and gas from virtually every section of the State, was now the greatest source of wealth, topping the older cattle and cotton industries in yearly value. The larger cities, Houston, Dallas, San Antonio and Fort Worth, were also becoming manufacturing centers of importance. By the same census Houston was disclosed as the largest city in Texas, with Dallas as a close runner-up in second place.

But the most striking revelation in official government figures lay in the fact that petroleum alone, in 1929, had toppled cotton from his throne as the largest single source of wealth in Texas. Oil, as has been seen, had been discovered as early as 1867 in Nacogdoches County. The discovery at Corsicana in 1895 introduced the State, however, into the circle of commercial producers. The strike of gusher proportions at Spindletop, near Beaumont, in 1901 was followed by other major oil discoveries on the Waggener Ranch in Wichita County in 1911, the great Ranger boom after 1917, the Burkburnett pool in 1919 and the opening up of other major pools from the Texas Panhandle to the Gulf in the 1920's. These successive discoveries had lifted the annual recovery of oil in the State from a mere dribble to staggering totals of hundreds of millions of barrels.

The year 1930 was to prove unforgettable in the history of the oil industry and Texas, however, for the unprecedented strike in East Texas. While President Hoover was struggling to offset the worst results of the stock market collapse and Texas farmers and business men were looking toward the Farm Board or some other miracle worker to halt the disastrous drop in cotton prices, a veteran oil prospector by the name of C. M. ("Dad") Joiner fought desperately to keep a rig drilling in Rusk County in the face of unbelievable financial trials. This former member of the Tennessee Legislature, later one of the builders of the new State of Oklahoma, had been interested in Southwestern oil exploration for twenty years. The East Texas area in which "Dad" Joiner was prospecting had been examined by leading geologists in the industry—and condemned as a dry field. The middle-aged wildcatter refused to be halted by the decision of the scientists, however, and in October he was rewarded finally in his discovery well near Overton. This opened up the world's largest oil field, a proven area now fifty-five miles long and four to eight miles wide, which extends into five Texas counties, has thus far yielded more than three-quarters of a billion barrels of oil and is computed to hold three and one-quarter billions more. With its 25,000 producing wells, the East Texas field has contributed heavily to the supremacy of Texas as the largest oil-producing State in the Union.

The emergence of oil as the chief revenue-producing element in Texas life—more than one-fifth of the population is now dependent upon it and more than half of the State's taxes are derived from it—did not reflect itself immediately in the political life of the State. In the year "Dad" Joiner brought in the East Texas field, the State political campaign reflected instead the unsettled aftermath of the Smith-Hoover campaign. Governor Moody was completing his second term, and though he was tempted to offer himself once more, he resisted out of deference to the tradition of no third term, and the field of candidates for Governor was thrown wide open. Eleven patriots offered themselves for the Democratic nomination, among whom were Congressman James Young of Kaufman, former Lieutenant-Governor Barry Miller of Dallas, State Senator Clint Small of Lubbock, Earle B. Mayfield, Mrs. Miriam A. Ferguson and former State Senator Thomas B. Love.

The issue in the forepart of 1930 was loyalty to the Democratic party. Old-line conservative Democrats had captured control of the State Executive Committee, and war was declared on party bolters who had enabled the Republican Hoover to win his victory in the State two years earlier. By a vote of 21 to 9 the State Executive Committee voted to bar from the ballot all candidates who had deserted Smith in 1928. This infuriated the Hoover-crats—as the bolters were termed—and Thomas B. Love took up the cudgel in behalf of the proscribed. Instituting a mandamus suit to require the Secretary of State to certify his name on the ballot, he won complete victory in the Supreme Court of Texas.

But the fight over party loyalty failed to hold the interest of the voters. A feeling of lessened confidence in elected officeholders gained temporary ascendancy; a business man not intimately associated with politics was thought by many to be the answer to the needs of the State. This ideal materialized in the person of Ross S. Sterling of Houston, formerly head of one of the largest oil companies in the State and the successful, appointed chairman of the Texas Highway Commission since 1926.

THE NEWS refused to endorse any candidate during the first stages of the primary campaign, but on July 14, less than two weeks before the election, E. M. (Ted) Dealey, experienced political analyst and member of the editorial staff, summarized his views after an extensive trip over the State. He predicted that sentiment would crystallize rapidly behind Sterling as the candidate with the best chance to defeat the Fergusons. Two days later THE NEWS announced its formal support of Sterling. "This was pivotal in the campaign," Paul Wakefield, political writer who later wrote the history of that campaign, commented. "There is widespread confidence in the disinterestedness and devotion of THE NEWS to the public welfare. This is particularly true in North and East Texas, those sections of the State where the contest was decided." And, as predicted, Sterling won the nomination and election as Governor of Texas. Although Mrs. Ferguson led in the first primary, Sterling reached second place, and in the run-off primary in August defeated the former woman Governor.

☆

Gathering and tabulating returns of elections in Texas proved a troublesome job for newspapers in former years, and THE NEWS was the first newspaper in the State to undertake this task. For the last twenty or more years the collection and tabulation of election returns has been accomplished through co-operative effort on the part of all the newspapers in the State through the Texas Election Bureau, an association incorporated in Texas as a non-profit-making organization, the purpose of which is to collect and to disseminate to newspapers information about elections.

Prior to the organization of the Texas Election Bureau, THE NEWS alone, through its corps of special correspondents in all parts of the State, collected returns and announced the results; for other elections at times other newspapers co-operated with THE NEWS, sharing the work and participating in the fruits of such labor.

Tom Finty, Jr., was in charge of gathering election returns in these pioneering days. From years of observation he had learned that in the majority of elections it was not necessary to count every vote cast in the State to determine who had been successful. To know the results of the voting in a few key counties was to know the result of balloting in the entire State. Thus in reporting elections prior to organization of the Texas Election Bureau, special correspondents in certain key counties were instructed to report the votes counted in those counties at stated intervals. The votes reported from these counties were tabulated and the totals thus obtained indicated to a surprisingly accurate degree the standing of the candidates in the various races for the State as a whole.

In the co-operative effort participated in by more than one newspaper, the State was divided into districts and certain counties were assigned to each newspaper as the territory from which it was expected to gather returns. Each newspaper then gathered returns from its counties, tabulated these returns and transmitted by telegraph the totals thus obtained to THE NEWS, where these various totals were assembled and the returns for the entire State announced. From this co-operative effort grew the Texas Election Bureau, which now has charge of gathering election returns for newspapers and news services in Texas.

☆

But if Governor Sterling was elected without reference to the oil situation or the general business depression, his one term of office was to be vitally affected by these factors. The vast flood of oil from the new East Texas field glutted the world market and the price of oil dropped from a dollar to as low as five cents a barrel. The Legislature of Texas attempted to shut off the suicidal flow by authorizing the Texas Railroad Commission to prorate production. This initial regulatory measure was defective and injunctions rendered it powerless. At the depths of the oil disaster, Governor Sterling on August 17, 1931, declared martial law in the oil field and, backed by State militia, personally curtailed production. When this control was relaxed, more orderly measures of proration through the Texas Railroad Commission were ready to take effect—by which means the State subsequently has been able to aid in the restoration of order and stability in the industry.

Increasing economic distress was felt in Texas in 1932, and, sharing the growing unrest of the country as a whole, the electorate returned the Fergusons to power after a single term by Governor Sterling. Another business man professing little knowledge of the ways of politics, President Hoover, was turned out in similar fashion that year. Texans were greatly interested in the choice of a Democratic candidate for President, all the more so since the times seemed ripe for a Democratic victory. A favorite son, Speaker John N. Garner of the House of Representatives, easily captured the Texas delegation to the national convention at Chicago. In combination with spokesmen of the Democracy at California, the Texans were able through a trade to secure the vice presidency for Garner by supporting Franklin D. Roosevelt for the first place on the ticket. In view of the subsequent course of American history, and the acute suffering among conservatives of all parties over the direction which President Roosevelt gave to his New Deal, it is perhaps amusing to recall that Republican strategists in 1932 hoped to re-elect Hoover on the issue of Garner's supposed "radicalism."

Texas passed into the darkest hours of the great depression, along with the nation, in the forepart of 1933. The banking crisis reached its apex at the very hour President Roosevelt took office. With a nation-wide paralysis of the banking system and untold misery and suffering throughout the land, the new President, as Cleveland forty years before, electrified the nation by his inaugural appeal; again it was the fear of fear that must be mastered, and again a nation took renewed hope under a vigorous and unified leadership. THE NEWS, and Texans generally, rallied to the banner of the nation's leader. Throughout the crucial phase of the emergency, the paper gave unquestioned support to the measures for its relief. Not until the crisis passed and until the New Deal veered, in the opinion of the newspaper, from emergency measures for recovery to more debatable questions of reform, did THE NEWS relax its editorial adherence to Roosevelt. While supporting many of the plans and programs of the Roosevelt Administration, THE NEWS subsequently felt it necessary to differ radically with Washington on specific policies, particularly opposing President Roosevelt's proposal to enlarge and reorganize the United States Supreme Court.

After 1934 the clouds on the economic horizon began to lift somewhat. Whether it was due to the Bankhead restriction act, to the devaluation of the dollar or to any other cause or causes, the price of cotton doubled in the first year of the Roosevelt Administration. Oil and other commodities improved in price. Texas was climbing out of the depression faster than in any previous period of economic distress. With its fellow-citizens, THE NEWS, therefore, felt that Texas was able to carry out a memorable celebration of its first hundred years of freedom in 1936.

The Texas Centennial had been foreshadowed as early as the first year of THE NEWS' existence in Dallas. Veterans of the Battle of San Jacinto met in Dallas for one of their last reunions, the semi-centennial celebration of April 21, 1886. They enjoined posterity to remember that date. Mercurial Governor Hogg in 1902 had suggested that plans be made well in advance and the movement had received some impetus before the World War. It was not, however, until 1923, at a convention of the Advertising Clubs of Texas at Corsicana, that the project took tangible form. There the late Theodore H. Price of New York, editor of *Commerce & Finance,* advocated a world's fair to celebrate Texas' century of freedom. By unanimous vote, the 4,000 delegates decided to lay the proposal before the people of Texas. By 1924 the State government had become interested, following the work of the special survey committee of the advertising clubs, which was headed by Lowry Martin of Corsicana. Governor Pat M. Neff then created the first State-wide centennial body, a group of 100 citizens of whom Cato Sells of Fort Worth was chairman. Later Sells resigned, and Jesse Jones of Houston became its chairman.

Throughout succeeding years, THE NEWS energetically cooperated with this committee of 100 in keeping the Centennial idea alive. The Legislature was persuaded in 1931 to give official standing to the Centennial Commission, and in 1932 an amendment to the State Constitution was submitted to the voters. This was adopted, thereby authorizing a Centennial celebration and instructing the Legislature to appropriate funds for it by the issuance and sale of necessary bonds. Two years later plans had matured to the point where the Legislature drew up regulations for the selection of the site for the Texas Centennial Central Exposition. The location was put up at public auction; by decree of the Legislature "the central exposition and principal celebration will be in that city or community that offers . . . the largest financial inducement and support thereof."

Dallasites now prepared their bid. The majority of business and civic leaders concurred in the view of THE NEWS that Dallas must make every honorable effort to secure this designation. As a result, the city's bid, opened by the Texas Centennial Commission at Austin on September 9, 1934, topped the best that the two other chief contenders, Houston and San Antonio, would offer. The State Fair of Texas, now having a valuation of $4,000,000 in grounds and structures, was offered as the location. Dallas in addition pledged $5,500,000 in cash, of which $3,500,000 was to be raised by municipal bond issue and the remainder by private subscription through the sale of exposition corporation bonds. The Commission, which was headed by Cullen F. Thomas of Dallas, promptly awarded the honor to the highest bidder.

Early in 1935 the Legislature appropriated $3,000,000 as the State's part in the celebration of a century of independence. It was decided, however, that a series of local festivals would be held in various parts of the State, and only half of this sum would be spent at the central exposition at Dallas. Thus, approximately $1,000,000 was set aside for the erection of the State of Texas building or Hall of State, the chief contribution to the exposition at Dallas by the State government. An advertising and publicity fund of $500,000 was set up to foster the exposition and all other celebrations. The Federal government joined Texans by appropriating $3,000,000, about half of which was pledged to the Dallas exposition. Private exhibitors augmented the capital outlay by several millions of dollars, so that when the big show opened on June 6, 1936, it was generally referred to as a $25,000,000 exposition.

The Texas Centennial Central Exposition, held during the six months of summer and early fall, attracted more than 6,000,000 visitors, chief among whom were President Franklin D. Roosevelt and Vice President John N. Garner. It was the culmination of a mighty, State-wide birthday party which began in Gonzales, site of the first battle of the Texan war for independence, continued through memorable celebrations at the Alamo in San Antonio and at the San Jacinto battlegrounds near Houston and concluded in Dallas. A frontier exposition emphasizing the old and the new West, with a generous portion of Broadway entertainment in the form of an open-air supper club, ran concurrently in Fort Worth. While the exposition at Dallas had its own amusement features, it was primarily an educational and patriotic celebration designed to commemorate the serious history and development of the State. In its dramatic outdoor spectacle, the Cavalcade of Texas, in its great historical museum in the State of Texas Building, and in a myriad of other public and commercial displays it portrayed this engrossing story. James V. Allred was Governor at the time.

As might have been expected, THE NEWS and its associated

E. M. (TED) DEALEY, VICE PRESIDENT
[1915–]

J. M. MORONEY, SECRETARY AND TREASURER
[1934–]

G. B. DEALEY, PRESIDENT

[1874-   ]

publications, as well as RADIO STATION WFAA, gave unstinted support to the Centennial celebration in news and editorial columns and on the air, and by generous purchase of the bonds of the corporation. The Centennial more than lived up to its chartered purpose of being a non-profit association; it became, in fact, a costly undertaking with a large financial loss chalked up at the conclusion. The Centennial attracted tens of thousands of visitors, many of them important citizens of the world, to Dallas and to Texas. They came from all parts of the United States and many foreign countries. For most of them Texas was discovered personally for the first time. THE NEWS, along with virtually all other backers, felt richly rewarded. Pride in the achievements of a century had called for as magnificent an observance of the occasion as the people of Texas could afford. It was a lavish birthday party, carried out in the open-hearted spirit of old-time Texan hospitality; the hosts, naturally, never stopped to consider the returns in dollars and cents.

Since 1926 THE NEWS has made its most significant gains, both as a journalistic institution and as a business property—this, in spite of the intervention of the severest depression in American history. Executive direction has continued under G. B. Dealey, who, on October 12, 1937, began his sixty-fourth year of continuous service with THE NEWS.

During the 1920's Walter A. Dealey accepted increasing responsibility in the direction of THE NEWS. Familiar with all phases of the business but particularly well schooled in the mechanics of publishing, he rendered invaluable assistance as second in command to his father. As has been pointed out, the development of the pioneering RADIO STATION WFAA resulted primarily from his foresight and constant supervision. His interest extended beyond the problems of newspaper making and distribution to that of salesmanship, and his energies contributed greatly toward the progress of the business during the years immediately succeeding the reorganization of 1926. As the depression of the early 1930's descended on Texas his experience and counsel were of incalculable aid to a harassed management. It was more than a tragic personal loss, therefore, when he was stricken fatally in 1934 at the very moment when THE NEWS had begun to emerge from its greatest trial, when the economic clouds were beginning to clear on the horizon ahead.

The death of Walter A. Dealey threw an unexpected burden in the management of THE NEWS upon his younger brother, E. M. (Ted) Dealey. A member of THE NEWS staff since 1915, Ted Dealey had received a thorough training in various departments, but his longest service had been in the news-gathering and editorial ends. As a staff correspondent he had acquired long and direct knowledge of the various economic, social and political phases of contemporary life in the Southwest. As editor of the Sunday Magazine of THE NEWS, inaugurated in 1922, he rapidly built this into one of the most significant depositories of historical and literary material in Texas, a popular and highly diverting weekly chronicle but one that had lasting importance in the cultural development of the State. He also found time to write independently, becoming one of the best-known writers of short stories and magazine articles in the Southwest. He was named assistant to the publisher in 1928. Called to the vice presidency of THE NEWS on his brother's death, Ted Dealey brought the same enthusiasm and energy to the expanded range of publishing problems that he had given to the purely editorial. It is significant that, as in the case of all his predecessors in the executive direction of THE NEWS, he holds the conviction that a newspaper must be first of all a news-gathering agency. Many of the important journalistic innovations and advances which have carried THE NEWS to new heights in recent years have owed much to his initiative.

Another important addition to the executive staff after 1934 has been the secretary and treasurer of the company, J. M. Moroney, member of a Dallas family long prominent in the mercantile world and himself an expert in the field of finance. Chief among his supervisory duties is assistance to the staff of STATION WFAA which, under the general managership of Martin B. Campbell

since 1932, has become one of the most important parts of THE
NEWS as well as an indispensable adjunct of popular education
and entertainment in the Southwest.

Strong editorial leadership has distinguished THE NEWS from
its earliest days. Since the resignation of Donaldson C. Jenkins,
last business associate of Willard Richardson, in 1901, the general
direction of editorial policy has, in fact, been chiefly answerable
to G. B. Dealey. The publisher's direct and constant concern with
this department has given the policy of the paper an unusual degree of consistency and steadfastness of purpose. But, charged with
immediate responsibility, have been several chief editors who
maintained this tradition. After the death of Luther Clark in
1920, Alonzo Wasson, former Washington correspondent of THE
NEWS and one of the ablest political analysts in the country, became chief editorial writer. He enjoyed the aid and counsel of the
late Tom Finty, Jr., who, although identified after 1914 with THE
DALLAS JOURNAL as its editor-in-chief, was equally available to
the parent publication.

James Quayle Dealey, brother of the publisher and one of the
nation's notable educators and social scientists, next succeeded to
the editorship of THE NEWS in 1929 when Alonzo Wasson removed to Austin to continue as a political commentator for THE
NEWS. A member of THE NEWS' organization at Galveston while
a youth, James Q. Dealey left to continue his education in the
East and soon began his long career in the academic world. Although he served for one year as a member of the first faculty of
what in later years became the North Texas State Teachers' College at Denton and subsequently was an instructor in certain other
institutions, his teaching career was identified principally with
Brown University. There his career extended over thirty-five
years, during which period he was head of the department of
political and social science for more than a quarter of a century.
As director of editorial policy, James Q. Dealey brought an unusually ripe and experienced viewpoint to the host of problems,
local, State, national and international, which beset America after
1929. His death, early in 1937, was a severe blow to the institution.

Succeeding him is J. J. Taylor, a member of the editorial staff since 1904, State Press editor since 1908 and one of the best-known journalists in the Southwest. The management at the same time designated William B. Ruggles, formerly sports editor of both THE NEWS at Galveston and THE NEWS at Dallas and an editorial writer since 1925, as associate editor-in-chief. A factor of great strength in the editorial department of THE NEWS is John F. Knott, a cartoonist of international repute, whose drawings have been a daily feature of the newspaper since 1914.

Modern journalism in Texas is subject to a highly complicated field of statutory law involving libel. Since the start of THE DALLAS NEWS in 1885, it has had but two attorneys representing it in this important matter, the late Col. W. L. Crawford and his successor, J. C. Muse, Sr., the recognized authority on the subject in Texas.

Direction of the news department today stems chiefly from the appointment in 1925 of John E. King as managing editor. Joining THE NEWS in 1911 at Galveston, he had served a well-rounded apprenticeship under older heads when he was called upon to lead in a program of expansion. He succeeded such outstanding journalists as Frank A. Briggs and George McQuaid, who served for relatively short periods as managing editor, following the death of D. Prescott Toomey in 1919.

Closely allied to THE NEWS is THE DALLAS (Evening) JOURNAL, which has been in existence since April 1, 1914. Its managing editor is Harry C. Withers, a veteran of THE NEWS organization and one of the best-known journalists of the State. The editor of THE JOURNAL is Lynn W. Landrum, an unusually forceful and widely read writer.

THE SEMI-WEEKLY FARM NEWS, largest publication of its kind in Texas, has been edited since 1894 by DeWitt McMurray. This publication, which continues in unbroken line from the original NEWS issued in Galveston first in 1842, has long carried to another large audience most of the news and features which are contained in the daily issues. In addition it contains a number of features specially adapted to its reading circles.

The second oldest unit of THE NEWS is THE TEXAS ALMANAC AND STATE INDUSTRIAL GUIDE, first published in 1857 at Galveston. It was issued annually from 1857 until 1861, and after the hiatus caused by the Civil War, was published from 1867 until 1873. It was revived at Dallas in 1904; issues were brought out for 1910, 1911, 1912 and 1914, when publication ceased on account of the World War. Tom Finty, Jr., and Frank A. Briggs were editors during those years. The present series of THE TEXAS ALMANAC dates from 1925 and has been continuously under the editorship of Stuart McGregor.

Time took a heavy toll in THE NEWS within less than twelve months, beginning with the death of James Quayle Dealey in 1937. E. B. Doran, one of the directing forces in the institution for more than forty years, died on January 1, 1938. Business manager in the last few years of active service, he had spent the greater part of his career, however, on the editorial side. First as city editor, then news editor of THE DALLAS NEWS, and later as managing editor of THE DALLAS JOURNAL from its founding in 1914, he made a lasting impression on journalism in the Southwest. In 1918 he was named director of news and telegraph for all publications, a post he held until his appointment as business manager in 1929.

The death of John F. Lubben at Dallas on January 30, 1938, terminated another notable career of service in the executive family. The son of a sea captain, Henry G. Lubben, and Ludovica Wessels, he was born in Galveston January 9, 1866. He entered the employ of THE NEWS on August 20, 1881, and subsequently held every desk in the Galveston office. On September 1, 1888, he was named business manager of the Galveston end of the business and, on the death of Thomas W. Dealey in 1906, became the second secretary and treasurer of the corporation. On the sale of THE

GALVESTON NEWS in 1923, John F. Lubben moved to Dallas to continue as secretary and treasurer and a member of the board of directors until his death.

☆

Today, as in the ninety-six years of its past, THE NEWS faces the future with the confidence born of achievement. Its record of pioneering in journalistic advances has been traced in these pages —a record of mechanical and technical advances in all spheres of publishing. Recognition of its part in the journalism of America has come in innumerable ways since before the Civil War. One of the strongest tributes to the ideals and policies of the institution was paid by Adolph S. Ochs, rehabilitator of the present-day New York *Times*. Speaking at Houston in 1924 at a dinner in his honor, the publisher said that when he bought *The Times* in 1895, he was determined to keep its columns as free of "the vulgar, the inane and the sensational" as was humanly possible. "I received my ideas and ideals from THE GALVESTON DAILY NEWS and THE DALLAS MORNING NEWS," he continued. "I had before me the beautiful example of those newspapers—the driving inspiration for me in those days."

In 1935 THE DALLAS NEWS was awarded a medal of honor for distinguished service in journalism by the School of Journalism of the University of Missouri. The social viewpoint of the institution both in its editorial and business departments was singled out in the citation in support of the belief that THE NEWS has made "an outstanding contribution in its area." But in the following sentence from the same award is to be found one of the more succinct histories of the institution: "In the midst of conflict both political and commercial, this newspaper has stood not to present prejudice, but to report and explain news sincerely and accurately."

As THE NEWS sails ahead into its second century, its great asset continues to be something more indestructible than matter— for all of its physical equipment of brick and steel and intricate machines, its hundreds of thousands of readers. That asset is, rather, the spirit which has animated a great company of men and women—literally, tens of thousands—since 1842. At first there were only Bangs and his brother-in-law, soon joined by Richardson and company. Under the regime of Colonel Belo the company became a brigade. Today, a personnel of some 800, inspired by a morale which is perhaps unique in American journalism, gives modern expression to the same ideas and ideals.

The most perfect expression of this spirit in one person is the man who himself is a link with the earliest days of the organization and who for more than half a century has been the greatest single influence in the destiny of the institution—G. B. Dealey. THE DALLAS MORNING NEWS celebrated its fiftieth anniversary with the issuance of a Golden Jubilee edition on October 1, 1935. At the conclusion of a first-page letter to the readers and patrons of THE NEWS, he said:

"With its predecessor on the Gulf, for more than ninety years, THE DALLAS MORNING NEWS has labored for the material and cultural development of the whole State. Its heart is a Texas heart, and its great desire is that Texas be known not only as the largest, but also as the finest State in the Union, a State renowned for its moral standards as well as for the happiness and contentment of its people.

"Always THE NEWS had aimed to be known primarily as a medium for gathering and disseminating reliable information. But beyond that primary duty, it has had further duties. From its beginning nearly a century ago it has sought to make known to its people the vastness of the natural resources left for their use by the Creator, only a small fraction of which has even yet been brought into use.

"It has spent time, money and effort in printing matter to inculcate a desire for attractiveness and beauty of every kind in its urban centers and its countryside. It has desired to be the champion of all kinds of wholesome education and to develop the finer things of life. Consistently it has been the champion of wholesome religion, no matter what the creed. All this has been 'a day's work,' multiplied by the number of days of a half century. The results

have come from the efforts of the entire NEWS staff, not alone
from the best efforts of those whose work and writings gained
reputation and recognition, but also from those whose compensation, beyond their salary, was the inward satisfaction of duty well
done and the pride of accomplishment for their newspaper, their
city and their State. . . .

"A half century of effort and labor of the management ended
last night. Today the curtain rises on a new day, another epoch of
service on the part of those who have the honor of comprising 'the
oldest business institution in Texas.' THE NEWS has done its best.
It has tried to serve faithfully and honestly. If its readers and
patrons can conscientiously say, 'Well done, thou good and faithful
servant,' its managers will feel amply rewarded and will confidently
turn their eyes to the rising sun."

SALE OF *THE EVENING JOURNAL*

Since this history was written and the matter in type,
ready for printing, negotiations for the purchase of *The
Evening Journal* were instituted. These negotiations culminated on June 20, 1938. Messrs. Karl Hoblitzelle and Alfred
O. Andersson, of Dallas, purchased *The (Evening) Journal*
and *The (Evening) Dallas Dispatch*. They formed a new
corporation to print a six-day-a-week afternoon newspaper
to be called *The Dispatch-Journal*. The last issues of *The
Journal* and of *The Dispatch* were on June 30, and the new
paper appeared on July 1, 1938.

S. H. A.

APPENDIX

Personnel of THE DALLAS NEWS and associated enterprises as of May 1, 1938, showing continuous employment with the company since:

1874	Dealey, G. B.—President
1885	Allen, Arthur M.—Mechanical Board
1886	Blake, Charles H.
1889	Seay, Charles M.—Mechanical Board
1891	Page, Warren A.
1892	Benners, W. H.—Assistant to Publisher
	Davis, William M.
	McMurray, DeWitt—Editor, Semi-Weekly Farm News
1896	Richmond, Frank B.
1897	Maynard, William L., Sr.—Assistant Foreman, Mailing Room
	Porter, Thomas W.—Foreman, Mailing Room
1898	Thornton, William M.—Head of Austin News Bureau
1900	Hamilton, L. E.
	Scott, H. C.—Superintendent of Transportation
1901	Hogg, Jennie
1902	Ward, Harold—Mechanical Board
1904	Deputy, Leven T.—Mechanical Superintendent
	Taylor, J. J.—Editor-in-Chief
	Thomas, Walter K.
	Withers, Harry C.—Managing Editor, The Journal
1905	Stephenson, Harvey R.
	Wasson, Alonzo—Special Staff Correspondent at Austin
1906	Goodwin, Mark L.—Washington Correspondent
	Ward, K. A.—Assistant Circulation Manager
1908	Moxley, Sam E., Sr.—Store Keeper
	Rheinlander, George H.—Day Foreman, Ad Room
1909	Norcom, Miles
	Rollins, Sam W.
1910	King, John E.—Managing Editor, The News
	Leggett, H. W.—Night Dispatcher, Circulation Dept.
1911	Hatton, E. W.—Day Assistant Foreman, Stereotype Dept.
	Knott, John F.—Cartoonist of The News
	Reed, Sherman C.—Assistant Circulation Manager
1912	Brown, Frank B.—Head of Stencil Department
	Hall, Edward K.

311

1913 Guy, Harry D.—Director of National Advertising
      Hill, Cecil O.—Night Assistant Foreman, Composing Room
      McMurray, G. Ray—Assistant Editor, Semi-Weekly Farm
            News
      Murray, R. J.—Cotton Exchange Special Correspondent
      Richardson, Will T.
      Shivers, Boykin
      Thomason, J. Leroy
      Weever, A. C.

1914 Brunts, Floyd L.
      Cherry, Robt. L.
      Greer, Hilton R.—Literary Editor, The Journal
      Hart, Sterling M.
      Reilly, Jos. H.
      Truax, Wm. W.—City Editor, The Journal

1915 Dealey, Edward M. (Ted)—Vice President
      Ponder, W. Wayne

1916 Bagwell, Oscar L.
      Crannell, K. B.
      Fox, Frank A.—Foreman, Press Room
      Hatchett, W. S.
      Hornaday, Walter C.—Political writer, The News
      Truly, J. Wilmer

1917 Buckner, Ruth
      Daniell, T. C.—Manager, Employees' Lunch Room
      Ely, Bess
      Fair, Nathan
      French, J. S.—Markets Editor, The News
      Jones, Mildred A.
      Schoffelmayer, Victor H.—Agricultural Editor, The News
      Tanner, Frank B.

1918 Bedell, Joe—Foreman, Stereotype Dept.
      Buckner, G. C.
      McAdams, Mrs. Lee J.
      Morris, E. H.
      Patton, Jack I.—Cartoonist of The Journal
      Pirtle, Mrs. Mattie C.
      Railey, Jas. R.—Zone Manager, City Circulation Dept.
      Travis, John C.
      Walker, Earley

1919 Adams, O. G.
      Dathe, Walter W.
      Davis, Victor E.—Radio Editor
      Ely, Vera C.
      Gentry, P. M.—Assistant Manager, Accounting Dept.
      Gillham, Ralph R.
      Gullette, Frank E.—Foreman, Power Department

1919 Hicks, Louis H.
Horn, W. F.
McClellan, W. J.
Millis, Tom C.
North, Henry B.
Prasifka, Charles
Renfro, Leland H.—Manager, Automotive Advertising Dept.
Swepston, Hershel C.—Chief of Telephone Operations
Taggart, James E.—Manager, Accounting Dept.
Whitehead, Benjamin V.
Wilson, W. H.—Traveling Representative, Circulation Dept.
Young, Leona D.

1920 Bateman, Talbot O.—Chief of Art Department
Crosby, A. B.
Cumming, E. R.—Assistant Day Foreman, Composing Room
Daniel, Chas. A.
Doyle, Patrick
Kelly, Walter L.—Cashier
Moxley, Wm. C.
Taylor, Noden W.—Assistant Director, National Advertising
Tompkins, Mrs. Mary Toomey
Trible, Mrs. Betty
Ward, Wm. Allen—Editor, Oak Cliff Journal

1921 Anderson, Cyrus C.
Buchanan, R. M.—Business Manager
Cason, Chas. S.
Colhoun, Adams—Office Manager, Radio Station WFAA
Elder, Arthur B.
Fowlkes, M. D.
Landrum, Lynn W.—Editor, The Journal
Lowry, Walter C.
Milliorn, J. H.
Murphy, Ben
Rosenfield, Henry—Assistant Day Foreman, Press Room
Smith, David W.—Assistant Director, Local Advertising
Treuer, Jack B.
Utley, Olga E.—Secretary to the President
Wimmer, Arthur L.—Telegraph Editor, The News

1922 Barrett, Theodore H.—City Editor, The News
Black, Chas. J.
Booth, L. E.
Campbell, Harvey M.
Carter, Leon
Davis, W. R.
Griffing, Aaron B.
Hicks, Ellis
McBeth, Arch R.

1922   McKey, C. D.
        Phillips, Mrs. Pauline—Supervisor, Classified Adv. Telephone
            Operations
        Smith, Herbert W.—Promotion Manager
        Toomey, Anna Prescott—Head of Adv. Copy and Art Dept.
        Trott, Arthur L.—Night Foreman, Ad Room •
1923   Caulk, Walter
        Ely, Julia Kate
        Fitzgerald, A. N.
        Geiser, George B.
        Haydon, Mrs. Dorothy
        Hopp, Anthony F.
        Howser, E. L.
        Kranebell, Mrs. Edith N.
        Laird, Thompson
        Luter, Elmer G.—Automobile Editor
        McGregor, Stuart M.—Editor, The Texas Almanac, and Staff
            Economist of The News
        McGinnis, John H.—Literary Editor, The News
        Morris, Harold M.
        Mosig, Carl—Head of Fort Worth News Bureau
        Ormsbee, Forrest C.
        Palmer, James M.
        Whitener, Stephen J.
        Willetts, Joseph F.—Assistant Managing Editor, The News
1924   Baldwin, Katherine
        Bearden, Avery
        Bearden, Mrs. Leta
        Cannon, P. H.
        Galloway, H. D.
        Hamlet, C. B.
        Humphrey, Frank H.
        Hunter, Mrs. Marion
        Jackson, Georgia A.
        Marable, Mrs. Verna
        Morrow, W. F.
        Moxley, I. A.
        Murphy, Walter W.—Advertising Manager, Semi-Weekly
            Farm News
        Peters, H. L.
        Rosenfield, John, Jr.—Drama, Art and Amusements Editor
        Sanders, Pete
        Vaughan, A. P.—Manager, Classified Advertising Dept.
1925   Acheson, Sam H.—Editorial Writer
        Anderson, Donald C.
        Davis, Binnie S.
        Echkenfels, Herman E.
        Estes, Jack—Circulation Manager

1925 Fenley, Relf N.
   Goebel, Evelyn
   Green, Mrs. Marian Snyder—Head of Biographical Dept.
   Josch, Martin—Assistant Day Foreman, Press Room
   Koegl, Max
   Lovell, Raymond
   Lunsford, Robert—Assistant City Editor, The News
   Maxwell, W. Kirk—Foreman, Composing Room
   Moore, James A.—Assistant Day Foreman, Stereotype Dept.
   Preston, J. W.—Telegraph Editor, The News
   Robinson, W. L.
1926 Alexander, Geo. A.—Zone Manager, City Circulation Dept.
   Armstrong, Mrs. Blanche
   Bishop, Barry Lee
   Braley, Henry
   Jones, Jno. Grover
   Leonard, Frank S.
   Lynch, Ola
   Maynard, Wm. L., Jr.
   Moxley, Sam E., Jr.
   Peters, Claud M.
   Rainwater, Ollie
   Ruggles, William B.—Associate Editor in Chief
   Russell, Mrs. Genevieve
   Smith, J. E.
   Wilson, Earle A.
1927 Berueffy, Oscar H.
   Black, Lee—Traveling Representative, Circulation Dept.
   Collins, Thelma
   Conkle, William H.—Day Foreman, Mailing Room
   Eastus, Harry T.—Night Foreman, Mailing Room
   Fee, J. E.—Manager, Waco News Bureau
   Hendrix, Homer R.
   Hester, Fred L.
   Johnston, Lowell W.
   Moses, Frank
   Mosteller, Clyde S.
   Murray, Joe J.—Assistant City Editor, The Journal
   Pressly, W. A.
   Shelby, J. E.
   Simmons, Alfred Coy
   Simmons, Walter Raymond
   Sorrels, Charlie
   Thomas, Alvin
   Turns, Annie
   Williams, Nev. H.
   Woods, Ervin
1928 Akers, F. M.

1928   Biondi, Mathew
Butters, Edwin B.—Head Machinist, Composing Room
Collins, Raymond—Technical Supervisor, Radio Station
    WFAA
Crump, Richard L.
Davis, Jno. A.
DuPre, Flint—Sports Editor, The Journal
Ford, L. J. (Jack)
Haughton, B. H.—Head Make-Up, The Journal
Hodges, E. H.
Lindberg, Dorothy
Lubben, Joe A.
Moore, Earl B.—Chief Photographer
Morrow, Hal M.
Newland, Otto H.
O'Connell, Edwin—City Circulation Manager
Owens, E. Harry—Merchandise Manager, National Adv.
    Dept.
Owens, Marguerite
Sharp, R. W.—Assistant Night Foreman, Press Room
White, Geo. W.—Sports Editor, The News
Wilson, W. B.

1929   Attebery, J. N.
Baldwin, Mrs. Hazel L.
Barnes, Paul C.—Chief Plant Engineer, Radio Station WFAA
Blasingame, Mrs. Mildred
Brice, Marguerite
Conkle, Roy L.
DeHay, Ted P.
Duckworth, Allen—Telegraph Editor, The Journal
Echols, Leslie—Street Circulator
Ellis, W. C.—Production Manager, Radio Station WFAA
Fussell, Mrs. Maurine Osburn
Hand, Kenneth N.
Hicks, Jesse C.
Jones, Mrs. Jennye V.
Knight, Geo. H.
Petersen, Mrs. Marie
Price, Thomas A.—State Editor, The Journal
Reynolds, John W.
Reynolds, George L.
White, Guy B.
Whitley, D. P.

1930   Brewer, J. Leonard
Cooper, Mrs. Lila Lindhe
Daniels, L. Lee, Jr.
Fair, Burnett
Fryman, Mrs. Clotilde

1930 Harris, Claxton A.
     Latimer, W. R.
     McClanahan, William J.
     Overstreet, Lula
     Phipps, William E.
     Riddell, El Jene C.
     Sanderson, J. W.
     Stewart, Mrs. Edith M.
     Williamson, Mrs. Bessie F.
     Wilson, Mary Alice—Head of Society Desk, News and Journal
     Winsett, M. A.

1931 Barnes, Carlton
     Crull, Elgin E.
     Dent, Ione
     Dowell, J. W.—Traveling Representative, Circulation Dept.
     Ely, Lewis
     Fenley, George W.
     Gilmore, Robert O.
     Lynch, Robert E., Jr.
     Odum, M. D.—Traveling Representative, Circulation Dept.
     Pemberton, Lewis E.
     Ranson, Mrs. Nancy Richey
     Reese, Billie T.
     Reynolds, Lloyd R.
     Simmons, Thomas J.—State Editor, The News
     Streater, Aubrey M.
     Watkins, W. L.—Zone Manager, City Circulation Dept.
     Young, Charles Edward

1932 Boyce, Mrs. Irene W.
     Campbell, Martin B.—General Manager, Radio Station WFAA
     Cleghorn, C. A.
     Ellis, Bonnie L.
     Hatch, Homer R.
     Hemley, John
     Hull, W. L.
     Johnson, Charles W.
     Katz, Sol—Zone Manager, City Circulation Dept.
     Keese, Alexander C.—Region Sales Manager, Radio Station WFAA
     Lloyd, Henry B.
     Phares, Don H.
     Raymey, Talmage—Zone Manager, City Circulation Dept.

1933 Bass, Louise
     Boyce, Velma
     Burleson, Roosevelt
     Burton, Chas. A.
     Chambers, C. R.

1933 Chenault, Thomas E., Jr.
      Crofford, George L., Jr.—Advertising Manager, Oak Cliff
            Journal
      Crotty, Willard
      Donosky, Myer M.—Assistant Secretary and Treasurer
      Doyle, Mildred K.
      Eastland, Willie
      Emerson, Mrs. Dorothy G.
      Finklea, Robert W.
      Fomby, Harold J.
      Foree, Kenneth, Jr.—Night City Editor, The News
      Foy, Raymond W.—Director, Local Advertising
      Gard, Wayne—Editorial Writer
      Green, Mrs. Gertrude
      Hudson, L. Banks—Zone Manager, City Circulation Dept.
      Jones, Jacqueline
      Jones, Robert
      Kirby, R. M.
      LeBlanc, Hilda T.
      Lockart, James E., Jr.
      Lowry, R. V.—Traveling Representative, Circulation Dept.
      Matthews, H. P.—Traveling Representative, Circulation Dept.
      Miller, R. K. (Joe)
      Morgan, E. C.
      Morris, H. H.
      Morrow, J. Edward
      Nisbet, Fairfax—Amusements Editor, The Journal
      Posey, Chas. I.
      Saunders, Hazel
      Scott, Mrs. Elizabeth King—Food Editor, News and Journal
      Scott, Isabel
      Sheppard, Sterling T.
      Snodgrass, Walter W.
      Swain, Jack C.
      Wallis, Eugene C.—Business News Editor
      Ward, Alex W.
      Wicker, L. J.
      Wilson, Charles M.
1934 Ard, Wilbur—Staff Conductor, Radio Station WFAA
      Bonta, Ray W.
      Brown, Olin S.
      Davis, James E.
      Engle, Parke F.
      Gaddis, Jack C.
      Gross, Irvin—Merchandise Manager, Radio Station WFAA
      Hall, Jay—Oil Editor, The News
      Hawpe, George A.—Assistant Building Superintendent
      Hill, Robert S.

1934   Hiser, O. D.
      Howard, Gerlad M.
      Johnson, Mrs. Lucille
      Kennedy, John S.
      Merritt, William S.
      Moffett, Ruth
      Monson, Clifford
      Moon, John R.
      Moroney, James M.—Secretary and Treasurer
      Morris, Otto J.
      Moses, Harry B.
      Neff, Raymond L.
      Newman, Raymond C.
      Page, Thomas W.
      Rice, Jack B.
      Robertson, Donald L.
      Trantham, Ira
      Vance, Julia
      Wofford, Lester

1935   Adams, Hal A.
      Batts, Aubrey C.
      Bogan, Allen B.
      Boylan, Elaine—Librarian
      Bradfield, James R.
      Bridges, Henry D.
      Brown, Gordon C.
      Burden, Hubert L.
      Burdette, Houston S.
      Burleson, Vernell
      Duncan, George H.
      Fudge, Arthur S.
      Hart, Hammond P.
      Hill, Dr. Robert T.—Special Writer
      Holcomb, Elbert C.
      Johnson, Herod
      Jones, Albert M.
      Keedy, Carlton
      Kirby, Eugene
      Lanham, Raymond
      Lewis, Kay
      McRee, Charles A.
      Moore, Thomas W., Jr.
      Nimmons, Ralph W.—Program Director, Radio Station
          WFAA
      Odom, Emmett W.
      Parks, Joe E.
      Peterson, D. A.
      Ponder, Mrs. Dorothy C.

1935 Robbins, Hugh—Building Superintendent
   Ruth, Mrs. Selma
   Sable, Donald E.
   Snell, Mrs. Jeannette
   Stanglin, Charlie W.
   Starr, Sayde Frances
   Stewart, Mrs. Pearl
   Suter, Allen K.
   Tucker, Elizabeth
   Vickers, Mrs. Bernice
   West, Richard—Assistant Agricultural Editor, The News
   Wilkinson, Mrs. Hazel
1936 Armentrout, Charles D.
   Bartley, James O.
   Bates, Byron A.
   Beckman, John B.
   Bedell, Ross
   Boyd, Charles H.
   Bradberry, Jesse C.
   Brawner, John B.
   Burks, Robert I.
   Buxton, Coburn A.
   Castleman, James W.
   Clark, Milo E.
   Connor, Thomas V.
   Cooley, Thornton
   Crofts, Mrs. Mary Elizabeth
   Crume, Paul
   Cunningham, Mrs. Alma
   Decherd, Ben
   DeLoach, James W.
   Doyle, James E.
   Dreesen, Donald S.
   Duncan, Dawson
   Eastland, Orange
   Echols, John S.
   Emery, E. W.
   Epperson, Jack L.
   Esry, Walter C.—Foreman, Job Department
   Fine, Earl M.
   Fish, Bennie L.
   Floyd, Glen L.
   Galm, Albert
   Georgs, Herman T.
   Greely, Joseph A.
   Hamilton, Jack
   Hartzell, Cecil Hale
   Hayes, Robert M.—Manager, East Texas News Bureau

1936   Hester, Mrs. Evelyn
Horn, Gladys
Johnson, Roy A.
Jones, John O.
Jones, Walter R.
Kelly, Sidney S.
Kuehn, Arthur C.
Lewis, Leo L.
McAnally, Jack L.
McCormick, Harry
McCune, Maureen
Martin, Eudell
Martwich, Lenora
Milam, Margaret—Society Editor, The News
Mills, Clifton B.
Mitchell, Eugene
Monroe, Barton C.
Montique, Robert
Moore, Glenn
Morris, Ben A.—Assistant Night Foreman, Press Room
Newnam, John
Osborne, Ray
Parker, Mrs. Winnifred
Perry, Reagan L.
Pouncey, Truman—Rotogravure Editor, The News
Proctor, Jack
Rice, Mrs. Bernice
Riley, Mrs. Thelma C.
Ripley, Glen A.
Routt, James O'Neal
Samuels, McKinley R.
Smith, Erwin J.
Steffy, Martin J.
Stewart, Leland S.
Storrs, Newell J.
Stout, Bess Inez
Thompson, Hal
Tidwell, Jack M.
Turner, J. G.
Warner, Charles L.
Wolf, Bob
Wright, Clifford L.
Wright, Henry H.
Zepp, Fred R.

1937   Alderman, James S.
Appleby, Alexander A.
Austin, John C.
Bates, Eugene

1937   Beauchamp, Mrs. Jennie V.
        Bennett, Lula Mae
        Bostaph, Paul E.
        Bowen, Fred J.
        Brittain, Roy R.
        Burke, James E.—Assistant Night Foreman, Stereotype Dept.
        Burns, Paul A.
        Campbell, Raymond, Jr.
        Chapman, Clovis
        Clasbey, Sam H.
        Clayton, James L.
        Cochran, Correll B.
        Cohen, Rosa
        Cook, Lucille
        Covington, Charles R.
        Crites, Emery D.
        Crocker, Mrs. Elizabeth Rea
        Crump, E. R. L.
        Davis, Luther E.
        Day, John H.
        Dealey, Al
        Debnam, Emerald
        Denney, Jesse W.
        Drake, Robert L.
        Dunn, Edward W.
        Embry, Joe B.
        Grant, Donald H.
        Gross, Louis R.
        Hardberger, Lawrence M.
        Harris, Ruth
        Hendrix, Cecil
        Jeter, John H.
        Johnson, Ora
        Jones, Dorothy Rea
        Jordan, Richard P.
        Julian, L. F.
        Kalusche, Earle J.
        Kemp, Ed L.
        King, J. E., Jr.
        Knott, Karl
        Lambertz, Karl J.—Musical Director, Radio Station WFAA
        MacIver, Donald J.
        Moncrief, Mrs. Bessie P.
        Nesbit, Alden C.
        Patrick, Billy
        Perkins, Arthur L.
        Price, Lloyd
        Ruggles, Dan G.

1937 Sanders, Oscar P., Jr.
Seale, Leon O.
Simms, John S.—Assistant Night Foreman, Stereotype Dept.
Simpson, Mrs. Gay
Smith, Reynolds
Snyder, Ada
South, Dorothy
Stewart, F. L.
Summers, Dan
Tesch, Melvin
Trott, Mrs. Lora
Walker, Emery
Webb, Jean
Woolsey, Clifford W.
Wyman, C. C.
1938 Carr, Harry F., Jr.
Chapman, Garland Mac
Chatelain, Paul
Dilg, Millard J.
Eastus, Harold

EXECUTIVE STAFF

G. B. Dealey, President
E. M. (Ted) Dealey, Vice President
James M. Moroney, Secretary-Treasurer

DIRECTORS

Briggs, George Waverley
Buchanan, R. M.
Dealey, E. M. (Ted)
Dealey, G. B.
Donosky, M. M.
Estes, Jack
King, John E.
Moroney, James M.
Withers, H. C.

INDEPENDENT TRANSPORTATION CONTRACTOR AND HIS EMPLOYEES

Edwards, Raymond J.—General Transportation Contractor,
engaged in delivery of The News since 1902

Aherns, T. D.	Lewis, R. L.
Akers, C. A.	Lindsey, L. L.
Burks, Ira	Perser, H. J.
Clark, J. C.	South, C. F.
Eury, E. J.	Stanberry, Ray
Goodlett, Bert	Tucker, George
Gusicke, Ralph	

NOTE

Obviously the basic, almost exclusive source of this book has been the files of THE NEWS from its origin in Galveston in 1842. There is no occasion, therefore, for any separate documentation, since all important references to the files have been given by dates in the text, or else are patent to the reader. For data on the life of Samuel Bangs (Chapter I), I am indebted to the scholarly research of Mrs. Lota M. Spell, whose *Samuel Bangs: First Printer in Texas* is invaluable. Mrs. Spell's article first appeared in the *Hispanic American Historical Review,* edited by Dr. J. A. Robertson, published by the Duke University Press and was reprinted in the *Southwestern Historical Quarterly,* Vol. XXXV, pp. 267-278. Bangs' part in the start of THE NEWS, however, is my own conclusion—based chiefly on an editorial of March 24, 1871, which quotes Wilbur Cherry relative to office matters of the period 1842-43. In Chapters I and II, use has also been made of the published papers of Mirabeau B. Lamar, edited by Miss Winnie Allen, Mr. Chas. A. Gulick, Jr., and Miss Harriet Smither. The letter of Louisa Blanche Murrel to President Lamar (quoted in Chapter II, pp. 17-18) is from Lamar Papers, Vol. V, pp. 422-23. For data on the military service of Col. A. H. Belo (Chapter V), I am indebted to *Histories of the Several Regiments and Battalions from North Carolina in the Great War 1861-'65,* edited by Walter Clark, Vol. III.

For indispensable assistance in the reading and helpful criticism of all or parts of the manuscript, the writer wishes to express his sincerest appreciation to Messrs. G. B. Dealey, E. M. (Ted) Dealey, who suggested the title of the book; Wayne Gard, John E. King, Lynn W. Landrum, Stuart McGregor, De Witt McMurray, J. M. Moroney, William B. Ruggles, Victor H. Schoffelmayer, J. J. Taylor, Joseph F. Willetts, Harry C. Withers, all of THE NEWS organization, and to Prof. Herbert P. Gambrell and Prof. John H. McGinnis of Southern Methodist University. The aid of Miss Anne Prescott Toomey, Mr. T. O. Bateman and Miss Olga E. Utley of THE NEWS is also gratefully acknowledged. Profound appreciation is likewise expressed to Mrs. Sarah Chokla Gross, who has compiled the index. In making these brief and inadequate acknowledgments, however, the writer wishes to emphasize that none of the above are responsible for any of the opinions expressed about matters in this book, complete responsibility for which rests solely upon the writer.

SAM ACHESON.

INDEX

325